Taking Charge
of Your Learning

A Guide to College Success

Dianna L. Van Blerkom

University of Pittsburgh at Johnstown

THOMSON

WADSWORTH

Australia • Brazil • Canada • Mexico • Singapore • Spain • United Kingdom • United

THOMSON

WADSWORTH

Taking Charge of Your Learning: A Guide to College Success
Dianna L. Van Blerkom

Editor in Chief: *PJ Boardman*
Publisher: *Lyn Uhl*
Director of Developmental English and College Success:
 Annie Todd
Editorial Assistant: *Daniel DeBonis*
Senior Technology Project Manager: *Stephanie Gregoire*
Executive Marketing Manager: *Stacy Best*
Marketing Assistant: *Kathleen Remsberg*
Marketing Communications Manager: *Darlene Amidon-Brent*
Associate Content Project Manager: *Jennifer Kostka*
Senior Art Director: *Cate Rickard Barr*

Print Buyer: *Betsy Donaghey*
Manager, Text Permission Acquisition: *Ron Montgomery*
Rights Acquisition Account Manager: *Mardell Glinski Schultz*
Senior Rights Acquisition Account Manager, Images: *Sheri Blaney*
Production Service/Compositor: *ICC Macmillan Inc.*
Text and Cover Designer: *Denise Hoffman*
Text and Cover Printer: *Edwards Brothers, Inc.*
Cover Photos: © left: *Photodisc/Barbara Penoyar/Getty;*
 top: *Photodisc/Getty;* right: *DigitalVision/Charlie*
 Edwards/Photodisc; bottom: *Fogstock LLC/*
 Index Open

ISBN-13: 978-0-534-53949-8
ISBN-10: 0-534-53949-1

Thomson Higher Education
25 Thomson Place
Boston, MA 02210-1202
USA

For more information about our products, contact us at:
Thomson Learning Academic Resource Center
1-800-423-0563

For permission to use material from this text or product, submit a request online at **http://www.thomsonrights.com** Any additional questions about permissions can be submitted by e-mail to **thomsonrights@thomson.com**

Printed in the United States of America
1 2 3 4 5 6 7 11 10 09 08 07

Library of Congress Control Number: 2006934851

Credits appear on page 283, which constitutes a continuation of the copyright page.

For Mal,
with love

Contents

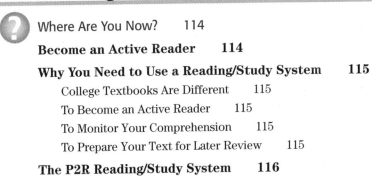

CHAPTER 5   Reading Your Textbook   113

CHAPTER **6**   **Marking Your Textbook**   **137**

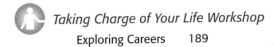

CHAPTER 10   Preparing for Finals   259

To the Instructor

Getting students actively involved in their own learning is one of the goals of all college success, orientation, and learning strategy courses. Most first-year students need new strategies to manage their time and become self-regulated learners, to learn from texts and lectures, and to prepare for and take exams. Many of them find out very quickly that what worked in high school doesn't work well in college. Some students who have been out of school for five or more years may feel some anxiety about what will work for them. They are returning to school unsure of what to expect and uncertain about what will be expected of them.

Students need to be actively engaged in their own learning to change the way they study and learn. When students know that a strategy will help them master their course material, they are more willing to use that strategy when completing their own course assignments. To help students make changes in the way they approach their courses and assignments, we, as instructors, need to do two things. We must provide them with new strategies that will help them be more successful in college and we must find ways to motivate them to use those strategies in their own coursework. We need to get students to become active participants in this task—they must become active learners. Active learners read and write, talk and listen, think and reflect, and apply what they are learning to their own lives. Although many students find college lectures interesting and informative, not all students benefit from the lecture format. There are many different learning styles and not all students learn best by simply hearing a lecture. Many students learn more effectively when they are actively involved in the classroom. In the real world they rarely sit back and watch someone else do things; they are actively engaged in life. Whether they are learning a new musical piece, competing in a sporting event, or even working on a new project at work, our students are active participants. Our students no longer just sit in front of the computer screen absorbing what's there. Instead they are actively involved in instant messaging, gaming, and surfing the net. They interact with the computer rather than just react to it. They don't just sit back and watch or listen; they get involved in the task, they try new techniques, and they make adjustments when the outcome is not what they wanted.

One of the objectives of college success and learning strategy courses is to teach students new strategies for learning. However, I think we all share the expectation that our students will then use those new strategies in their own coursework to be more successful in college. Knowing what to do is not enough; students must actually do it. Very early in my teaching career, I discovered that not all of my students were applying what they were learning in my course to their other coursework. I was shocked. I always thought that if they learned new strategies for reading their texts, taking lecture notes, and preparing for exams, just to name a few of the topics I presented, they would use those strategies in their own courses to be more successful in college. That discovery forced me to make changes in the way I taught, and it resulted in much more success for my students. I began to incorporate workshops into my course to help students learn how to apply the strategies they were learning to their own course material. I later realized that those workshops served other purposes. They motivated my students to use the strategies because in the process of using the strategies in class, many of the students realized that they worked. Knowing how to use the strategy and that it did help them made a huge difference in the transfer to their own coursework. It also allowed me as an instructor to monitor their use of the strategies (to be sure they were using them correctly) and provide them with feedback to ensure a better outcome.

During the past fifteen years, I have developed many workshops that provide students with the opportunity to learn how to use new strategies, practice using those strategies, and discover that the strategies do work. I wrote *Taking Charge of Your Learning: A Guide to College Success* so that I could share those workshops with other students. This book shifts the focus of learning strategy, college success, and orientation courses from passive to active learning.

What are workshops? In many ways these workshops are similar to the workshops that we as professionals enjoy (and learn from) at conferences. I refer to them as workshops because the students actually do the work during each of them—they are active participants in their own learning. In many of the workshops, a new strategy is presented at the beginning of the period and then the students are provided with materials—from real college texts—on which to use that strategy. They are then given feedback on their use of the strategy and subsequently have an opportunity to reflect on how well that strategy worked for them. In other workshops, the students are given a "case study" or scenario and asked what they would do in that situation. Some of the workshops allow students to discover more about themselves—how they learn best, the strategies they use to learn and remember information, and how they use their time, for example.

The text incorporates both the essential study strategies and the key life skills for college success. Each chapter includes text material and four "Taking Charge of Your Learning" workshops that allow students to become actively engaged in using the strategies that were presented in the chapter. Through their participation in the workshops, students will have an opportunity to talk and listen, think and reflect, write and read, and test and monitor their learning. In addition to chapters on time management, text reading, taking lecture notes, and preparing for exams, just to name a few, *Taking Charge of Your Learning: A Guide to College Success* also includes nine "Taking Charge of Your Life" workshops designed to help students make a successful transition to college. Each of these short workshops provides students with essential information about topics such as clarifying values, making wise decisions, managing stress, setting goals, celebrating diversity, and exploring careers. Students are asked to evaluate their own knowledge and current practices on the first page of each workshop in the "Where Are You Now?" activity. The remaining pages are packed with information and further resources on each of the topics. At the end of the workshop, students are asked to decide what they would do in a specific situation in the "What Would You Do Now?" activity. They are provided with a scenario related to the topics that were presented and asked to apply what they learned to their own lives. Because the text is perforated, the students will be able to tear out the pages to complete the workshops and turn them in afterward for feedback and/or grading.

Many of the workshops within the text focus on collaborative learning because many students learn best when working with others. Collaborative learning by its very structure provides students with many opportunities for growth and development. Other students seem to learn best when working alone—they benefit most by being actively engaged in their own learning. A variety of workshops are provided in each of the chapters, some involving independent learning and others incorporating collaborative learning, so that students can experience opportunities for growth and development in both areas. Some of the workshops are designed for in-class use and require the instructor's guidance and feedback; others can be done outside of class.

This text lends itself well to any type of course designed to help students improve their success in college. Instructors can begin by discussing some of the strategies that are presented in the text portion of the chapter and then incorporate one or more of the workshops into the class. Because there are several workshops to choose from, course instructors have some choices. Instructors can also assess the needs of the students in the course and then choose the workshop(s) that best fits the needs of that particular class. You can do several of the workshops from each chapter in class if you are teaching a two- or three-credit course or alternate workshops from term to term in one-credit courses. Some of the workshops can be done outside of class for additional practice. Each of the workshops contains clear, specific directions and all of the materials the students will need. Step-by-step instructions for presenting the workshop are available in the Instructor's Manual, and all of the materials that you, as an instructor, will need are available instantly (password protected) on the Instructor Website.

Unique Features of the Text

- Student assessment activities in each chapter
- Clear, in-depth explanations for each of the skills presented
- Step-by-step approach to success in college
- Learning strategies that transfer to students' own coursework
- Emphasis on active learning
- Workshops to get students actively engaged in learning
- Excerpts from other college textbooks for practice
- Student examples that model how to use the strategies
- Activities for reflection and self-monitoring
- Case studies for evaluation and discussion

Taking Charge of Your Learning Workshops

 Each chapter includes four "Taking Charge of Your Learning" workshops that provide students with an opportunity to apply what they learned in the chapter to their own coursework and their own life. They allow students to try new strategies and to see which ones work best for them. The workshops include all of the student materials necessary to complete the activities. Directions for completing the workshop, practice materials to use (including time management calendars, text excerpts, and sample tests to take, for example), and questions for self-reflection and monitoring are included. Some of the workshops may take an entire period to complete and others take as little as 10 to 15 minutes. A variety of workshops is included to allow for both in-class and out-of-class practice.

Taking Charge of Your Life Workshops

 The "Taking Charge of Your Life" workshops are located between each of the chapters. They are designed to help students make a successful transition to college and they focus on topics such as clarifying values, working collaboratively, staying healthy, and building relationships. By completing these workshops, students have an opportunity to explore their attitudes and feelings about many of the social issues they must deal with during their college years. Each workshop begins with a "Where Are You Now?" assessment to allow students to reflect on what they currently believe and do. This activity is followed by information and resources that help students gain new insights into the topics that are presented. At the end of each workshop, students are given a scenario and asked to respond to a "What Would You Do Now?" question. By applying what they learned in each of these workshops to their own lives, they can grow into mature individuals who can better navigate the college landscape.

Instructor's Manual and Test Bank

The Instructor's Manual includes suggestions for teaching the course, step-by-step instructions for presenting each workshop, approximate time frames for the workshops, answer keys for some of the activities, quiz and test questions, and a list of slides related to each workshop, which are available on the Instructor Website.

Workshop Materials on the Instructor Website

 The Instructor Website contains a copy of the Piaget video for use with the lecture note workshop and electronic versions of the "teachers' editions" of the transparencies that demonstrate various steps in the use of the strategies for many of the workshops. In addition, "final" versions of transparencies (in electronic form) will also be included. Instructors who adopt the text will have all of the materials that they will need to run the workshops. Additionally, PowerPoint slides that reinforce many of the essential strategies will be included. The password for the Instructor Website is available from your local Thomson Wadsworth sales representative upon the adoption of the textbook.

Acknowledgments

Many people contributed their time, energy, ideas, and assistance in making *Taking Charge of Your Learning: A Guide to College Success* possible. I am very grateful to Carolyn Merrill for sharing my vision for a college success book that focused on active learning both in and out of the classroom. Thank you, Carolyn. I am also so pleased to be working with my new editor, Annie Todd, who has jumped in to help complete the process of turning a manuscript into a textbook. Thank you, Annie. I couldn't have done this without both you and Carolyn. I also am appreciative of the wonderful support of Eden Kram and Dan DeBonis. Thank you both for helping make this book a reality. Many others have helped in the process of taking a vision to a manuscript to a book. I am also very appreciative of the assistance of Elise Kaiser, Jennifer Kostka, Lynn Lustberg, Stacy Best, and Kate Remsberg, who helped make this text possible. Thank you also to Stephanie Gregoire and Sean O'Keefe for their help in creating the Instructor Website for the text. As always, my husband, Mal, has been very supportive. Thanks, Mal, for all of your help in brainstorming, proofreading, copying, and reminding me that I should be working. I am also grateful to Katherine Stall Kinsinger for her collaboration in writing the "Taking Charge of Your Life" workshops. Thanks, Kate. It was great working with you on this project. I am always appreciative of the support and feedback from my own students who have over the years participated in many of these workshops and shared their ideas for how to make them more effective, interesting, and fun.

I also have been very fortunate to have had a wonderful group of reviewers who have been both enthusiastic about the idea of a book that focuses on active learning and shared their own ideas for how to make it even better. Thank you for your insight, your suggestions, and your support in making this book possible.

Suzanne Ashe, *Cerritos College*
Alicia Dunphy-Culp, *Curry College*
Arthur Lizie, *Bridgewater State College*
Deborah J. Lotsof, *Mount Union College*
Sheryl Hartman, *Miami Dade College*
Connie Hunt, *Arapahoe Community College*
Deborah Mapp-Embry, *Kentucky State University*
Teresa Massey, *Chemeketa Community College*
Bridgett L. McGowen, *Prairie View A&M University*
Amanda Stone Norton, *University of Denver*
Patricia Parks, *Reading Area Community College*
Nancy Wood, *University of Arkansas, Little Rock*
Elaine Wright, *University of Southern Maine*

To the Student

As you begin your college career, think about the last few classes you attended. Were you an active participant in your own learning, or did you simply sit back and let the instructor do all the work? Many college classes are lecture-based, but that doesn't mean you can't be actively involved throughout the period. In much the same way, you can be actively engaged as you read your texts, complete your assignments, and prepare for exams. Are you? *Taking Charge of Your Learning: A Guide to College Success* was designed to help you become an active learner—an active participant in the learning process. Throughout the text, you will find many new strategies for managing your time, taking notes, reading your texts, preparing for and taking tests, and many others. Rather than just reading about strategies that you may find helpful, you'll have the opportunity to participate in workshops that will help you learn to use the strategies and find out which ones work best for you. By learning and applying these new strategies to your own course work, you can improve your academic performance.

Once you put your newly learned strategies into practice, you should see your grades begin to improve in each of your courses. This kind of improvement does not result from just being told what to do differently, but rather from hard work and persistence in applying effective learning strategies to your own course material. Becoming a successful student takes time and effort—there are no miracles involved. However, if you are willing to try new strategies and practice using them when completing your other course assignments, you can achieve your goals.

How to Use This Book

There are many resources in this text designed to help you be more successful in college. Each of the text resources will provide you with the information and practice you need to help you achieve your goals.

 ### Where Are You Now? Activities

By completing the "Where Are You Now?" activities before reading the chapter, you can evaluate your current use of strategies related to the topics in each chapter. Once you identify your strengths and weaknesses, you can focus on those areas in which you need the most assistance. You may notice that completing these assessments also provides you with an overview of some of the strategies that will be discussed in the chapter. After completing the chapter and the related workshop activities, go back and redo the activity again using a different color to mark your answers. You may find that your responses have changed because you have changed the way you approach some of your tasks.

Student Examples

The student examples included in the text serve as models for many of the strategies that are presented in the chapter. Although it has become almost a cliché, a picture is worth a thousand words to students who are not quite sure how to take lecture notes, create recall questions, and create study sheets, just to name a few of the applications you may find useful in this text. Occasionally, some examples are included in the workshops that contain common errors that students make. These examples are designed to help you better evaluate your strategy use and keep you from making the same mistakes.

Taking Charge of Your Learning Workshops

Each chapter includes four "Taking Charge of Your Learning" workshops. Some of them are designed to provide you with an opportunity to practice and get feedback on the correct use of the strategies that were described earlier in the chapter. Others give you an opportunity to apply what you have learned in the chapter to your own coursework and/or your own life. They give you a chance to try new strategies and see which ones work best for you. My hope is that once you prove to yourself that a strategy is effective, you will be more willing to use that strategy in your own coursework.

Many of the strategies involve individual effort because some students learn best working independently. In many cases you need to reflect on your own strategy use and then evaluate the effectiveness of a variety of strategies to find out which ones are the most effective for your course work and for the way you learn best. Other workshops are designed for collaborative learning. Many students learn best when working in a group. By working together, you may find that you can accomplish more in less time. You may also be surprised to find that two or three heads are better than one. Many students find that brainstorming with others helps them learn more effectively. Others find that seeing how someone else approaches a task gives them new ideas that are more helpful than the original strategies they were using. Finally, many of you may find that working individually on a task and then comparing your work with that of one of your classmates or with your instructor will provide you with feedback that helps you become a more active and successful student.

The "What Would You Do?" workshop in each chapter provides you with a case study to think about and discuss. As you read about each student's difficulties, think about whether you know someone who has experienced the same or similar problems. By analyzing the mistakes that each student made and developing strategies that could be used to help resolve those problems, you may develop new ways to deal with the problems that you may face during your own college career.

Taking Charge of Your Life Workshops

The "Taking Charge of Your Life" workshops, located between the chapters, are designed to help you make a more successful transition to college. They focus on topics such as clarifying values, working collaboratively, staying healthy, building relationships and others. By completing these workshops, you'll have an opportunity to explore your attitudes and feelings about many of the social issues you must deal with during your college years. At the end of each workshop, you'll be given a scenario and asked to respond to a "What Would You Do Now?" question. By applying what you learned in each of these workshops to your own lives, you can develop and grow as students who can better navigate the college landscape.

Becoming a Successful Student

CHAPTER 1

In this chapter you will learn more about:

- How to become an active learner
- How to become a strategic learner
- How to become motivated to learn
- How you learn best

? Where Are You Now?

Take a few minutes to answer *yes* or *no* to the following questions.

		YES	NO
1.	Do you know how to increase your motivation?	___	___
2.	Do you use active strategies to prepare for exams?	___	___
3.	If you miss class, do you expect your professor to go over the material with you at a later date?	___	___
4.	Do you know your preferred learning style?	___	___
5.	Do you monitor your learning by asking yourself questions after reading?	___	___
6.	Do you attend class regularly and stay up-to-date with your assignments?	___	___
7.	Do you set specific goals to get assignments done on time?	___	___
8.	Do you do some assignments without putting in much effort?	___	___
9.	Have you really thought about why you are in college?	___	___
10.	Do you expect college to be the same as high school?	___	___
	Total Points	___	

Give yourself 1 point for each *yes* answer to all questions except 3, 8, and 10, and 1 point for each *no* answer to questions 3, 8, and 10. Now total up your points. A low score indicates that you need some help adjusting to college. A high score indicates that you already know how to become a successful student.

What Is a Successful Student?

If you ask different people to define a successful student, you'll get many different answers. Who are successful students? College administrators might argue that students are successful if they graduate within a reasonable time frame (four, five, or even six years). College instructors might say that students are successful if they successfully master the course material. Some students would define success as earning a good grade in a course, whereas others might define success as having successfully participated in extracurricular activities, service projects, or social events. I'm sure that some students consider themselves successful students when they graduate with a good job already lined up. All of these definitions are valid—all contribute to the mission of a college. What is your definition? How will you know when you are successful? To be a successful student, you need to learn the skills and strategies that will help you master course material; find time to participate in college activities and still have time for your friends, family, and work; and develop skills within your field of study. To do this you need to become an active learner, a strategic learner, and an independent learner. You need to know how you learn best and then apply that knowledge to achieve your academic goals.

The Taking Charge of Your Learning Workshops within each of the chapters will help you develop many of the academic skills you will need to be a successful student. However, becoming a successful student also involves growing as an individual. The Taking Charge of Your Life Workshops, found between each of the chapters, will help you explore many of the non-academic topics that will contribute to your college success.

Become an Active Learner

What is an active learner? Active learners talk and listen, read, and reflect on (think about) what they are learning.[1] Active learners get actively involved in their academic assignments. They think about the material they are working on; ask and answer questions in class; talk about the material with friends, family, and classmates; and generate study materials such as text notes, edited lecture notes, study sheets, and flash cards. Active learners quiz themselves after reading a chapter by answering the review questions, taking online tests, or predicting their own questions and practicing answering them. As you progress through the chapters in this text, you'll learn new strategies to become actively engaged during class, as you complete your assignments, and when you prepare for and take exams. You'll also have the opportunity to practice many active learning strategies in the workshops in each chapter.

Increase your level of involvement. What did you do when you completed your last reading assignment? Did you:

- Skim it?
- Read it?
- Read and highlight?
- Read, highlight, and take notes?
- Read, highlight, take notes, and predict questions?
- Read, highlight, take notes, predict questions, and do the exercises?
- Read, highlight, take notes, predict questions, do the exercises, and quiz yourself on the material?

Put a checkmark at your level of interaction. If it was near the beginning of the list, you weren't very actively involved with the material. If your checkmark was in the middle or near the bottom of the list, you were more actively involved in the task. As you increase your level of involvement, you also increase your comprehension of the material, your interest in the task, and your learning. You'll probably find that you also improve your ability to concentrate during reading and study tasks when you use active strategies. Taking notes, predicting questions, doing exercises or problems, and self-testing all keep you focused on the material. As you complete your assignments this week, get actively involved in your learning by moving to a higher level of active involvement.

---

[1] Chet Meyers and Thomas B. Jones, *Promoting Active Learning: Strategies for the College Classroom* (San Francisco: Jossey-Bass, 1993).

Use active strategies to prepare for exams. How do you typically prepare for a quiz or an exam? Do you just read over the text and your notes a few times? You may be thinking that reading over the material worked well for your high school exams. Unfortunately, it won't work as well for college exams. You need to know the information at the recall level of learning. That means, for completion, short answer, and essay questions, you need to supply the correct answer from memory. Even though many of your college exams will be made up of multiple-choice questions, most instructors rephrase the answers—they use different words than those presented in your text and notes. You won't be able to just recognize the correct answer because it won't be there. To learn information at the recall level, you need to be actively involved in the process. You need to identify the important information, organize it, and condense it so that it will be easier to learn. Then you need to practice the information a number of times (over several days) to embed it in long-term memory (see Chapter 4). Finally, you need to quiz yourself to see if you really do know the material before the exam.

Become a Strategic Learner

Another way to become more successful in college is to become a strategic learner. According to Weinstein and Hume, "Strategic learners are students who view studying and learning as a systematic process that is, to a good degree, under their control."[2] Weinstein's model of strategic learning involves three main components: *skill*, *will*, and *self-regulation*.

Strategic learners possess a wide variety of skills. Strategic learners have a great deal of prior content knowledge as well as knowledge about themselves as learners, about different types of academic tasks, about different strategies for learning, and about the contexts in which that knowledge could be useful.[3] After twelve years of formal schooling, you have a great deal of knowledge about yourself as a learner and about completing academic tasks. However, some of the tasks that you'll be asked to complete in college are different from anything you've done before. You'll be asked to learn much more information in a shorter time frame than you've ever done before. You'll also be expected to understand the information rather than just memorize it. To achieve these goals, you'll have to complete new tasks, complete some tasks differently, and apply new strategies for learning.

Strategic learners possess the will to be successful. Strategic learners set goals, select appropriate study strategies to fit the task, and believe in their own ability and the strategies that they have chosen. Strategic learners are motivated—they are willing to work hard to achieve their goals. In Workshop 1-1, you'll have an opportunity to set some academic goals. How hard are you willing to work to achieve your goals? Many students are surprised by the workload in college. College is like a full-time job—you need to put in a great deal of time and effort if you want to be successful. Do you have the will to succeed in college? Just having skills isn't enough—you must have the will to succeed.

---

[2] Claire E. Weinstein and Laura M. Hume, *Study Strategies for Lifelong Learning* (Washington, DC: American Psychological Association, 1998).

[3] Claire E. Weinstein, "Strategic Learning/Strategic Teaching: Flip Sides of a Coin," in Pintrich, Brown, and Weinstein, Eds., *Student Motivation, Cognition, and Learning: Essays in Honor of Wilbert J. McKeachie* (Hillsdale, NJ: Lawrence Erlbaum, 1994).

Strategic learners are self-regulated learners. Strategic learners manage their time, monitor their learning, and evaluate the results of their effort. They approach learning in a systematic way.[4] Self-regulated learners plan before starting a task, select strategies that they know are appropriate for the task, and monitor their own learning as they are completing the task and after the task is completed. Self-regulated learners schedule their study tasks, know about how long it takes them to complete routine assignments, and use strategies to motivate themselves to get their work done on time. They are self-directed, not other-directed. Self-regulated learners don't have to depend on someone else to tell them what to do and when to do it. They are aware of what must be done and set goals and design plans to help them succeed. Self-regulated learners monitor their learning. They pause to check their understanding when reading, ask questions in class when they don't understand something, compare lecture notes with friends, and self-test before exams. Self-regulated learners also monitor their learning strategies and make adjustments when they find that specific strategies are not working. You may find that one of the most important transitions you'll have to make in college is learning to become a self-regulated learner.

Get Motivated to Learn

Psychologists have been trying to explain why some people work hard at a task while others choose not to do so. Many believe that motivation is the determining factor. Motivation can be described as something that energizes, directs, and sustains behavior toward a particular goal.

Motivation affects your college success. Motivation affects whether or not you do your work, whether or not you complete your work, when you do your work, and where you do your work. Motivation also has an impact on how long you work on a task, how much effort you expend doing it, and how well you concentrate while working on the task. Finally, motivation affects how you do the task (which learning strategies you use) and how much you learn in the process of completing the task. In Workshop 1-2, you'll have an opportunity to learn more about your level of motivation.

Three main factors influence your motivation. *Goals, self-efficacy,* and *effort* play an important role in how motivated you are to complete your academic tasks.

● *Your goals influence your motivation level.* Without challenging, realistic goals, you may not be very motivated to do your work. You may have noticed that your motivation (or lack of motivation) varies depending on the task that you need to complete. Many students find that they are more motivated to work on a task when they have a personal interest in completing it or find it challenging to do so. You may choose to work on a task because you want to learn or do something (*intrinsic motivation*) or because you expect an external gain such as money, grades, or praise from another (*extrinsic motivation*). In high school you were

---

[4] Claire E. Weinstein and Laura M. Hume, *Study Strategies for Lifelong Learning* (Washington, DC: American Psychological Association, 1998).

probably motivated by extrinsic rewards like promised money or gifts, grades, or recognition from others. In college you need to develop more intrinsic motivation, because intrinsic motivators (feeling satisfaction at a job well done, pride in your work, interest, and challenge) are more powerful motivators that help you persist and complete the task when it is difficult or boring. Many students begin a task because they want to be able to answer questions in class, complete the homework assignment, or do well on a quiz or test. Do you? It's okay if you said yes because you may finish the task because of intrinsic motivation.

● *Your self-efficacy influences your motivation.* Self-efficacy refers to your belief in your ability to successfully complete a task. Are you good at math? Writing papers? History? If you believe that you can successfully complete a task, you'll be more motivated to work on it. Each time you're successful in accomplishing one of your goals (completing a task), it increases your self-efficacy (self-confidence) so that you can complete a similar or even more difficult task in the future. For these reasons, many psychologists believe that past successes lead to future successes.

● *Your belief that effort makes a difference influences your motivation.* If you believe that the amount of effort you put into a task will affect your performance, you'll be more motivated to complete the task. On the other hand, if you believe that your performance depends on something over which you have no control, such as luck or whether or not your professor or teaching assistant likes you, you won't be very motivated to work on the task. Unlike luck, which is out of your control, you can exert a lot of effort, very little effort, or no effort when completing a task. If you work hard at the beginning of the semester, you'll see that the amount of effort you put into your academic tasks does have a positive effect on your performance. When you know that your effort is worthwhile, you'll be more motivated to work hard, which will lead to even more success.

Use strategies to increase your motivation. There are hundreds of strategies that you can use to increase your motivation. You can find books on increasing motivation in the self-help section of your local bookstore or from online booksellers. You can also find many strategies on the Internet by searching websites from college learning centers, journals, and magazines. Some strategies that you may find useful are listed here.

● *Set challenging but realistic goals.* You'll be more motivated to complete tasks when you feel that they are within your reach. You may also find that thinking of each task as a step toward achieving your long-term personal or career goals can also motivate you.

● *Set learning goals.* Instead of thinking about how many pages you have to read for your next assignment, decide what facts, concepts, or ideas you want to learn before you begin working on a task. When you know what you want to accomplish and have a personal stake in completing the assignment, you'll be more motivated to put more effort into the task.

● *See the value in every task.* Understanding why you're doing the task—seeing the importance of the task—can help motivate you to complete it.

● *Have a positive attitude.* You'll be more motivated if you have a positive attitude toward the task. Similarly, believing you can successfully complete the task will increase your motivation. For that reason, you need to use positive self-talk.

Tell yourself the task is important, think about how it will benefit you, and remind yourself that you can do it and that you've successfully completed similar tasks before.

● *Work hard.* One of the most important steps in getting motivated is to work hard—exert effort—on a task. Putting time and effort into each task (with the right strategies) will help you be more successful. That success motivates you to continue working hard.

● *Use active learning strategies.* Using strategies that work can also help you successfully complete a task. You may also find that using a study strategy that you like (such as taking notes or predicting questions) can make completing a reading assignment more interesting. For example, if you like predicting questions more than reading sociology, you may be more motivated to work on the task.

● *Break tasks down.* Some students have trouble getting started when tasks are long or difficult. Which would you rather read: ten pages or sixty pages? If you said ten pages, why do you try to read a sixty-page chapter at one time? Instead, break long tasks into chunks. By breaking tasks down into smaller chunks (and completing them one at a time), you can increase your motivation.

● *Monitor your learning.* When you know that your time, effort, and strategies are working to help you learn, you'll be more motivated to continue working. Answering your own self-test questions, taking end-of-chapter or online tests, or reciting from memory are just a few ways to monitor your learning. When you quiz yourself and know the information, you feel good and that motivates you to continue studying. If you quiz yourself and don't know some of the answers, you may be motivated to work even harder to prepare for your exam.

Discover Your Learning Style

Knowing how you learn best can help you be more successful in college. The term *learning style* refers to the preferred way that you acquire, process, and retain information—the way you learn best. We learn new tasks in different ways; we each have our own style or preference for learning. The time of day you study, the kinds of strategies you use, whether you work best alone or with a group, and even the place you study are all aspects of your learning style. Your personality type can also have an impact on how you study and learn.

What kind of learner are you? In Workshop 1-3, you'll have an opportunity to discover a number of things about your learning style. Do you learn best in the morning or late at night? Are you an impulsive or reflective learner? Do you prefer to outline a paper or just start writing and let your ideas develop spontaneously? Are you a visual learner, an auditory learner, or a kinesthetic learner?

● *Are you a visual learner?* Visual learners learn best by seeing things. You may find that you understand new information best when you read about it or watch videos and demonstrations. If reading the chapter before the lecture helps you understand your professor's lecture, you're probably a visual learner. Look at the list of active strategies for visual learners in Figure 1.1. How many of those strategies do you use? If you find that you're a visual learner, you may find that taking notes, making concept maps, writing questions in the margin of your text and notes, and creating study sheets may help you learn better.

Figure 1.1 ● Active Learning Strategies for Visual, Auditory, and Kinesthetic Learners

VISUAL	AUDITORY	KINESTHETIC
• Read and highlight your text	• Read difficult passages out loud	• Take notes as you read your text assignments
• Visualize pictures, charts, and diagrams	• Recite the main points at the end of every headed section of the text	• Predict questions in the margin at the end of each headed section
• Outline information	• Explain information out loud	• Create word, question, and problem cards and practice them in groups of ten or fifteen
• Map information	• Discuss the text assignment or lecture material with a study partner or study group	• Make up puzzles or games to learn text and lecture material
• Create charts and study sheets	• Tape the lectures from your most difficult class and play them again when you commute or do household chores	• Practice labeling diagrams, recreating maps, and filling in charts to learn information for exams
• Read related material		
• Rewrite your lecture notes		
• Color code your notes and study sheets	• Cover the details in your lecture notes and recite from the headings	• Construct diagrams, models, and problem cards to practice math and science material
• Write out steps in a process for solving math and science problems	• Recite the answers out loud to questions in the margin or word and question cards	• Create self-tests in the same format as the actual test and take them
• Create study sheets	• Teach the material to someone or something else	• Participate in study groups and review sessions
• Write word and question cards	• Create a taped self-test and recite the answers before listening to the correct ones	• Re-do math problems
• Write questions in the margin and underline the answers	• Explain the steps for solving math and science problems	• Take end-of-chapter and online tests to prepare for exams
• Create visual images to connect information to acronyms and acrostics	• Create rhymes, poems, and songs to recall information	• Develop acronyms and acrostics to recall information and practice using them

● *Are you an auditory learner?* Auditory learners learn best by hearing the information. You probably have found that you understand the text chapter better after you hear the professor's lecture. Look at the list of active strategies for auditory learners in Figure 1.1. How many of them do you use now? Are you reading difficult sections of text out loud? Do you talk about the course material with a classmate or study group? Do you answer questions aloud or recite the information in your notes when studying for an exam? Listening to yourself or others talk will help you learn the information better.

● *Are you a kinesthetic learner?* Kinesthetic learners learn best by doing. They prefer hands-on tasks that allow them to touch and feel. Many of the strategies used by visual and auditory learners also appeal to kinesthetic learners. Which of the strategies in Figure 1.1 do you use now? Do you like to make study sheets, take notes, predict questions, do experiments, take self-tests, or do chapter or online tests? These are all kinesthetic tasks because you are making or doing something in order to learn the information.

Learn to use multiple learning styles. Although each of us has a preferred learning style, most of us learn information by using a combination of learning styles. In fact, some courses, assignments, or exams may require you to use one or more of your less preferred learning styles to complete the task successfully. When you're forced to complete a hands-on task such as orally identifying the bones on a skeleton, you may find that using a kinesthetic approach (practicing saying the names of each bone as you point to it) may help you complete the oral exam better than reading about the bones or practicing their names aloud. Even though it may not be your preferred style for learning, it may be the best way to learn that information for that kind of exam. The most successful students are often the ones who can use a variety of strategies from all of the ways they learn or those who can switch to different strategies depending on the demands of the course or the assignment.

What's your personality type? The Myers-Briggs Type Inventory (MBTI) can tell you more about how you learn best. The MBTI measures four different groups of indicators.

● *Introverts vs. Extroverts.* Introverts tend to feel more comfortable working alone or with one other person. They prefer to listen rather than talk. They study best by themselves or with a study partner. Although they may know the answers to the professor's questions in class, they usually aren't the ones who answer. Extroverts prefer working with others and enjoy and benefit from working in groups. They like to talk and participate in class. They prefer group projects and like working in study groups. Extroverts enjoy discussion classes and learn by active participation.

● *Sensing vs. Intuiting.* Sensing types are interested in facts, details, and what can be proven. They are very practical, realistic, and solve problems using established methods. They like solving problems and seeing that their solutions are correct. They like studying by memorizing facts and details and do well in classes that involve practical applications. Intuitive types, on the other hand, prefer to think about things and consider various possibilities. They tend to be imaginative and often quite creative. Intuitive types look at information in a more global way. They see beyond the facts and details to the whole picture.

● *Thinking vs. Feeling.* Thinkers tend to make decisions based on logical reasoning. They seek out truth and focus on the objective. Thinking types are analytical and make decisions based on information rather than emotions. Feeling types instead focus more on personal feelings. They seek balance and care about how others may feel more than themselves. Feeling types make decisions based on their sense of right or wrong and their emotions rather than objective facts or details.

● *Judging vs. Perceiving.* Judging types like to plan in advance. They tend to be very organized and enjoy working on one task at a time before moving on to another. They are very task-oriented and work well with planners, lists, and calendars. Perceiving types are more flexible and spontaneous. They don't like to schedule things too far in advance so that they can be flexible if other things come up. Perceiving types are comfortable working on multiple projects, moving easily from one task to another.

In Workshop 1-3, you'll find the websites of two different online Myers-Briggs Type Indicators. After completing the indicators, review the material on each website to learn more about your learning style. Then read the descriptions listed previously to learn more about your personality style. All of the personality styles are composed of four-letter combinations (there are sixteen possible variations), and all are normal. There are no right or wrong combinations. However, each is unique.

WORKSHOP 1-1   Characteristics of Successful Students

In this workshop, you'll have a chance to develop a list of characteristics of successful students. As you complete the workshop, think of some successful students you know. What makes them more successful than other students? What personal characteristics do they have that helps them achieve their goals? What do they do differently?

1. List ten characteristics of successful students. Use key terms or phrases to describe their personal characteristics or actions.

   1. _____   6. _____
   2. _____   7. _____
   3. _____   8. _____
   4. _____   9. _____
   5. _____   10. _____

2. Form a group with two or three of your classmates and compare your responses to theirs. How many of them are the same? Talk about your responses until you can agree on one list of ten. Write these characteristics below.

   1. _____   6. _____
   2. _____   7. _____
   3. _____   8. _____
   4. _____   9. _____
   5. _____   10. _____

3. Share your list with the entire class by writing it on a transparency or the chalkboard or reading it aloud. Following a short discussion, develop a list of the ten best characteristics of successful students and write the class list below.

   1. _____   6. _____
   2. _____   7. _____
   3. _____   8. _____
   4. _____   9. _____
   5. _____   10. _____

4. Put a checkmark next to the characteristics that describe you now. List them below.

   _____   _____

   _____   _____

   _____

5. Put a star next to the characteristics that you wish described you. List them below.

_____   _____

_____   _____

_____   _____

_____   _____

6. How do you plan to become a successful student? What personal characteristics or actions do you plan to adopt to increase your chances for success? How will you do that? Continue on your own paper if necessary.

_____

_____

_____

_____

_____

_____

_____

_____

_____

_____

_____

_____

_____

_____

7. List your academic goals for this semester.

1. _____   6. _____

2. _____   7. _____

3. _____   8. _____

4. _____   9. _____

5. _____   10. _____

8. List your academic goals for this week.

1. _____   6. _____

2. _____   7. _____

3. _____   8. _____

4. _____   9. _____

5. _____   10. _____

WORKSHOP 1-2   **How Motivated Are You?**

In this workshop, you'll have a chance to learn more about how motivated you are by evaluating how you complete your assignments.

1. List three to five academic tasks that you completed this week, such as reading assignments, math assignments, writing assignments, or similar tasks. Leave the short lines blank for now.

Task	E	B	D	C
1. _____	___	___	___	___
2. _____	___	___	___	___
3. _____	___	___	___	___
4. _____	___	___	___	___
5. _____	___	___	___	___

2. On a scale of 1 to 10, how much *effort* (E) did you exert when completing each of the tasks? Think of 1 as the lowest amount of effort that you ever put into an academic task and 10 as the highest amount of effort you put into an academic task. Write a number between 1 and 10 on the E line next to each of the tasks.

3. Go back and look at your list of tasks again. Were any of them *boring* (B)? If so, put a checkmark in the B column. Did you complete the tasks even though they were boring? Why?

_____

_____

_____

_____

_____

_____

4. Go back to your list again. Were any of the tasks *difficult* (D)? If so, put a checkmark in the D column. Did you complete the tasks even though they were difficult? Why?

_____

_____

_____

_____

_____

_____

5. Go back to your list again. Did you have trouble *concentrating* (C) as you completed any of the tasks? If so, put a checkmark in the C column. What may have caused your concentration problems?

_____

_____

_____

_____

6. Now look at the numbers that you wrote down to describe your effort.

   a. Were any of them high (7, 8, 9, or 10)? Which ones?

   _____

   _____

   b. Were any of them low (1, 2, 3, or 4)? Which ones?

   _____

   _____

   c. Were they all the same or did you have some high scores and some low scores?

   _____

   _____

   d. What differences did you find in the amount of effort you expended on the tasks when they were difficult or boring?

   _____

   _____

7. How motivated are you?

_____

_____

_____

_____

_____

_____

8. What do you plan to do to increase your motivation to succeed in college?

_____

_____

_____

_____

WORKSHOP 1-3   **What's Your Learning Style?**

In this workshop, you'll learn more about your learning style—about how you learn best. Complete each of the inventories, answering each question honestly.

Study Preference Inventory

Rank the four responses to each item according to the following scale: 4 = best, 3 = good, 2 = fair, 1 = poor.

1. I learn best when I study

   _____ in the morning.

   _____ in the afternoon.

   _____ in the evening.

   _____ late at night.

2. I learn best when I study

   _____ in complete quiet.

   _____ with soft background noise.

   _____ with moderate levels of noise.

   _____ in a noisy environment.

3. I learn best when I study

   _____ by myself.

   _____ with my regular study partner.

   _____ with a small group.

   _____ in a large group such as a review session or recitation class.

4. When I take exams, I generally

   _____ just guess to get done.

   _____ pick the first answer that looks right.

   _____ read all possible answers before I choose one.

   _____ eliminate incorrect responses before I select the correct answer.

Learning Style Inventory

As you read each of the following statements, put a check mark for *yes* or *no* to indicate the response that describes you best.

		YES	NO
1.	I remember things better if someone tells me about them than if I read about them.	_____	_____
2.	I'd rather read about "tapping" (extracting the sap from) trees than take a field trip and actually tap a tree.	_____	_____
3.	I enjoy watching the news on television more than reading the newspaper.	_____	_____
4.	I'd rather build a model of a volcano than read an article about famous volcanoes.	_____	_____
5.	When I'm having trouble understanding my text chapter, I find that reading it out loud helps improve my comprehension.	_____	_____
6.	If I had to identify specific locations on a map for an exam, I would rather practice by drawing and labeling a map than reciting the locations out loud.	_____	_____
7.	I tend to better understand my professor's lecture when I read the chapter before class.	_____	_____
8.	I would rather take part in a demonstration on how to use a new computer program than read a set of directions on its use.	_____	_____
9.	If someone asked me to make a model for a class project, I would rather have someone explain how to make it than rely on written directions.	_____	_____
10.	If I were preparing for an exam, I'd rather listen to a summary of the chapter than write my own summary.	_____	_____
11.	I would prefer that my professor give me written directions rather than oral directions when I have to do a writing assignment.	_____	_____
12.	I'd rather listen to the professor's lecture before I read the chapter.	_____	_____
13.	If I had to learn to use a new software program, I'd rather read the written directions than have a friend describe how to use it.	_____	_____
14.	If I have trouble understanding how to complete a writing assignment, I prefer to have written directions than have someone explain how to do it.	_____	_____
15.	I like to listen to books on tape more than I like to read books.	_____	_____
16.	When I have to learn spelling or vocabulary lists, I prefer to practice by reciting them out loud rather than writing them over and over again.	_____	_____

17. If I had a choice, I would prefer to watch a video of someone
else doing a chemistry experiment than actually do it myself.

        _____   _____

18. When I have trouble with a math problem, I prefer to work through the
sample problem rather than have someone tell me how to do it.

        _____   _____

Your responses to both the *yes* and *no* columns are important in determining your preferred learning style. Tally your responses using the following scoring key and then use the chart to total your responses.

1. Circle your *yes* and *no* responses as they appear in the boxes below. Not all numbers will be circled.

Auditory	Visual	Kinesthetic
YES:	YES:	YES:
1 3 5 9 10 12 15 16	2 7 11 13 14 17	4 6 8 18
NO:	NO:	NO:
6 7 11 13 14 18	1 3 4 5 8 9 12 15	2 10 16 17

2. Now total your circled *yes* answers and *no* answers in the chart below.

	A (Auditory)	V (Visual)	K (Kinesthetic)
Number of *yes* responses			
Number of *no* responses			
Total points			
Cutoff score	8	8	5

3. Total your score for each column. Your total for all three columns should add up to eighteen.

4. Compare your total to the cutoff score.

5. If your score is equal to or higher than the cutoff score, then you show a preference for that style of learning.

6. The higher your score is, the stronger your preference for that learning style. You may find that you have high scores in two areas; that's okay. You may learn well using more than one learning style.

Myers-Briggs Type Indicator

1. There are many websites devoted to the Myers-Briggs Type Indicator. Some contain information and others feature the tests themselves. Although the original MBTI is unavailable online in a free version, many free forms of the indicator are available in other formats.

 2. Go to the Humanmetrics website: **www.humanmetrics.com/cgi-win/JTypes2.asp** and complete the inventory. This inventory takes a few minutes to complete but is easy and self-scoring.

3. What type are you?

   _____   _____   _____   _____

 4. Go to the Personality Pathways website: **www.personalitypathways.com/type_inventory.html** and complete the inventory. This inventory is extremely quick and self-scoring.

5. What type are you?

   _____   _____   _____   _____

6. Did you get the same results from both indicators? If not, what differences did you notice?

   _____

   _____

   _____

   _____

   _____

7. Go back to the text material and read the descriptions of each of the indicators. What changes do you plan to make in the way you study and participate in class now that you know more about your personality type?

   _____

   _____

   _____

   _____

   _____

8. Using your own paper, write a description of what you found out about yourself as a learner. Discuss also how this information will impact your academic performance. What changes do you plan to make in the way you work in class, complete assignments, or prepare for exams?

WORKSHOP 1-4   **What Would You Do?**

In this workshop, you'll have a chance to consider a case study and make suggestions that Maria could use to improve her chances for college success.

Maria is having a hard time understanding and learning the material for her U.S. History course. She reads her text assignment while lying in bed and then closes the book and goes to sleep. The next morning, however, she is upset because she can't remember anything she read. In class, she sits near the back of the room with her friends and tries to listen to the lecture, but it is so boring that she tends to daydream a lot. Maria crammed for her exam, putting in three hours the night before the test. She tried to reread her textbook, but there were so many chapters on the exam that she knew she couldn't read them all. She looked over her notes a few times and thought about some questions the professor might ask. When Maria took her first exam in the course, she thought she knew most of the answers, but found out the next week that she had failed the exam. She doesn't want to give up, but she doesn't know what she should do. Her strategies worked in high school and she can't figure out why they don't work now.

1. What contributed to Maria's exam failure?

_____

_____

_____

_____

_____

_____

_____

_____

_____

_____

_____

_____

_____

_____

_____

_____

_____

_____

_____

_____

_____

2. What should Maria do differently to be better prepared for her next exam? List at least five suggestions that will help her be more successful on the second exam.

_____

_____

_____

_____

_____

_____

_____

_____

_____

_____

_____

_____

_____

_____

_____

_____

_____

Now think about a class in which you experienced difficulty.

3. What was the situation? What did you do that may have contributed to the problem? What would you do differently now?

_____

_____

_____

_____

_____

_____

_____

_____

_____

_____

_____

_____

_____

_____

Taking Charge of Your Life Workshop

Clarifying Values

Your values should be the signposts along your journey through life, pointing you in a positive direction. In this workshop, you will examine personal values, explore reasons why students cheat, and review examples of cheating in the college classroom. You will also learn tips to help you keep your academic integrity.

Where Are You Now?

Take a few minutes to answer *yes* or *no* to the following questions.

	YES	NO
1. Do you consistently act according to your values system?	___	___
2. Do you believe that outside influences dictate your personal beliefs?	___	___
3. Are there times when it is okay to cheat?	___	___
4. Are you certain about your personal values in regard to cheating?	___	___
5. Do you end or withdraw from discussions that challenge personal viewpoints?	___	___
6. Is it okay to hand in a paper that has already received a grade in a different class?	___	___
7. Is it okay to use another person's words as long as you cite appropriately?	___	___
8. Are your goals to achieve certain grades realistic?	___	___
9. Do you seek academic and personal help as soon as you need it?	___	___
10. Do you know your college's academic integrity policy?	___	___
Total Points		___

Give yourself one point for each *yes* answer you gave to questions 1, 4, 7, 8, 9, and 10 and one point for each *no* answer you gave to questions 2, 3, 5, and 6. Now total your points. A low score indicates that you could benefit from clarifying personal values and becoming more informed about academic integrity. A high score indicates you have a good perspective on your own values and academic integrity.

Your Values Define Who You Are

Each of us possesses a unique set of values—our important beliefs. Some of your values are probably rather clear to you, while you may be more uncertain about some of your other beliefs. Either way, your values define who you are, the decisions you make, the friends that you choose, and much more. Let's take some time to consider some basic information about values.

- **Just where do your values come from?** Your have accumulated your set of beliefs throughout your journey in life up until this point. Some of the influences on your beliefs are probably apparent to you, such as your parents, friends, and religious background. Keep in mind, though, that we are products of the sum of our experiences (for better or worse). You have been influenced more subtly by additional factors, like your hometown, the music you listen to, and more. Despite the power of external influences, your values system is your own. You ultimately choose which values you hold.

- **How will college shape your values?** It is possible that your values are challenged during this time period more than at any other point in your life. Your new environment, new interactions, and exposure to a variety of subjects and opinions will prompt you to do some soul-searching. Regardless of the views you hold, the process of having your values challenged is a positive one. As a result of this process, you will continue to develop your purpose in life—certainly a worthwhile endeavor.

- **Being challenged is a healthy and normal process.** There may be times when you hear an opposing viewpoint and feel offended or angry—particularly when that value in question is important to you. Try to keep an open mind and focus on the merits of being involved in a lively debate. The outcome of being challenged is that you become educated on an opposing viewpoint. As a result, your own value is strengthened—or you may shift your perspective.

- **Is your behavior consistent with your values system?** When students use their values to guide their behavior, they tend to experience a sense of well-being. In contrast, if your behavior is consistently out-of-sync with your values, you are likely to feel conflicted. At these moments, you need to examine the value you hold, how important it is to you, and why you are going against what you believe in. You may find that you regret your actions, or you may find that your value has shifted and you have changed your mind about what you believe.

- **If you shift your values, make sure your new views support your well-being.** Let's look at an example: Joe did not consume alcohol in high school, believing that underage students should not drink and feeling confident and comfortable with his value to remain a non-drinker until age 21. As Joe is experiencing his first few weeks of college, he goes against his value and drinks to the point of intoxication a couple of times. At this point, Joe has a choice: to adapt his behavior to align with his value that underage drinking is wrong or to change his value in regard to drinking to fit his behavior. College students typically experience some shifting in their values system while at college, which can be a healthy process as long as the new value supports overall well-being.

- **Turning down "the noise" of life will help define your values.** Current college students are the most "plugged-in" generation yet—from instant messaging and video games to texting and blogging—little time is left at the end of day for quiet introspection. Obviously, there are positive and negative role models in our society, and breaches of integrity consistently become public. How are you influenced by these instances of cheating in society? Take a break every once in a while to explore how you respond to challenges to your integrity. You might talk with a trusted support person in your life to help you keep on track.

Why Students Cheat

As previously discussed, students are confronted with a multitude of difficult decisions. Therefore, a solid values system is essential as you sort through the various challenges of college life. Your ethics consist of your beliefs about what is right and wrong. What are your own ethics when it comes to cheating in school? Whether you have cheated on academic tasks in the past or not, examining the reasons why students cheat and the risks involved can help you maintain your academic integrity.

- **Cheating is easier for current students than for past generations.** While the Internet has created a wonderful opportunity to seek out resources, it also has increased the means to cheat. Consider first the sheer volume of information available to you and then ponder the existence of Internet papermills, whose businesses rely on selling papers to students. You are expected to resist the temptation to cheat despite being inundated with opportunities to take the easy way out.

- **But what is the harm every once in a while?** Some students feel that there are some cases when it is okay to cheat. Have you heard any of the following? "Everyone in my class does it." "My instructor is so unfair." "There is just too much work to do." "My professor doesn't care." Each of these efforts to legitimize cheating is just an excuse, attempting to shift responsibility away from the individual. We run the risk of being desensitized to the wrongness of cheating as we hear of instances of wrongdoing, both in the classroom and in society.

Just believing that cheating is commonplace can lead to more people doing it. When it comes to cheating in the classroom, students find themselves succumbing to the behavior for additional reasons.

- **The drive to succeed clouds some students' judgment.** Feeling pressure to succeed can lead some students to cheat, fearing that their best just isn't going to be enough to garner desired results. Striving to get into certain majors, attain specific GPAs, or gain entrance into graduate school can feel overwhelming. As a result some students will cheat in an attempt to achieve their goals.

- **Other students may feel overwhelmed as a result of poor planning.** Cheating becomes a "quick fix" for students who don't put enough time and effort into their work. They wait until the last minute to begin writing a paper or studying for a test and then feel overwhelmed by the tremendous amount of work in front of them. For other students, the burden of balancing a myriad of responsibilities becomes too difficult, and they resort to cheating for temporary relief.

- **Others are looking for the easy way out.** These students are looking to the beat the system, refusing to recognize the benefit of putting in the necessary work to complete assignments. "Why do the work when I can just cheat and get good results?" For these students, cheating usually is not isolated to one incident, and they end up being poorly prepared for their desired careers.

What Constitutes Cheating?

In some circumstances, students may not even realize that they are cheating. Policies in higher education are likely to differ from the usually more relaxed rules of high school. Each college and university should have a set of policies regarding academic integrity. The following examples are some broad guidelines on behaviors that could constitute cheating. Check with your university's specific policy.

- **Plagiarism takes on many forms.** Whether paying for and downloading a paper from the Internet or not attributing a source adequately, plagiarism involves submitting someone else's work as your own. Obviously, everyone knows that handing in another person's paper is cheating. The line can seem blurrier for other acts, such as including ideas without citation or using a source too closely without adequate paraphrasing. You should always access feedback from your professor or a writing tutor when uncertain about integrating someone's work into your own.

- **I got a good grade on the paper—why not hand it in for a different class?** Actually, submitting a piece that has received a grade in a different class is a considered a breach of academic integrity policies at most colleges. Again, check out your specific policy and seek the guidance of your professor if you have any questions.

- **Collaborate only when it has been cleared by the professor.** Working together on an assignment seems like a good way to be efficient. However, unless specified as a group project, collaboration on assignments is usually prohibited. Your work should not reflect someone else's—it should be solely your own.

- **Smuggling answers into the classroom for exams is more overt.** It is likely to garner serious consequences. Passing answers to a buddy, copying from a friend's exam, or peeking at answers on your baseball cap or cell phone are all considered cheating. Your professors are probably pretty savvy at picking up on the various techniques for smuggling answers. Also keep in mind that both the student copying answers as well as the student giving answers are likely to be charged.

Keeping Your Academic Integrity

Cheating spans a variety of behaviors, each involving a devious means of obtaining a grade on an exam, paper, homework, speech, and so on without doing the required work. Each of you may reach a point at which you are tempted to cheat. Whether the opportunity just presents itself or you are experiencing a great deal of pressure, doing your best to adhere to the following guidelines can help you maintain your integrity.

- **Stick to or tweak your ethics.** Consider how you truly feel about cheating. Make sure your actions align with your beliefs about what is right and wrong. If you find that your values concerning cheating have eroded as a result of your misperceptions that everyone is doing it or no one cares, it is time for some real introspection. Make sure your values support your well-being and worth and guide you to make positive choices.

- **Know your institution's policies—and the consequences of not adhering to them.** Make sure you are informed in terms of what constitutes cheating, so that you avoid any "accidental" cheating. Consult the academic integrity policy at your school for more specific information. If you can find no other motivator to avoid cheating, consider the consequences, which are likely much more severe than those of your high school. Penalties will vary depending on the nature of the incident and your school's policies, but be aware that you risk expulsion each time you cheat.

- **Be prepared.** The idea is to avoid unnecessary pressure and stress. Manage your academic and personal responsibilities so you are not overwhelmed. Effective time management and a strong work ethic will go a long way in being well-prepared for the challenges of college life and beyond.

- **Be realistic.** Let's face it—college presents a great deal of challenges, both personal and academic. Given the various dynamics (course difficulty, major, credit load, and so on), decide upon a reasonable grade to achieve for each of your classes. Set a goal and work toward it—do not put yourself in a position where you have to live up to impossible expectations.

- **Seek help.** Another strategy to avoid feeling overwhelmed is to seek out the support of others before you reach a crisis point. Your first stop should be your course instructor. He or she is interested in helping you succeed in college and is willing to help you. Apply for a tutor as soon as possible if you anticipate you will have difficulty in a particular class. Talk with a counselor to help develop skills to improve the way you deal with stress in your life.

 RESOURCES

- Check out the *Journal of College and Character*'s website for resources and information about character development in college, including students' reflections on moral conflict. Go to **www.collegevalues.org/articles.cfm**

- Need a comprehensive reference to help you avoid plagiarism? *The Little, Brown Essential Handbook for Writers* by Jane E. Adams is the resource for you.

- Need the quick lowdown on citing sources? The Purdue University Online Writing Lab (OWL) at **owl.english.purdue.edu/** offers concise handouts regarding citation, paraphrasing, and more.

What Do You Do Now?

Clarifying Values Scenario

Joe, a sophomore Business major, is struggling to balance his academics and his social life. He wants to have a career in International Business and has picked up Spanish as a minor because it will help him become more marketable to prospective employers. Joe also is a member of a fraternity and student government. Joe has an eight-page research paper due tomorrow and is considering purchasing a paper online.

1. What are the dynamics contributing to Joe's temptation to cheat?

_____

_____

_____
_____
_____
_____
_____

2. What should he do? What factors should enter into his decision?

_____
_____
_____
_____
_____
_____
_____

3. What would you do? Why?

_____
_____
_____
_____
_____
_____
_____

Now think about an occasion when you were tempted to cheat.

4. What was the situation? What did you decide to do? What entered into your decision? What could you have done differently?

_____
_____
_____
_____
_____
_____

Managing Your Time

CHAPTER 2

In this chapter you will learn more about:

- How to evaluate your time use now
- How to identify time available for study
- How to identify time needed for study
- How to organize your time
- How to schedule your study tasks

? Where Are You Now?

Take a few minutes to answer *yes* or *no* to the following questions.

		YES	NO
1.	Have you estimated how many hours you need to study this semester?	____	____
2.	Do you tend to complete your assignments on time?	____	____
3.	Do you know how long it takes you to read ten pages in each of your textbooks?	____	____
4.	Do you begin working on long-term assignments early in the semester?	____	____
5.	Do you make lists of things to do in your head rather than on paper?	____	____
6.	Do you find that you go out even when you know you should be studying?	____	____
7.	Do you schedule time to study for exams?	____	____
8.	Do you study in a room surrounded by noise?	____	____
9.	Do you know exactly what you are going to work on when you sit down to study?	____	____
10.	Do you do the assignments from your favorite class first?	____	____
	Total Points	____	

Give yourself 1 point for each *yes* answer to all questions except 5, 6, 8, and 10, and 1 point for each *no* answer to questions 5, 6, 8, and 10. Now total up your points. A low score indicates that you need some help in managing your time now. A high score indicates that you are already using many good time-management techniques.

Why Is Time Management Important?

Time management is the way you regulate or schedule your time. You can make much more efficient use of your study time and complete your work in less time by using good time-management strategies. Some students have to juggle classes, full-time jobs, and home responsibilities. Others have part-time jobs and/or are actively involved in sports or campus activities. For most college students, learning to balance their time use is critical to their college success. Although you're in class about 12 to 15 hours a week, you need an additional 30 to 45 hours to complete your work. Many researchers believe that the amount of time you spend working on your assignments (and preparing for exams) has a major impact on your success.

If you don't have enough time to complete your work, you can't be successful in college. The amount of time you spend reading your text assignments can make the difference between whether or not you understand the material or even remember what you read. In the same way, the amount of time you spend working on a paper or solving math (or math-related) problems can affect how well you complete the task. If you spend three hours studying for an exam in history, you probably won't do as well as the student who spends ten hours preparing for the same exam. Of course, just spending time on a task isn't the only factor that affects your success. In Chapter 1, you learned that the strategies you use make a difference in your performance. You may have also discovered that how well you use your time is a factor, too. In this chapter, you'll learn how to monitor your time use now, how to calculate how much time you have available for study, and how much time you need for study. You'll also learn how to organize and schedule your study time. Using good time-management strategies can help you achieve both your academic and personal goals.

Evaluate Your Time Use Now

The first step in good time management is to find out how you use your time now. In Workshop 2-1, you'll have an opportunity to compare your own ideas for how you as a college student should use your time to how you actually do use your time. You may be surprised at where your time is really going. How much time should you spend on academic tasks? Sleeping? On the rest of your life? If you're a full-time student, you should spend about one third of your time on each category. That means that in a week (168 hours), you should spend about 56 hours sleeping, 56 hours in and out of class on academics, and 56 hours on the rest of your life (personal chores and responsibilities, commuting, working, socializing, and relaxing).

Complete a Time Log.   There are many ways that you can monitor your time use, but one of the most effective is to complete a Time Log (see Workshop 2-1). Like a check register helps you keep track of your spending, your Time Log can tell you where your time is going. Pick a typical week during the term and keep track of what you do every hour of the day (a Time Log is included with the workshop). Write in the times that you're sleeping, eating, attending class, working, commuting, watching TV, surfing the net, chatting online, or talking on the phone. Include social activities and any personal chores or responsibilities. Finally, include your study tasks. Don't worry about the five minutes you spent checking your e-mail; track half-hour or longer tasks. At the end of the week, it's important to count the number of hours you spent on each type of activity. Then evaluate your use of time by determining how closely your actual use of time matches with your expectations of how you thought you should or would have used your time. Looking realistically at how you're using your time can help you make some necessary changes to be more successful in college.

Monitor your study time by keeping a Study Log.   You'll also find it helpful to keep track of how much time you spend studying (reading, taking notes, editing lecture notes, doing math and writing assignments, preparing for exams, and so on). One way to do it is to keep a Study Log. Create a chart with the names of each of your classes down the left side and the days of the week across the top. As you work on your assignments, time yourself. Write down how much time (hours or fractions of an hour) you spend on each class each day. You may be surprised to find that you're spending a lot of time on one or two of your classes and very little on the others. If you also realize that you're earning lower grades in the classes in which you're studying less, you may need to make some changes in your time use.

Many students don't realize that they are short-changing some of their classes until they see the numbers on paper. Are you spending enough time studying in all of your classes?

Identify Time Available for Study

A key step in learning to manage your time is to find out how much time you actually have available for study. Some college students think they should do all of their assignments in the evening after dinner, much as they did in high school. Unfortunately in college you don't have enough time to get all of your study tasks done if you work for a few hours every evening. Some students find that they are staying up late at night trying to complete their work. Are you? Instead you need to find out how much time you have available for study.

How much time do you have available for study? One way to identify time available for study is to find out how much of your time is already committed to other activities. The amount of time you have available for study won't be the same as that of your friends or classmates. Some students may have only 20 hours available for study and other students could have seventy or more. The difference depends on how many fixed commitments each student has.

What is a fixed commitment? Fixed commitments are things that you do at the same time every day or every week. All students share some fixed commitments such as sleep, class, meals, and time needed to get ready in the morning. Some students work, participate in sports or exercise programs, are involved in clubs and organizations on campus, have household responsibilities, watch television (specific shows they always watch), check their e-mail, spend time commuting, attend religious services, or spend time socializing; however, they don't all share all of their fixed commitments.

Complete a Fixed Commitment Calendar. To determine how much of your time you have available for study, you need to complete a Fixed Commitment Calendar. In Workshop 2-2, you'll have an opportunity to do just that. Once you fill in all of your fixed commitments, you'll be able to see clearly when you do have time to complete your academic study tasks. You'll probably have some short study blocks (perhaps an hour between classes or an hour before dinner) and some long study blocks in the evening or on weekends. Think of these time blocks as time available for study rather than as free time. If you aren't working or involved in extracurricular activities, you may find that you have more hours available for study than you will need. That doesn't mean you have to study during all of those blocks of time; instead, you'll be able to be more selective about when you want to complete your work. You may notice that you have a lot of time to study some days and very little time on other days. Being able to see at a glance when you have time to study can be very helpful when scheduling your study tasks (see Greg's Fixed Commitment Calendar in Figure 2.1). If you have a full-time job, you'll have less time available for study than someone working only 10 to 15 hours a week. For example, Juanita works during the day and takes classes three evenings a week. As you can see from her Fixed Commitment Calendar (Figure 2.2), most of her available study hours fall during the weekend. As a final step, count the total number of hours you have available for study and list it at the bottom of your calendar.

Figure 2.1 ● Greg's Fixed Commitment Calendar

	Monday	Tuesday	Wednesday	Thursday	Friday	Saturday	Sunday
7:00 A.M.	sleep	sleep	sleep	sleep	sleep	sleep	sleep
8:00 A.M.	shower/dress/eat	shower/dress/eat	shower/dress/eat	shower/dress/eat	shower/dress/eat	sleep	sleep
9:00 A.M.	Algebra class	lift weights	Algebra class	lift weights	Algebra class	sleep	sleep
10:00 A.M.	lift weights	lift weights		lift weights	lift weights	shower/dress	shower/dress
11:00 A.M.	English class	History class	English class	History class	English class	eat	eat
12:00 P.M.		eat		eat		work	watch football
1:00 P.M.	eat		eat		eat	work	watch football
2:00 P.M.	Sociology class		Sociology class		Sociology class	work	watch football
3:00 P.M.						work	watch football
4:00 P.M.	practice	practice	practice	practice	practice	work	watch football
5:00 P.M.	practice	practice	practice	practice	practice		work
6:00 P.M.	eat	eat	eat	eat	eat	eat	work
7:00 P.M.							work
8:00 P.M.					out	out	work
9:00 P.M.					out	out	work
10:00 P.M.					out	out	
11:00 P.M.	TV	TV	TV	TV	out	out	
12:00 A.M.	sleep	sleep	sleep	sleep	out	out	sleep
1:00 A.M.	sleep	sleep	sleep	sleep	out	out	sleep
2:00 A.M.	sleep	sleep	sleep	sleep	sleep	sleep	sleep

Hours Available for Study __34__   Hours Needed for Study __32__

Figure 2.2 ● Juanita's Fixed Commitment Calendar

	Monday	Tuesday	Wednesday	Thursday	Friday	Saturday	Sunday
7:00 A.M.	breakfast/ commute	breakfast/ commute	breakfast/ commute	breakfast/ commute	breakfast/ commute	sleep	sleep
8:00 A.M.	work	work	work	work	work	shower/ dress	shower/ dress
9:00 A.M.	work	work	work	work	work		church
10:00 A.M.	work	work	work	work	work		groceries
11:00 A.M.	work	work	work	work	work		clean
12:00 P.M.	lunch	lunch	lunch	lunch	lunch	lunch	lunch
1:00 P.M.	work	work	work	work	work		
2:00 P.M.	work	work	work	work	work		
3:00 P.M.	work	work	work	work	work		
4:00 P.M.	work	work	work	work	work		
5:00 P.M.	dinner/ commute	dinner/ commute	commute	dinner/ commute	commute		
6:00 P.M.	College Algebra	English Composition	dinner	Study Strategies	dinner	dinner	dinner
7:00 P.M.	College Algebra	English Composition	laundry	Study Strategies	out	out	
8:00 P.M.	College Algebra	English Composition		Study Strategies	out	out	
9:00 P.M.	drive home/ snack	drive home/ snack		drive home/ snack	out	out	
10:00 P.M.					out	out	
11:00 P.M.	sleep	sleep	sleep	sleep	sleep	out	sleep
12:00 A.M.	sleep	sleep	sleep	sleep	sleep	out	sleep
1:00 A.M.	sleep	sleep	sleep	sleep	sleep	out	sleep
2:00 A.M.	sleep	sleep	sleep	sleep	sleep	sleep	sleep

Hours Available for Study __24__   Hours Needed for Study __22__

Identify Time Needed for Study

Knowing how much time you have available for study is important, but you also need to know how much time you need for study. You may have heard that the average student studies 2 hours outside of class for every hour spent in class. According to that formula, a student with fifteen credits should spend 30 hours a week on academic tasks (reading, writing and math assignments, projects, and test preparation). However, it's not quite as simple as that. To get an accurate measure of how much time you need for study, you need to consider your credit load, the difficulty level of your classes, your grade goals, and how much time it takes you as an individual to complete your work.

Consider your credit load. The first indicator of how much time you need for study is your credit load. If you're taking twelve credits, you should begin with a two-to-one study ratio—remember though that this is a minimum and will change when you consider other factors. If you're taking fifteen credits, you'll need more time for study than someone taking only twelve credits. The more classes you take, the more work you'll have to do.

Consider the difficulty level of your classes. You'll need to increase your study ratio (the hours you spend outside of class compared to the hours spent in class) when you're taking difficult courses. Some courses at every school seem to have a reputation for being "killer" classes. If you're enrolled in a "killer" class, you'll need to increase your study ratio to three-to-one (3 hours outside of class for every hour in class) or even four-to-one. Even if you're not taking a killer class, you may be taking a class that is difficult for you. If you aren't good at math (or haven't taken math for ten years), you may find that College Algebra is tough. When you're taking a demanding course, you'll need more time to complete the assignments because you may have to read portions of the chapter several times; you may need to work with a tutor, your professor, or teaching assistant to clarify the material you don't understand; or you may need to spend more time learning the material when you aren't familiar with it.

Consider your grade goals. If you want to earn high grades in your classes (As or Bs), you'll have to put more time into your work. The two-to-one study ratio was the average time that students spent on study. Something conveniently omitted from that statement is that the average grade students earn in college is a C. To achieve high grades, you need to do better than average work. You may need to take notes as you read or predict questions in your text and lecture notes before an exam (see Chapters 3 and 7). You'll need to study 8 to 10 hours for an exam (see the Five-Day Study Plan in Chapter 8) rather than 3 or 4. Many students work together in study groups to excel in college. Others work with tutors or meet with their instructors to ensure their mastery of the material. Did you sit down and just write a rough draft of your last paper or did you brainstorm, outline, draft, revise, and then get a friend or someone in your writing center to review your paper before you turned it in? If you have high grade goals, if you want to do the very best job you can on each assignment, you'll need more time for study.

Consider how much time it takes you to do your work. Not everyone reads, writes papers, works problems, or learns information at the same speed. Time yourself the next time you read each of your textbook chapters. How long did it take you to read ten pages in each of your texts? If you're a slow reader, it's going to take you longer to complete the same reading assignment than other students in your class. In the same way, you may be able to complete a math assignment (because you're good at math) much faster than a classmate who struggles with math. To accurately measure how much time you need for study, you need to have an accurate understanding of how long it takes you to complete your work. Keep track on your Study Log as you do your assignments over the next two weeks. You may need to increase your study ratio again (perhaps from three-to-one to four-to-one) if it takes you a long time to complete the assignments for one of your classes. Let's say you have World History, which involves tons of reading, and you read rather slowly. If you'd be happy earning a C and it's an easy class for you, you may have decided that a two-to-one study ratio would be fine (6 hours a week if it's a 3-credit course). After keeping track of how long it took you to do the reading for a week or two, you may realize that you spent more than 6 hours just reading the text assignments for each week. You then would need to increase your study ratio to three-to-one or even four-to-one if you also had to answer end-of-chapter questions for homework, write a short paper every couple of weeks, and study for exams.

Do you have enough time available for study? After you complete the Time Needed for Study Chart in Workshop 2-2, compare the time you need for study to the time you have available for study. Then count up the hours you used for a week or two from the Study Log you completed. Does the time you think you need for study match the time you're actually spending on your work? Did you leave any tasks undone? Did you do your best on all of your work or did you sometimes only do the minimum just to get the job done? Do you have enough time to complete your work?

Revise your time use when necessary. If you find that you actually require more time than you have, you may need to make some changes in the way you're using your time. Some students think that they can sleep until noon on Tuesdays and Thursdays if they don't have morning classes. You may have listed those hours as fixed commitments or listed similar time blocks as fixed commitments thinking that you had the time to socialize all day Saturday and Sunday or watch television every night from 9 P.M. to 11 P.M. If you need more time for study, you'll have to either reduce your credit load or give up some of your fixed or not-so-fixed commitments. Many students attend college today on a full-time basis and work full-time, too. To have enough time to study and do well in college, they may have to give up television or social time, for example, and drastically reduce their other commitments. With only 168 hours in a week, you have to make some choices if you're going to sleep for 56 hours (and you need 7 to 8 hours of sleep a night to function well); work for 40 hours; attend class and study for another 50 or more hours (15 hours in class and 35 or more hours outside of class); and still find a little time to get ready in the morning, eat, and commute to and from work and school. If you're fortunate and are working ten hours a week or less, you should find that you have enough time to complete your work and still have time for personal tasks and social activities.

Organize Your Study Time

Once you've set up a plan that allows you enough time to complete all of your work, you need to learn to organize your time so that it can be used effectively and efficiently. By learning to organize your study time, you can begin to make better use of your time.

Create an Assignment Calendar. One of the best ways to organize your study time is to make an Assignment Calendar. Just take a blank block calendar and fill in the dates for each of the months of the term or semester. Then refer to each of your syllabi and copy the assignments due onto the calendar (see Figures 2.3a and b).

Figure 2.3a ● Sample Assignment Calendar for September

Month _____ September _____

Sunday	Monday	Tuesday	Wednesday	Thursday	Friday	Saturday
2	3	4 H - Ch 1 SS - Ch 1	5 A - 1.1 & 1.2 E - 1-35 Journal	6 H - Ch 2 SS - Ch 2	7 A - 1.3 & 1.4 E - 38-52 Journal Soc - Ch 1 (2-24)	8
9	10 A - 1.5 & 1.6 E - Experience essay-draft	11 H - Ch 3	12 A - 2.1 & 2.2 Soc - Ch 2 (26-48)	13 SS - Goal statements	14 A - 2.3 & 2.4 E - Experience essay	15
16	17 A - 2.5 & 2.6 E - 53-56 Soc - Ch 3 (52-74)	18 H - Ch 4 SS - Ch 3 To Do lists	19 A - 3.1 & 3.2 E - Observation essay-draft	20 SS - Ch 4 & H.O. Calendars due	21 A - 3.3 & 3.4 E - Observation essay due	22
23	24 A - 3.5 & 3.6 SOC-EXAM 1	25 H - Ch 5 SS - Ch 5 Notes due	26 A - 4.1 & 4.2 Soc - Ch 4 (75-103)	27	28 A - 4.3 & 4.4 E - 65-81	29
30						

A = College Algebra   H = Western Civilization   SS = Study Strategies
E = English Composition   Soc = Sociology

Use either a letter code (for example, H for History and E for English) or a different color pen for each course. You may find that you have a lot of assignments due on some days and very few on other days. Be sure to make quizzes and exams stand out by putting a box or circle around them. After you've completed your calendars, hang them on your bulletin board or refrigerator so that you can see two months at a time (one below the other, not behind it). Look again at the calendars in Figures 2.3a and b. The last week of September (Figure 2.3a) looks pretty easy after the Sociology exam on Monday. If you didn't look ahead to the first week of October (Figure 2.3b), however, you might decide you could take a break for a few days. If you don't get a semester (or term) view (looking ahead for two or three weeks instead of checking your syllabi each night), you won't be able to prepare for the exams in History, Algebra, and Study Strategies, complete the three writing assignments due in English, and stay up to date on your regular reading and math assignments. If you knew that such a tough week was ahead of you, what would you do after the Sociology exam? You could have started on your papers, you might have done some of your reading in advance, and you should have started studying for your exams. By seeing all of your upcoming assignments in one place, you can plan your time use much more effectively.

Prepare a running task list. Another good way to organize your study time is to keep a running list. You may want to do this in a planner, in a notebook, or even on your computer. Each week, look ahead at your Assignment Calendar and jot down the tasks you need to complete for the next two weeks. An easy way to organize

Figure 2.3b ● Sample Assignment Calendar for October

Month _____ *October* _____

Sunday	Monday	Tuesday	Wednesday	Thursday	Friday	Saturday
	1 A - 4.5 & 4.6 E - Exposition essay-draft	2 H - EXAM 1 SS - Text marking due	3 A - EXAM 1 E - Revision Soc - Ch 5 (105-130)	4 H - Ch 6 SS - EXAM 1	5 A - 5.1 & 5.2 E - Exposition essay due	6
7	8 A - 5.3 & 5.4 E - 82-111 Soc - Ch 7 (162-189)	9 H - Ch 7 SS - Ch 9 text notes	10 A - 5.5 & 5.6 E - Revision due	11 SS - Predicted questions	12 A - 6.1 & 6.2	13
14	15 A - 6.3 & 6.4 E - Portfolio due	16 H - Ch 8 SS - Ch 6 & H.O.	17 A - 6.5 & 6.6 Soc - Ch 8 (191-240)	18 SS - Ch 7	19 A - 7.1 & 7.2 E - 112-125	20
21	22 A - 7.3 & 7.4 E - Definition essay-draft SOC - EXAM II	23 H - Ch 9 SS - Ch 10	24 A - 7.5 & 7.6 E - 127-140	25 H - Ch 10 SS - Study plan due	26 A - EXAM II E - Definition essay due Soc - Ch 11 (278-310)	27
28	29 A - 8.1 & 8.2 E - Argument essay due	30 H - EXAM II SS - EXAM II	31 A - 8.3 & 8.4 E - 141-162			

A = College Algebra   H = Western Civilization   SS = Study Strategies
E = English Composition   Soc = Sociology

them is by course name. Have a category for each class and have one for miscellaneous, too. (If you keep track of the personal tasks you need to complete, they won't unexpectedly interrupt your study time.) You can put your study tasks on your list in order of due date or you can add the due date after each task. If your professor gives you an assignment in class that's not listed on the syllabus, just add it to your running list and write it on your calendar so you can see ahead what other tasks may be competing with it for your time. The running task list is great because it allows you to keep track of upcoming study tasks and takes so little time to complete.

Make a daily "To Do" list. Each afternoon or evening, take a look at your running list and make out a "To Do" list for the next day. You can make a "To Do" list on an index card, on notebook paper, in your planner, or make up a template on your computer. To be the most effective, write your study goals at the top of your "To Do" list and write your personal goals at the bottom. You may even want to use those terms as separators on your list. It's also a good idea to set priorities on your "To Do" list. Simply look over the tasks you've listed and number them with 1 being the top priority and a larger number showing a lower priority. You'll probably find that if you break tasks down as you write them on your list, you'll be more motivated to achieve them. After all, would you rather read fifteen pages of History or sixty? Although you may find that you have four fifteen-page History tasks on your list, you'll also find that you can complete the tasks more quickly when they are smaller. Writing very specific study goals—ones that include exactly what you plan to accomplish during each study session—will help you complete your work. Don't just list: *Read history.* Instead write: *Read pages 105 to 120 in history.* You'll know exactly what you want to accomplish and that will motivate you to do your work. It's also important to be realistic about what you can accomplish in one day. If you list much more than you can actually do (in the time you have available for study), you may be disappointed with yourself at the end of the day. You may also begin to do some tasks with minimal effort just to get them done. When you keep track of how long it typically takes you to do your work, you'll have a better idea of what you can accomplish in each of your available study blocks. As you complete the tasks on your "To Do" list, cross them off both your "To Do" list and your running list. It's really easy to stay organized when you have a semester (or term) view of your workload, when you know what you need to accomplish in the next week to ten days, and when you set daily goals for yourself on your "To Do" list.

Set Up Your Study Schedule

To make the best use of your study time, it's important to set up a study schedule. In college, you can't get all of your work done in a few hours at night. You need to make use of all of your available study time—you need to do work during the day and even on weekends. Using your time well is not just about deciding when you should study, but also about deciding what you will do when. Getting in the habit of actually assigning your study tasks to specific time blocks will help you make the most efficient and effective use of your study time. In Workshop 2-3, you'll have an opportunity to try out some new strategies for scheduling study tasks. As you review the strategies that are presented in this section, think about how many you're using now and which others may help you make more effective use of your study time.

Use your daytime study hours. Look at your Fixed Commitment Calendar. How many study hours do you have available if you only count your evening study blocks? You'll probably find that you don't have enough to complete all of your work. You need to use some of your daytime hours. In fact, by starting your assignments early in the day, you'll be able to complete some of your assignments before you settle in for a long evening of study. Setting a goal to complete one or two assignments (or parts of them) before dinner is very motivating. Most students find that once they get started on a task (reading the first ten pages of a chapter, completing half of the math problems, or even planning out or writing a draft of a paper), they are more likely to complete the task. Look back at the Learning Style Inventories you completed in Chapter 1. Did you find that you learn better early in the day? If so, you'll find that you can accomplish more when you study during daytime hours.

Create a good study environment. You'll also find that you can complete more work in less time when you can concentrate on your work. By eliminating or at least reducing your distractions, you'll make better use of your time. You need to evaluate your study environment. Are you constantly interrupted? Do you stop working to check your instant messages or e-mail every time you hear a "beep"? Are you constantly annoyed by the noise that surrounds you? If you answered yes to any of these questions, you may need to find a better place to study. The tips for setting up a good study environment (Figure 2.4) will help you maximize the time you spend studying. Which ones do you use now?

Figure 2.4 ● Tips for Setting Up a Good Study Environment

- **Find a quiet study space.** Find a place to study that is away from the "center" of household activities. It's almost impossible to concentrate if you're surrounded by distractions. A card table in the basement may not look pretty, but the quiet will make up for it. If you can't study at home, try the library or a quiet study room.
- **Study in the library.** The library is a great place to get work done. Find a quiet place away from regular traffic areas. Take only what you plan to do with you so you have to do it.
- **Limit your distractions.** Put your desk against the wall and remove all photos, mementos, and decorations. When you look up from your work, you won't be distracted by reminders of your friends or family or other responsibilities.
- **Use your desk only for studying.** If you use your desk only for studying, you will automatically think about studying when you sit down.
- **Save instant messaging and e-mail for breaks.** Turn off or mute your phone and computer during study time. When you complete your work, check your messages and send your responses.
- **Screen your phone calls.** If you're constantly interrupted by phone calls, let an answering machine or voice mail pick up your calls.

- **Never study lying down in bed.** You'll have trouble concentrating and may get so comfortable that you fall asleep.
- **Turn off the television, stereo, and radio.** If you need some sound to serve as a "white noise" to block out the other noises around you, use soft music. Save that new CD as a reward for completing your work.
- **Do your work when your house is quiet.** Study when family members are asleep or out. Schedule study hours before your children get up and after they go to bed. If you get home from work or school an hour before they do, use that time to do course work.
- **Consider studying at school.** If you can't concentrate at home, you may have to do your work at school, before or after class. You can often find an empty classroom, quiet corner in the library, or study area in the student union. Compare your distractions when studying on campus and at home.
- **Get help when you need it.** Ask a family member or friend to stay with your children when you're trying to study for exams or complete major assignments. If necessary, hire a sitter or a mother's helper to entertain or care for your children.

Use one-hour time blocks. Many students think that they can't really accomplish very much in an hour between two classes. How do you use that time? You can actually accomplish a lot in a 1-hour study block. You can read ten or fifteen pages of a text assignment, get a good start on a math assignment, or complete a short writing assignment. The time after a class is the best time to edit your lecture notes (see Chapter 3) or start your next assignment because you'll have a good memory of the material that was covered. You may also find that it's a great time to do a review before the next class, especially if you're going to have a quiz or exam.

Tackle difficult assignments first. Which do you do first: the assignments that are the easiest or the most difficult? Most students start with their easiest tasks—not the best strategy for making the most effective use of your time. Because you can do the easy assignments even when you're tired, it's better to do the difficult assignments first when you're most alert. Planning to do them first is also a good way to make sure you get them done. Many students who save their most difficult tasks for late in the day don't do them at all. Has that ever happened to you?

Do your favorite assignments as a reward for completing the ones you don't like. Which do you do first: assignments for classes you like or the ones for classes you dislike? Most students tend to do their favorite assignments first. If you do the assignments you like first, you have nothing to look forward to except things you don't want to do. It's actually more motivating to do something you like as a reward for completing a task you don't like. If you only have one or two assignments that you really enjoy completing, break them into chunks so that you can use them to keep you motivated throughout the day. Do one assignment (or part of one) that you don't like and then do part of one of your favorite assignments. Continue alternating one you dislike with one you like as you complete all of your work.

Break tasks down into manageable units. The thought of reading a fifty- or sixty-page chapter is enough to make most students want to do something else instead. If you have long reading assignments, break them into ten- or fifteen-page chunks on your "To Do" list and then schedule them into different time blocks when you set up your study schedule. In fact, start thinking across days and not just across hours when completing your assignments. If you have a Monday/Wednesday/Friday class, you really could start working on the chapter due for Wednesday on Monday. You could read ten pages Monday after class, the next ten Monday evening, ten more pages Tuesday afternoon, another ten Tuesday evening, and the final ten pages Wednesday morning before class. By breaking tasks down and spacing your work across several days, you can complete each of your tasks without becoming bored, losing comprehension, or procrastinating.

Switch subjects when you have long study blocks. When you have a 3- to 4-hour study block, you'll find that you can maintain your motivation and your comprehension by alternating between reading and writing or math assignments. If you find that you're having trouble staying interested in the material or maintaining your concentration, stop after about 50 minutes and take a 10-minute break. Then switch to a different type of task. If you find that you're moving well on a task, you don't have to stop or switch subjects. However, most students find that after an hour, they're only too willing to work on something else for a while.

Schedule time to complete each task. There are a number of ways to schedule your study tasks. You could write the time you plan to do each task next to it on your "To Do" list. You could use a daily planner and write in your assignments as if each were an appointment you had made. You also could make copies of your Fixed Commitment Calendar and actually write each task in one of the study blocks. Scheduling each assignment helps you plan your day and motivates you to complete your work. You'll also find that you'll feel more relaxed because you'll know that you have time to complete your work and know exactly what you need to do and when to do it each day.

Avoid the procrastination trap. Many students procrastinate. Do you? There are many reasons that students procrastinate when they should be completing their assignments. Some students procrastinate because they are overwhelmed by the amount of work they have to complete. With so much to do, they just don't know where to begin and feel that they can't possibly get it all done. Instead they put off their work. Others procrastinate because they don't know how to plan realistically. They overestimate the amount of work they can complete in a 1-hour study block. A number of other reasons students procrastinate are:

- The assignment seems too difficult. (They don't think they can do it.)
- The assignment seems too big. (It's too much work or will take too much time.)

- The assignment seems irrelevant. (It seems like busy work.)
- The assignment seems confusing. (They aren't sure how to do it.)
- The assignment seems unfair. (Perhaps they only have one week to complete a twelve-page research paper.)
- The assignment seems really boring.
- The class is irrelevant. ("It's not my major.")
- They lack motivation. (They don't care.)
- There are "better things" to do instead.

Many of the strategies described in this section will help you reduce your tendency to procrastinate. Learning to schedule your study tasks realistically is a first step in reducing procrastination. Some other strategies that you may find helpful are listed in Figure 2.5. Which ones do you already use? Which do you think may be helpful?

Figure 2.5 ● Strategies to Reduce Procrastination

- **Just get started.** The best way to overcome procrastination is simply to get started—to take action. Do anything. Take out paper and write anything. Work for five to ten minutes. At the end of that time, you can decide whether you want to work for another ten minutes.

- **Set realistic goals.** If you set reasonable expectations for yourself, you're more likely to accomplish your goals and less likely to have negative feelings about your capabilities.

- **Clarify the directions.** Make sure that you know how to do the assignment before you begin. If you're unsure, check with the professor, a tutor, or another classmate.

- **Start with the easiest part of the task.** Do the easiest part of the assignment or only a small part of it. Once you start the assignment, you're likely to continue. Remember, getting started is half the battle.

- **Avoid overscheduling.** Estimate how much time it will take to complete your daily tasks. If you plan only what you can accomplish in the time you have available for study, you won't have a long list of tasks to carry over to the next day.

- **Create "To Do" lists.** Putting your tasks in writing helps you see exactly what you must accomplish and strengthens your commitment to complete your work.

- **Set priorities.** If you complete your most important tasks first, you won't feel as though you have failed or let yourself down.

- **Break down large tasks.** Breaking down large tasks makes them appear less difficult and less time-consuming. It's always easier to get yourself motivated to do a small task.

- **Recognize that not all assignments are easy.** You will have to do some assignments that are difficult or time-consuming. Accepting that in advance will keep you from procrastinating.

- **Recognize that all courses are relevant.** Learning to see the relevance of your courses and assignments also can motivate you to do your work. A college education will help prepare you for a career, but it is also your opportunity to become an educated person (something that will serve you well in *any* career).

- **Use positive self-talk.** Tell yourself that you can complete the task, that you want to do it, and that you can be successful. Don't tell yourself that it's too hard, too big, or that you probably won't do it right. Making excuses for not working on the task leads to procrastination; using positive self-talk helps you get started now.

- **Identify escapist techniques.** You also can help yourself avoid procrastination by identifying your *escapist techniques*—things you do to keep from doing your work.

- **Plan rewards.** Planning to do something you really enjoy after completing the task may help you overcome your tendency to procrastinate.

WORKSHOP 2-1 Consider Your Use of Time

In this workshop, you'll have a chance to consider how college students should use their time and how you think you will use your time. After monitoring your actual time use, you'll be able to compare your predicted time use to your real use of time.

1. As a group, talk about how much time you think students should spend in various activities during a typical week in college. Then record your results in column A of the Consider Your Use of Time chart on the next page. You may add a couple more categories or substitute the names of a few if you need to. Remember that the column should total 168 hours.

2. Next, think about how you as an individual will spend your time. Complete column B individually. What differences did you find between your expected time use and your group's responses?

_____

_____

_____

_____

3. Complete a Time Log (Figure 2.6) for one week. Using the Time Log calendar for this workshop, keep track of your own time use for one week. Write down how you spent each hour of the day. Be as specific as possible. Track your time by hours or half-hours. Draw a diagonal line to split an hour when you use it for several tasks. You don't need to list the 5 minutes you spend checking e-mail, but should record the hour you spend surfing the net. List the names of the classes you attend, the time you spend working, eating, studying (include the study task you complete), commuting, exercising, socializing, and so on.

4. Complete the Time Use Chart (Figure 2.7) to evaluate your time use. Write in the names for the categories across the top of the chart by referring to your Time Log. You need a category for each way you use time. Everyone will share some categories: sleeping, eating, getting ready, attending class, and studying. Some of you will add working, commuting, socializing, Internet, phone, e-mail, and watching TV. If you only do something for 1 hour or so a week (like laundry or cleaning), you can lump them together under a Miscellaneous column. Be sure to limit the total number of hours of miscellaneous, though, to about 10 for the week. If you put too many things in that category, you won't have a clear picture of your actual use of time. Complete the three boxes at the bottom of your chart by totaling your sleep time, your time spent on academics (class, studying, meeting with tutors, teaching assistants, or professors), and on the rest of your life. If you're a full-time student, you should see a balance in your time use.

5. Record your totals for column C, and compare your time estimates to how you actually spent your time.

6. Using your own paper, write a paragraph or two describing what you found after comparing your group's responses to your own expectations for your time use. Include also a comparison of your expectations to your actual time use. What changes do you plan to make in your use of time?

Consider Your Use of Time

	A How many hours **should** students . . .?	**B** How many hours do you think you **will** . . .?	**C** How many hours **did** you . . .?
Sleep			
Attend class			
Study			
Eat			
Get ready			
Commute			
Work			
Watch TV			
Socialize			
Surf the net			
Exercise/work out			
Attend sports practice			
Talk on the phone			
Chat/e-mail/instant message			
Play games			
Total hours (168/week)			

Figure 2.6 ● Time Log

	Monday	Tuesday	Wednesday	Thursday	Friday	Saturday	Sunday
6:00 A.M.							
7:00 A.M.							
8:00 A.M.							
9:00 A.M.							
10:00 A.M.							
11:00 A.M.							
12:00 P.M.							
1:00 P.M.							
2:00 P.M.							
3:00 P.M.							
4:00 P.M.							
5:00 P.M.							

(continued)

Figure 2.6 ● *Continued*

	Monday	Tuesday	Wednesday	Thursday	Friday	Saturday	Sunday
6:00 P.M.							
7:00 P.M.							
8:00 P.M.							
9:00 P.M.							
10:00 P.M.							
11:00 P.M.							
12:00 A.M.							
1:00 A.M.							
2:00 A.M.							
3:00 A.M.							
4:00 A.M.							
5:00 A.M.							

Figure 2.7 ● Time Use Chart

	Sleep	Get ready	Meals	Class	Study							Misc.	Total Hours
Monday													
Tuesday													
Wednesday													
Thursday													
Friday													
Saturday													
Sunday													
Total Hours													

Sleep ☐   Academics ☐   The Rest of My Life ☐

WORKSHOP 2-2 Identify Time Available/Needed for Study

In this workshop, you'll learn how to determine how much time you have available for study and how much time you need for study. In order to schedule your study time effectively, you need to know when you have time available for study.

1. Complete the Fixed Commitment Calendar (Figure 2.8) in this workshop to determine your time available for study. Write in all of your fixed commitments—your regularly scheduled activities.

2. Using a colored highlighter or marker, draw a box around the study blocks you have available. Some will be small 1-hour blocks and others could be longer blocks of 2, 3, or 4 hours.

3. Count the number of hours you have available for study and write that number at the bottom of the calendar.

4. You also need to determine how much time you need for study. Use the Time Needed for Study Chart (Figure 2.9) included with this workshop to calculate that total.

5. List the names of each of your classes and the number of credits for each. If you were using a simple formula to determine the amount of time you need for study, you would multiply the number of credits you have by two or three (the number of hours outside of class you need to study for each hour in class).

6. To get a more accurate total, you should consider your grade goals (you'd need more study time to earn an A than a C), the difficulty level of the course (let's say that 1 represents easy and 5 represents very difficult), and the speed you read, write papers, or do math (it takes longer to read ten pages if you're a slow reader).

7. Fill out the chart listing your grade goals for each class, the difficulty level of the course for you (Physics is a difficult course for many students but not for all), and how quickly or slowly you tend to do the assignments related to the course (use terms like slow, average, or fast, if you like).

8. Then calculate the study ratio for each class (two-to-one, three-to-one, four-to-one, or even five-to-one). Finally, multiply the first number in the study ratio by the number of credits to calculate the number of hours you need to study for each class each week. For example:

   3 credit course with a 2-to-1 study ratio = 6 hrs/wk
   3 credit course with a 3-to-1 study ratio = 9 hrs/wk
   4 credit course with a 3-to-1 study ratio = 12 hrs/wk

Total those to get your time needed for study and write it at the bottom of your Fixed Commitment Calendar. If your time needed for study is lower than your time available for study, you should have enough time to complete your work and achieve your grade goals. However, if the time needed for study is higher than the time available for study, you will need to reconsider some of your fixed commitments.

Figure 2.8 ● Fixed Commitment Calendar

	Monday	Tuesday	Wednesday	Thursday	Friday	Saturday	Sunday
5:00 A.M.							
6:00 A.M.							
7:00 A.M.							
8:00 A.M.							
9:00 A.M.							
10:00 A.M.							
11:00 A.M.							
12:00 P.M.							
1:00 P.M.							
2:00 P.M.							
3:00 P.M.							
4:00 P.M.							
5:00 P.M.							
6:00 P.M.							
7:00 P.M.							
8:00 P.M.							
9:00 P.M.							
10:00 P.M.							
11:00 P.M.							
12:00 A.M.							
1:00 A.M.							
2:00 A.M.							
3:00 A.M.							
4:00 A.M.							

Hours Available for Study _____   Hours Needed for Study _____

Figure 2.9 ● Time Needed for Study Chart

Course Name	Credits	Grade Goal	Difficulty Level	How Slowly or Quickly You Work	Study Ratio	Hours per Week
					Total Hours	

WORKSHOP 2-3 Learn to Schedule Your Study Tasks

In this workshop, you'll learn to use new strategies to schedule your study tasks. Learning how to schedule your study tasks can help you get your assignments done on time, have time to relax and get some sleep, and reduce the stress in your life.

1. Below is a list of the study tasks that Greg needs to complete for his Tuesday and Wednesday classes.

   - Write a comparison/contrast essay for English (final copy due on Friday).
   - Read Chapter 4 (pages 80 to 120) in Sociology.
   - Read the first three articles on reserve in the library for Sociology (each is about ten pages long).
   - Read Chapter 3 (pages 60 to 91) and Chapter 4 (pages 92 to 122) in History. (*Note:* Greg should have completed Chapter 3 for Monday, but is behind in his reading because he hates the class.)
   - Do grammar exercises 3, 4, and 5 in Chapter 5 and study for a quiz in English.
   - Do problems 1 to 50 in Algebra on page 42.

2. Greg is an average reader. He plans to highlight as he reads but does not plan to take notes or do any questions in the margin unless he has extra time available. Greg is good at math but has never done well in English.

3. Greg never timed himself to see how long it would take to complete his reading, math, or English assignments. Because of this, Greg's time frames for completing specific study tasks may be incorrect. How long do you think it will realistically take Greg to do each of the assignments?

4. Refer to the copy of Greg's Study Schedule in Figure 2.10 and discuss it with the other members of your group. It should be fairly obvious that Greg didn't do much planning when he set up this schedule. What mistakes did he make? List them in the chart provided.

5. Using Greg's Revised Study Schedule (Figure 2.11), work with your group to set up a more effective and efficient study schedule for Greg. Consider the errors that you identified earlier as you write in a new study schedule for Greg. Remember that he needs to complete all of these assignments in time for his Wednesday classes (except for the English paper that is due on Friday).

6. What mistakes are you making now in scheduling your study tasks? Make a copy of your Fixed Commitment Calendar to schedule your own study tasks for the remainder of the week. What changes do you plan to make in how you schedule your study tasks now that you've completed this workshop?

_____

_____

_____

Figure 2.10 ● Greg's Study Schedule

	Monday	Tuesday	Wednesday	Thursday	Friday	Saturday	Sunday
7:00 A.M.	sleep	sleep	sleep	sleep	sleep	sleep	sleep
8:00 A.M.	shower/dress/eat	shower/dress/eat	shower/dress/eat	shower/dress/eat	shower/dress/eat	sleep	sleep
9:00 A.M.	Algebra class	lift weights	Algebra class	lift weights	Algebra class	sleep	sleep
10:00 A.M.	lift weights	lift weights	Start English essay	lift weights	lift weights	shower/dress	shower/dress
11:00 A.M.	English class	History class	English class	History class	English class	eat	eat
12:00 P.M.	go to lunch early	eat	Read Sociology articles in lib	eat		work	watch football
1:00 P.M.	eat	Do Algebra HW	eat		eat	work	watch football
2:00 P.M.	Sociology class	Do Algebra HW	Sociology class		Sociology class	work	watch football
3:00 P.M.	take a nap	Do Algebra HW	take a nap			work	watch football
4:00 P.M.	practice	practice	practice	practice	practice	work	watch football
5:00 P.M.	practice	practice	practice	practice	practice		work
6:00 P.M.	eat	eat	eat	eat	eat	eat	work
7:00 P.M.	Read Ch 4 Sociology	Do English grammar exercises					work
8:00 P.M.	Read Ch 4 Sociology	Study for English quiz			out	out	work
9:00 P.M.	Read Ch 3 History	Read Ch 4 History			out	out	work
10:00 P.M.	Read Ch 3 History	Read Ch 4 History			out	out	
11:00 P.M.	TV	TV	TV	TV	out	out	
12:00 A.M.	sleep	sleep	sleep	sleep	out	out	sleep
1:00 A.M.	sleep	sleep	sleep	sleep	out	out	sleep
2:00 A.M.	sleep	sleep	sleep	sleep	sleep	sleep	sleep

Hours Available for Study __34__   Hours Needed for Study __32__

Identify Greg's Scheduling Mistakes

What mistakes did Greg make? You should be able to find at least ten mistakes that Greg made in his study schedule. Identity each one and explain why it was a poor choice for that time slot. The first one is done for you.

Day/Time	Study Task	Explanation of Error
1. M/noon	go to lunch early	Greg really needs all of the time he has available for study. He is already behind in his work.
2.		
3.		
4.		
5.		
6.		
7.		
8.		
9.		
10.		

Figure 2.11 ● Greg's Revised Study Schedule

	Monday	Tuesday	Wednesday	Thursday	Friday	Saturday	Sunday
7:00 A.M.	sleep	sleep	sleep	sleep	sleep	sleep	sleep
8:00 A.M.	shower/dress/eat	shower/dress/eat	shower/dress/eat	shower/dress/eat	shower/dress/eat	sleep	sleep
9:00 A.M.	Algebra class	lift weights	Algebra class	lift weights	Algebra class	sleep	sleep
10:00 A.M.	lift weights	lift weights		lift weights	lift weights	shower/dress	shower/dress
11:00 A.M.	English class	History class	English class	History class	English class	eat	eat
12:00 P.M.		eat		eat		work	watch football
1:00 P.M.	eat		eat		eat	work	watch football
2:00 P.M.	Sociology class		Sociology class		Sociology class	work	watch football
3:00 P.M.						work	watch football
4:00 P.M.	practice	practice	practice	practice	practice	work	watch football
5:00 P.M.	practice	practice	practice	practice	practice		work
6:00 P.M.	eat	eat	eat	eat	eat	eat	work
7:00 P.M.							work
8:00 P.M.					out	out	work
9:00 P.M.					out	out	work
10:00 P.M.					out	out	
11:00 P.M.	TV	TV	TV	TV	out	out	
12:00 A.M.	sleep	sleep	sleep	sleep	out	out	sleep
1:00 A.M.	sleep	sleep	sleep	sleep	out	out	sleep
2:00 A.M.	sleep	sleep	sleep	sleep	sleep	sleep	sleep

Hours Available for Study __34__   Hours Needed for Study __32__

WORKSHOP 2-4   What Would You Do?

In this workshop, you'll have a chance to consider a case study and make suggestions that Lee could use to improve his chances for college success.

Lee is a Biology major taking fifteen credits this term. He hopes to become a physical therapist and knows that he needs to get good grades in college. Lee also wants to have fun and make new friends this year. A week before his first round of tests, Lee made out a study plan to catch up on his reading and prepare for his tests. His "To Do" list for Monday included reading seven chapters in Biology, two in History, and one in English. He also planned to begin to study for his English exam, which is scheduled for Wednesday. Lee went to his room right after lunch and started on his Biology reading. After about an hour, his roommate, Ross, came in and started to complain about one of his classes. Lee and Ross talked for a while about their classes and Lee complained that he had three exams in one week. Ross wanted to play a little basketball and asked Lee to come with him. Lee welcomed the chance to get to know some of the guys and decided that a short game of basketball might be just what he needed. After all, he thought, I can read the English chapter tomorrow and my Bio test isn't until Friday. On Tuesday, Lee wrote another "To Do" list that was even longer than the first. Most of the tasks were ones he didn't do on Monday. On Wednesday, after his English test, Lee wrote a new "To Do" list. This one was shorter. He decided that he didn't have time to read all of his Bio chapters and would instead work on studying his lecture notes. Lee got a D on his first Biology exam. His grade on the English exam was a C and he failed his History exam. When Lee got his exams back, he was shocked by his grades. He decided that he would do better on his next round of exams.

1. How did Lee's pattern of procrastination lead to his low exam grades?

_____

_____

_____

_____

_____

_____

_____

_____

_____

_____

_____

_____

_____

2. What should Lee do differently to be better prepared for his next round of exams? What suggestions would you give Lee to avoid the procrastination problems he is experiencing?

_____

_____

_____

_____

_____

_____

_____

_____

_____

_____

_____

_____

Now think about a time when you procrastinated on a task.

3. What was the situation? What did you do that may have contributed to the problem? What would you do differently now?

_____

_____

_____

_____

_____

_____

_____

_____

_____

_____

_____

_____

_____

Taking Charge of Your Life Workshop

Setting Goals

Goals—anything that you wish to accomplish—can help students be successful, both academically and personally. Goal-setting is a skill that can benefit you throughout your life, helping you to have direction, stay motivated, and fulfill dreams. Is goal-setting currently a part of your life?

? Where Are You Now?

Take a few minutes to answer *yes* or *no* to the following questions.

		YES	NO
1.	Do you consistently set academic goals?	_____	_____
2.	Do you consistently set personal goals?	_____	_____
3.	Do you sometimes allow distractions to interfere with your goals?	_____	_____
4.	Do you know how developing an action plan can help you attain your first job after graduation?	_____	_____
5.	Do you know the correct way to write goal statements?	_____	_____
6.	Do you sometimes set goals that are unrealistic?	_____	_____
7.	Do you often feel overwhelmed when you sit down to study?	_____	_____
8.	Do you feel that other people are setting your goals for you?	_____	_____
9.	Do you have a plan for overcoming any obstacles that might come up as you pursue your goals?	_____	_____
10.	Are you reluctant to ask for help when you need it?	_____	_____
	Total Points	_____	

Give yourself one point for each *yes* answer you gave to questions 1, 2, 4, 5, and 9 and one point for each *no* answer you gave to questions 3, 6, 7, 8, and 10. Now total your points. A low score indicates that you could benefit from learning more about the advantages and steps involved in effective goal-setting. A high score indicates you are aware of the benefits of goal-setting and consistently use the practice in your life.

For some of you, being accepted into college was a goal that you consciously and conscientiously worked toward. For others, coming to college just happened—perhaps it was a foregone conclusion for most of your life that you would pursue a college degree. The goal-setting process can be of great value now that you are in college; it can vary from setting goals that you want to achieve over the course of a given day to developing a detailed plan for establishing a career after graduation.

While sitting down and forming goals may feel more natural for some people, everyone can benefit from taking the time to focus on the things they wish to achieve—as well as on a path for getting there. Research indicates that people who set goals perform at a higher level than those who do not.[1] In fact, students can experience several positive outcomes related to goal-setting.

Goal-Setting Helps You Stay on Track

Think about the student who commutes to school—her goal each morning is to make it to campus on time for her first class. As a result, when she gets in her car, she knows that she will take the necessary roads and make the correct turns to get her into the parking lot. She is focused on making it to class—and if she isn't, she may get sidetracked and end up at a different destination altogether. So it goes with goal-setting in general: You create a map for yourself that provides direction and helps you stay on track and resist distractions.

So What's the Big Deal about Distractions?

You can probably easily answer this question. At any given moment throughout your day, you are faced with a multitude of potential distractions vying for your attention. Your cell phone rings, someone pings you with an IM, a friend down the hall stops by, you get a craving for your favorite ice cream . . . and on and on. Having a set plan of goals you want to accomplish each day can help you stick to the task at hand. In addition, maintaining a clear vision of what you want and need to accomplish in the long term (achieving a certain GPA to enter a major, obtaining a scholarship, and so on) can help strengthen your resolve. Another way to handle distractions is to incorporate rewards into your daily plan. For example, if you can check all the items off your daily "To Do" list (a mini-set of goals), you can go get that favorite ice cream.

Goals Can Help When the Going Gets Tough

Let's face it—keeping a high level of motivation day in and day out at college is rough on any student. Given the set of demands placed on you (combined with the latest illness floating through the residence hall or within your family), you may lose your momentum from time to time. Maintaining goals can help boost and push you through difficult times. Staying motivated is much more difficult for students who do not have a clear idea of what they want to accomplish.

The goal-setting process can assist you in all aspects of your life and need not be limited to academic desires. You can make a plan for almost anything you wish to accomplish. Goals can take the following forms.

---

[1] Locke, E.A. "Toward a theory of task motivation and incentives." *Organizational Behavior and Human Performance, 5*, 135–138, 1970.

Personal Goals

Where do you want to be in your personal life now and in the future? Do you have habits and relationships that contribute to your happiness and well-being? Are you leading the kind of life you desire? Setting personal goals helps you grow and develop and can enhance your enjoyment of life. Whether you want to start exercising or you've always dreamed of going on an African safari, writing down a specific plan will help make your wishes become reality.

Career Goals

Developing a plan to help you reach your desired career is also worth pursuing. Even if you are unsure of a major or job to pursue, developing a set of goals to assist you in career exploration can be very worthwhile. Likewise, if you are confident about your major, you can benefit from developing a plan that could include attaining a certain GPA, finishing general education requirements, finding a great internship, and so on.

Study Goals

Setting goals to accomplish within a study session holds many advantages for college students. The sheer volume of work that you need to complete can feel overwhelming. Having a plan laid out in front of you will keep you organized and on task. What subjects do you need to hit? Be sure to take care of the assignments you perceive as the most boring or difficult first to help ensure you will follow through with all tasks. If you have a reading assignment, think about how many pages you can reasonably expect to complete within the given time frame. Writing out your study goals takes only a couple of minutes but has many advantages.

Use the SMART System for Setting Goals

Hopefully, you've been persuaded to give goal-setting a try. The next step is to learn to develop well-written goals that truly represent your desires. Poorly written goals can pull you off course as you attempt to attain an impossible goal. Different systems exist to aid in the goal-writing process. One of the most basic—and helpful—is SMART, an acronym that stands for the following guidelines.

Specific

A goal statement that is too vague does not provide a clear direction on what exactly is to be accomplished. You will always know where you stand and what you are working toward if your goal is specific enough. For example, much is left up in the air if your goals states, "I will start exercising this week." On the other hand, you give yourself a set of specific instructions if you write the goal, "This week I will walk on the treadmill at 4 miles per hour on Monday, Wednesday, and Friday, from 4:00 P.M. to 4:45 P.M."

Measurable

Goals should also serve as a means to evaluate your progress. Therefore, writing a goal that can be measured is valuable. Consider the second of the two goals stated previously. You are able to measure progress by asking yourself the following questions, which are based upon your goal: Are you walking at 4 miles per hour? Did you exercise each of the days for the allotted time period? Measurable goals allow you to evaluate your performance and make changes as necessary.

Achievable

What can you reasonably expect to attain within the given time frame? If you aspire to a certain cumulative GPA, can you make it happen mathematically this semester? If weight loss is your goal, losing ten pounds in two weeks just in time for Spring Break is not an achievable (or smart) goal. Goals should be moderately challenging—not too simple (which won't benefit you) or too lofty (leading to disappointment). Students who choose goals that are moderately difficult are more likely to maintain the necessary level of motivation to follow through.[2]

Realistic

This is where the reality check needs to occur. Do some honest introspection. If you want to achieve that GPA, you need to take into consideration your course load, class difficulty, your ability, other commitments, and so on. Again, being reasonable in terms of what you can expect to achieve is vital to actual goal attainment. Setting a goal that just is not realistic for you does more harm than good.

Timely

You need to set time parameters within which to work. Giving yourself an end time or date for goal completion helps to keep you on track. Let's say you have a five-page paper to write in your Political Science class. To hand in a quality paper, you need to brainstorm ideas, do your research, write a rough draft, visit a writing tutor, and do your final edit. Setting specific time frames for each of the steps will assist you in accomplishing your goal of writing an "A" paper in a timely fashion.

An Effective Action Plan Will Help You Achieve Your Goals

The SMART system of goal-writing can be a helpful framework to help you get started. When developing your goals you should also make sure that your goal is truly your own—not the desire or dream of someone else. Self-set goals actually produce higher commitment.[3] Furthermore, your years in college should be a time for you to make discoveries about yourself and what you want in life. Try to stay true to your values, passions, and interests, and develop your goals correspondingly. Doing so will lead you down an enjoyable and rewarding path. Unfortunately, writing a solitary goal doesn't ensure that you are going to accomplish it. Through your intentions, effort, and work, you ultimately are responsible for attaining what you desire. While this reality can seem daunting, there are some techniques for developing a comprehensive plan to make your goals happen. An effective action plan will include the following.

Strategies

You should develop a series of strategies that, upon completion, will lead to the fulfillment of your goal. Think about strategies as the "how" in goal-planning. For example, if you wish to attain a certain GPA, list the steps you need to follow in

---

[2] Locke, E.A., and Latham, G.P. *A theory of goal setting and task performance.* (Englewood Cliffs, NJ: Prentice Hall, 1990).

[3] Schunk, D.H. "Self-efficacy and education and instruction." In J. E. Maddux (ed.), *Self-Efficacy, Adaptation, and Adjustment: Theory, Research, and Application* (pp. 281–303). (New York: Plenum Press, 1995).

order to make it happen. What study strategies will you use? What time-management tools will benefit you? Do you need to get a tutor or attend a supplemental instruction session? Writing down strategies makes your plan clear to you and gives up step-by-step instructions to follow.

Obstacles

Because life doesn't always run as smoothly as we plan, you need to anticipate any challenges that might arise. What might interfere with your pursuit of a certain GPA? Your work hours? Distractions from friends? A tendency to take naps during breaks from class? Articulating obstacles helps you anticipate and combat any potential interference to attaining your goal.

Resources

Likewise, list all the factors that exist to support you. Depending on your goal, resources can take the form of people offering moral support or expertise or could be any material item that helps you pursue your goal. Successful students are very adept at seeking out help when needed because they understand that doing so increases the odds of fulfilling their goals.

Finally, when developing an action plan, always keep in mind that your goal doesn't have to be set in stone. If something in your plan is not working, rework your goal so that it fits your current situation. That is the great thing about the goal-writing process: You create your plan to fit your needs and desires in order to create the kind of life you want.

 RESOURCES

- Check out Montgomery College's website at **www.montgomerycollege.edu/Departments/studev/skills.htm** for goal-setting guidance and other college success tips.
- For tips on career-related goal-setting, visit **www.uwec.edu/career/students/explore/plan.htm** for great goal-setting worksheets.

What Do You Do Now?

Setting Goals Scenario

Renee is a first-semester sophomore who has not declared a major. She is anxious to choose a field of study and a career path, but is unsure of how to get started.

1. Write a goal for Renee, given her situation, that meets SMART guidelines.

Goal:

_____

_____

_____

_____

2. Now write three strategies that Renee can use to achieve her goal.

   a. _____

   b. _____

   c. _____

3. List any obstacles that could keep Renee from achieving her goal, and then brainstorm resources she could use to overcome these obstacles.

Obstacles   Resources

_____   _____

_____   _____

_____   _____

_____   _____

_____   _____

4. How can this action plan benefit Renee? Could a similar plan benefit you?

_____

_____

_____

_____

_____

_____

5. Write out one personal goal and one academic goal that you would like to achieve, incorporating the SMART guidelines.

Personal Goal:

_____

_____

_____

_____

_____

Academic Goal:

_____

_____

_____

_____

_____

Taking Lecture Notes

CHAPTER **3**

In this chapter you will learn more about:

- Why you need to take lecture notes
- How to become an active listener
- How to take lecture notes
- How to edit your lecture notes
- How to review your lecture notes

Where Are You Now?

Take a few minutes to answer *yes* or *no* to the following questions.

	YES	NO
1. Do you review and edit your notes within 24 hours after each of your classes?	_____	_____
2. Do you try to write down exactly what your professor says in class?	_____	_____
3. Do you separate the main points from supporting information in your notes?	_____	_____
4. Are you able to read and understand your notes when you study for your exam?	_____	_____
5. Do you sometimes find that your notes don't make sense when you review them before an exam?	_____	_____
6. Do you tend to write down only key words when you take notes?	_____	_____
7. Do you review your notes by reciting them out loud?	_____	_____
8. Do you tend to miss a lot of information when you take notes?	_____	_____
9. Are you actively involved in the lecture?	_____	_____
10. Do you read your textbook assignment before you go to your lecture class?	_____	_____
Total Points	_____	

Give yourself 1 point for each *yes* answer to questions 1, 3, 4, 7, 9, and 10, and 1 point for each *no* answer to questions 2, 5, 6, and 8. Now total up your points. A low score indicates that you need some help in note taking. A high score indicates that you are already using many good note-taking strategies.

What Is Note Taking?

Taking notes during lecture classes is a way to become actively involved in class. You may have already found that the vast majority of college classes involve lecture. The instructor presents information and you, the student, are expected to record it for later review. Some new college students believe that if they sit back and pay careful attention, they will remember all of the information when test time rolls around. As you may have discovered, that doesn't work. So much information is presented in a college lecture that without an accurate and complete record of the information (notes), you won't be able to review it for an exam. As you'll see in Chapter 4, we forget rapidly. This chapter will provide you with strategies for taking notes, editing your notes, and reviewing your notes.

Why You Should Take Notes

Promotes active listening. Taking notes in class promotes active listening by helping you concentrate on the lecture. How many of your classes are lecture classes? If you're like most college students, you probably said most of them. Do you ever find that you have difficulty staying focused on the lecture? Do you daydream and miss what the professor is saying? Do you look out the window, think about other things, get bored, or feel that the class will never end? If you said *yes* to one or more of these questions, you have a problem staying actively involved in the lecture. Taking notes can help you generate a high level of involvement—it can get you actively involved in the learning process. When you're planning to take notes, you have a purpose for listening that helps you focus your attention. Taking notes keeps you involved in class because you're constantly making decisions. You have to decide what's important and what isn't—what to write and what to leave out. Taking notes involves listening to what the professor is saying, determining what's important, recognizing how different points relate to each other, and organizing the information as you write it down.

Provides an accurate record of the information. The most important reason for taking lecture notes is to get an accurate record of the information presented during the lecture. Most exam questions tend to come from lecture. College exams are spaced much further apart than they were in high school. You simply can't remember all of the information by test time. Even if you were to pay complete attention to the lecture, you still couldn't put all of that information into your long-term memory just by listening to it. You need to work on material to store it in memory. You'll learn more about that in the next chapter. Research studies have shown that we forget rapidly. Without rehearsal, you may forget 50 percent of what you hear in only 24 hours and 80 percent in just two weeks.[1] In fact, you may forget 95 percent within one month. You may also have noticed that each of your class lectures is packed with information that you're expected to learn for an exam. Without an accurate and complete set of notes, you won't have access to that information when test time rolls around.

Other benefits of taking notes. When you take lecture notes, you'll also have an opportunity to organize the information in a way that makes sense to you. As you take notes, you can separate the main points and their related details. You can also group all of the details about one topic together, even if the professor occasionally drifts from one point to another. You'll also find that taking notes helps improve your concentration—your ability to focus on the material. Because you have a purpose (writing down the information), you'll be able to stay focused more on the lecture. You'll also get some repetition of the material. Instead of simply sitting back and listening, you'll be listening, thinking about the material, interpreting it (putting the information into your own words as much as possible), and writing it. Of course, as you edit and review your notes, you'll get even more repetition of the material.

---

[1] H. Spitzer, "Studies in Retention," *Journal of Educational Psychology* 30 (1939): 641–656.

Become an Active Listener

What is active listening? If your ears receive sounds or you watch a sign language interpreter or real-time reporter, you will "hear" the lecture; however, you won't be listening if you're thinking about something else. Listening is "an active process that involves receiving, attending to, and assigning meaning to aural [verbal] and visual [non-verbal] stimuli"[2] (material in brackets not in the original definition). Listening involves paying attention to and interpreting what we hear. If you aren't actively engaged in processing the information, you aren't really listening.

Characteristics of active listeners. Active listeners are physically and mentally focused on the lecture. They sit up straight, may lean forward slightly (indicating interest), and make the lecturer the center of their attention. They often sit near the front of the room to avoid distractions, make eye contact with the professor, and ask and answer questions during class. Active listeners also evaluate what they hear and think about how this new information connects with their prior knowledge or with the information in the textbook.

How can you improve your listening skills? As you read through the list of strategies, put a checkmark next to the ones you use now.

- Read the text chapter before the lecture to build background.
- Review your last set of notes so you can connect the information from the last lecture to the current one.
- Decide that you want to listen.
- Focus your attention by physically sitting up and making eye contact with the speaker.
- Focus your attention mentally by eliminating and avoiding distractions.
- Listen with an open mind, setting aside your own biases.
- Listen for main points (topics) and related details and take notes.
- Hold yourself accountable for the material being presented.

How to Take Lecture Notes

Set up your note page. The Cornell System (developed at Cornell University) includes an excellent format for setting up your note page (Figure 3.1). To set up your page, use a ruler to create a wider margin (2 ½ to 3 inches) or purchase a summary margin notebook. If you're taking notes on your laptop, set your tab to create a wider margin. You'll need a wider margin so that you can write recall questions in your notes. At the bottom of each sheet, leave a two-inch margin so that you can write a summary of the important points in your notes. Don't forget to write the topic of each lecture at the top and date each set of notes in the top right corner. Take your notes in the 6-inch space to the right of the margin.

---

[2]A. D. Wolvin and C. G. Coakley, *Listening* 5th ed. (Dubuque, IA: Brown and Benchmark, 1996), p. 69.

Figure 3.1 ● Cornell Note Page

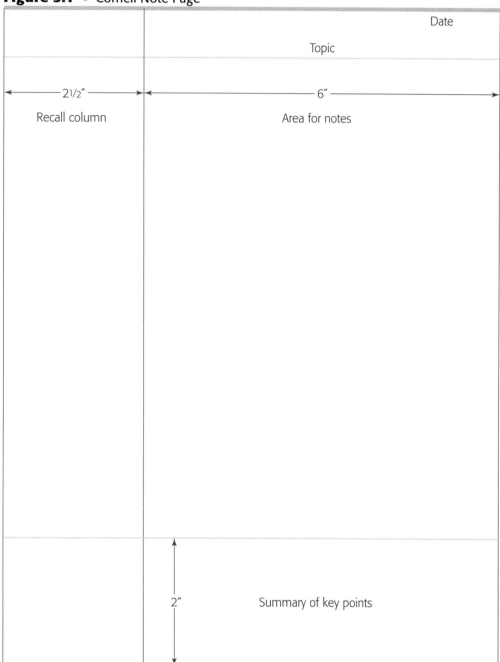

Use an effective note-taking system. You can use a variety of methods to take your notes, but most students find that outline, block, or modified-block notes work well for them.

● *Outline method.* Outlining involves indenting each level of supporting details under the preceding heading, subheading, or detail. You don't need to use letters and numbers in your notes. While you're trying to decide how to label each of the points in your notes, you might miss one of the points that the professor is making. Of course, if your instructor provides you with number or letter cues, use them.

Figure 3.2 ● Bryan's Informal Outline

Starting pts. for an economic system
    All people act selfishly (economically)
    Two Broad Types of Markets
        Product Markets (output) Market Activity
        Selfish
        Factor Market (input)
    Product Market
        Seller → firms (bus organ.) such as corporations
            → Maximize profits
        Consumers → buyers
            – Maximize utility
            – as prices increase, less is bought
    Factor Market
        Sellers – laborers, workers
            – maximize wages, minimize effort
        Buyers – firms (bus organ.)
            – maximize profits
    All markets structural
        Market is competitive
        No single buyer or seller influences outcome
        Great #s of buyers & sellers

Write the heading (the topic) next to the margin and indent about a half-inch on the next line to write down the details. Continue to indent for additional information that relates to the point above it. A sample of Bryan's notes using an informal outline format is shown in Figure 3.2. Be sure to include meaningful phrases as you take notes, though. It's easy when outlining to simply write down keywords. Unfortunately, they won't mean much when you go back to study for your exam.

● *Block method.* Block notes work especially well for classes in which the instructor talks very fast because you'll be able to get the information down very quickly. After writing the heading next to the margin, move to the next line and indent slightly. Now write down all of the details (in meaningful phrases) across the line separating the details by dashes (—) or slashes (/). Figure 3.3 contains a set of notes that Kyle wrote in block form. As you can see, you don't have to take time to think about how to label the details or even where to put them. You simply keep writing. Another advantage of block notes is that they are all grouped closely together under one heading. As you'll see later in the chapter, that makes them easier to review.

● *Modified-block method.* If you like the idea of writing all of the information grouped under one heading without showing various levels of support, you may find that modified-block notes work well for you. Here you write the heading next to the margin, move to the next line and indent slightly and then list each of the details on its own line. An example of Carrie's modified-block notes is shown in Figure 3.4. Some students like the idea of putting a dash or bullet in front of each detail. If you do, be sure to indent the dash (or bullet) about one-half inch from the

Figure 3.3 ● Kyle's Block Notes

Coal

General Info

    Problems w/ coal pollution similar to oil – coal
more widespread – most coal consumed where
produced – created in same way as oil – mined on
surface or underground – surface mines scrape dirt
off to mine coal – underground mines dominant in
PA – surface mining more economical & efficient –
surface mining affects landscape – underground
mines create acid mine drainage – underground
mines labor intensive

Types of coal

    Anthracite is solid coal – good coal – used for
heating – not as commonly used – Bituminous is
used in plants to produce electricity – Lignite –
"brown coal" used to produce energy – but BTU is
very low.

Figure 3.4 ● Carrie's Modified-Block Notes

Learning from Simple Behavioral Changes

Learning

    – a change in behavior resulting from experience

Habituation

    – simplest form of learning
    – no response to a stimulus after repeated exposure
    – ex: bird that is no longer afraid of a scarecrow
    – highly adaptive
    – allows animals to focus on relevant things

Imprinting

    – learning that is irreversible
    – results in strong bond between offspring & mother
    – occurs at specific period in animal's life
    – involves both innate behavior & experience

margin so that the headings still stand out. Modified-block notes are nicely organized and provide you with ample space to generate recall cues in the margin. You'll have an opportunity to practice taking notes in Workshop 3-1.

What to include in your notes. Since you want to get an accurate record of information that was presented in the lecture, you need to write as much down as you possibly can. That doesn't mean that you should try to write down every word the lecturer says—you can't. However, you need to record as much of the information as you can in meaningful phrases. Your fingers may feel sore from typing or you may even leave the lecture room with a sore hand. The following list will give you a good idea of the types of information you should record.

● *Headings.* The headings are the main topics that are presented. Listen for hints that a heading is coming. Your professor may say things like, "The next thing we're going to talk about is . . . ," "Another reason is . . . ," "What about vision?" or "First of all, . . ."

● *Details.* Anything that the lecturer says about the headings can be considered a detail. Details can be facts, reasons, examples, definitions, lists of things, or anything that explains or adds information about the heading. Once you hear the heading, "What about vision?" listen for anything the lecturer says about vision.

● *Discussion points.* You need to take notes during discussion classes, too. The question that the professor asks is the same thing as a heading in a regular lecture. The various comments made by the students and the professor's responses are the details. A good way to differentiate the discussion comments is to put an *S* in front of a student response and a *P* in front of the professor's response.

● *Math or science classes.* You need to take notes in math and science classes, too. Divide your note page with a margin line down the center in classes that focus on problems. Copy the problem on the left side of your note page and then write down everything the professor says about how to solve the problem on the right side. If the professor takes you through various steps to solve a problem, record the comments directly across from each step in the problem. If the problems are long and complex, use the left side of the page (back of the previous page) for the problem and use the right side of the page for the explanation.

● *PowerPoint presentations.* Many instructors use PowerPoint presentations in their lectures. You may even be given a copy of the "slides" with some space for taking notes. Instead of writing on the note spaces on the slides, use them to "set up" your notes. Copy each of the headings from the slide into your notes as your instructor presents it and then record all of the details. One problem with these handouts is that they really don't contain enough space to record all of the information about the topics presented. They do provide you with a nice record of the main points, so put them in your notebook, but take your own notes during the lecture.

Tips for taking better notes. There are many strategies that you can use to take better notes in class. Some tips that may help you are included here.

● *Use a full-size, single-subject notebook.* If you use a small notebook, you may unconsciously write less. You can also use a loose-leaf notebook with separate sections for each course.

● *Use common abbreviations in your notes.* You'll be able to get more information down more quickly if you abbreviate some of the words. Use some of the same short cuts you now use for IM or e-mail.

● *Skip a few lines if you miss information.* You'll have room to fill in the gaps when you edit your notes.

● *Draw a line if you miss a word or two.* Sometimes you miss a key word when recording a definition or explanation. Instead of trying to think of it, which will result in missing even more information, draw a line for each word missed and just keep writing. Ask a classmate or your instructor after class to help you fill in what you missed.

● *Skip a few lines before each new heading.* If your professor later mentions something he or she forgot, you can fill it in under the correct heading.

● *Find a note-taking "buddy."* If you miss a class, you'll know that your note-taking buddy will take great notes and share them with you.

● *Use a recorder with a counter.* Until you learn to take better notes, record the lecture (with the professor's permission), but use a recorder with a counter. Take notes in class using one of the formats described earlier. When you realize that you've missed something in your notes, check the counter number and jot it down in the margin. When you edit your notes, fast forward to that spot to fill in the missing information. If you're an auditory learner, you may want to play the lecture again as you commute to class or do household chores. Remember that using a recorder is only a temporary aid—once you learn to take better notes, leave it at home.

How to Edit Your Notes

Why you should edit your notes. Editing your notes actually helps you become a better note-taker. When you edit, you get feedback on the types of mistakes you make or problems you have when taking notes. If you find that you miss a lot of information, you may hold yourself a bit more accountable during the lecture—you may force yourself to pay closer attention to the lecture. Editing your notes also helps you make your notes more accurate and more complete, giving you a better set of notes to study for exams. In the process of editing, you'll also have an opportunity to review the information in both your notes and your text, helping you reinforce the information and move some of it into long-term memory. Writing recall questions prepares your notes for later review. By making up self-test questions before you even begin to study for an exam, you'll have more time to learn the information. Finally, you'll improve the organization of your notes when you edit, making your notes easier to study. As you'll learn in Chapter 4, when information is well organized, you can learn it and remember it more easily.

How to edit your notes. You need to edit within 24 hours of the lecture, because after that, you simply won't remember enough of the lecture. However, you really should edit your notes as soon as possible after the lecture, certainly the same day. There are four main steps in editing notes.

● *Fill in gaps.* Go through your notes and your text and fill in any missing information. You may need to add headings if you didn't catch them during the lecture or add details that you missed. Only include information that was actually presented in class; don't add material from the text that you know the professor did not discuss. All of the material highlighted in blue was added when Amy edited her notes (Figure 3.5).

● *Check for accuracy.* Go through your notes to look for errors. Many students make mistakes when recording dates, statistics, or other numerical data. You may also find that you confused closely related terms or misunderstood some of the material (especially if you didn't read the chapter before the lecture).

● *Improve organization.* If you have information under the wrong headings, arrows drawn in your notes, or details written in the margin because your professor

Figure 3.5 ● Amy's Revised Geography Notes

	2/21
◐	Canada
What rank (in order of land size) is Canada?	General Information 2nd-largest country in world
When did Canada become self-governed?	Became self-governed in 1901 after French & Indian War
In the 1960s which city became the capital?	Constitution recognized Ottawa as capital in 1960s
? % of population lives on	Population
? % of the land?	60% of population lives on 2.2% of land
How many people occupy Canada?	30.6 million people ex: less than state of Calif (33 million)
What % of pop. lives w/in 185 mi of U.S.?	85% lives w/in 185 mi of U.S.
What bodies of water do	Most of pop. in S. Quebec & Ontario/
◐ *most Canadians*	Middle Manitoba/Saskatchewan, &
live by?	Alberta/S. British Columbia/All along Great Lakes & St. Lawrence River
The province Nunavut was created for what purpose?	1999 – New province – Nunavut/created for Aboriginal Canadians (Eskimos)/called "First Peoples"
	Language

What % of Canadians speak English? French?	English as Mother Tongue/many French 59%
	    speak English/24% French/16% other
	      (primarily Chinese)/1% speak First
	      Peoples

	Land
How much of Canada is permafrost?	$^1/3$ land is permafrost part of inhabited land is permafrost 10%/yr
What type of forest has coniferous trees?	Boreal Forest – coniferous trees
◐	

jumped from topic to topic, you need to rewrite your notes to reorganize the information or cut and paste the information on your computer. Grouping all of the details under the proper headings is crucial for learning the information for an exam.

● *Add recall questions in the margin.* The last step in editing is to add recall words or questions about the material in the margin. Some students prefer to add key words in the margin to cue their memory for the information. If you do, be sure that the key words you choose actually prompt your memory for the important information within your notes. Writing recall questions requires you to target specific information and then recite the important points in your notes as the answers. Write broad questions that force you to think about and explain how the information is connected and specific questions that target the details in your notes. Look again at Amy's edited notes (Figure 3.5). She added recall questions in the margin. Can you locate the answers to each of her questions? You'll learn more about how to write recall questions in Workshop 3-3.

How to Review Your Notes

There are three main ways to review lecture notes, and reading over them is not one. To learn the information in your lecture notes, you should recite from the headings, recite from your recall questions, and talk about the information with others.

Recite from the headings. Put your hand over the details in your notes and use the heading as a cue to prompt your memory for the material. Recite the details related to the heading and then move your hand to check your memory. Continue practicing until you can recite all of the details. Not only do you get practice on the material, but you can monitor your learning at the same time. This review method helps you learn the material in an *integrated* (connected) way. You'll be able to answer essay, short-answer, multiple-choice, matching, and true/false questions.

Recite from the recall questions. Cover your notes with your hand or a piece of paper and recite the answers to each of the questions in your recall column. Then slide the paper down to check to see if you were correct. Continue to practice answering your questions from memory until you know them all. This method of review helps you learn the material in an *isolated* way—you learn specific answers to specific questions. Although you may not be able to answer an essay or short-answer question, you will know the answers to completion, multiple-choice, true/false, and matching questions.

Talk about the information with others. Look down at your notes and then look away and talk about the information with someone else. When you discuss the material in your notes, you generally put the information in your own words. That helps you both better understand it and learn it. If you're in a study group or have a study partner, you'll also be able to get another classmate's perspective on the topic. You may find that you can help each other.

WORKSHOP 3-1 **Practice Taking Lecture Notes**

In this workshop, you'll have a chance to practice taking lecture notes. As you watch the video, "Piaget: Intellectual Development" (available on the Instructor Website), take notes using the note sheet in Figure 3.6 or use your own paper. Then answer the questions below.

1. What was the main topic of the lecture?

_____

_____

2. What were the headings?

_____

_____

_____

_____

3. What signals did the professor use to let you know a new heading was coming?

_____

_____

_____

_____

4. What problems did you have recording the details?

_____

_____

_____

_____

5. What note-taking system did you use?

_____

_____

_____

6. How would evaluate your note-taking skills?

_____

_____

_____

_____

_____

Figure 3.6 ● Note Page

WORKSHOP 3-2 Evaluate and Edit Your Lecture Notes

In this workshop, you'll have a chance to evaluate the notes you took on the Piaget lecture and compare them to those of some of your classmates. Work together as a group to evaluate and edit your notes. Fill in gaps, correct errors, and rewrite the material to improve organization.

1. Compare the headings in your notes to each of the headings in the notes of the other members of your group. Jot down any headings that you missed below.

   _____

   _____

2. Compare the details for the first heading in your notes to the details in the notes of the other group members. Are you missing any details? Write them in the space below.

   _____

   _____

   _____

3. Are all of the details meaningful? Do they make sense? _____

   _____

4. Check the accuracy of the information in your notes with the others in your group. Did you have any incorrect information? List any errors in your notes below.

   _____

   _____

5. How did you organize your notes? What format did you use?

   _____

   _____

6. Check the organization of your notes. Are all of the details grouped properly under the correct heading? Do you need to move any of the information around to make it more organized?_____

   _____

   _____

7. Continue to compare headings and details and work with your group to create a new set of notes using the note sheet in Figure 3.7.

8. Compare your group's edited notes to those of your instructor or to those of the other groups in your class. How did your group's notes compare?

   _____

   _____

Figure 3.7 ● Note Page

WORKSHOP 3-3   Develop Recall Questions

In this workshop, you'll have an opportunity to practice writing recall questions in the margin of your notes. Use the set of notes in Figure 3.8 or use the set developed by your group in Workshops 3-1 and 3-2. Develop a set of questions in your notes, and then practice answering them to review the information.

1. You should be able to write fifteen to twenty questions for the information on this page of notes.

2. Be sure to write small so that you can write more questions. You may need to write two lines in one space on your note paper.

3. Be sure to put your questions directly across from the answer in your notes.

4. Phrase each of your questions so that you have to recite the important information in your notes as the answer.

5. Don't use yes/no or true/false questions because you won't have to prompt your memory for the material in order to answer them.

6. Underline or highlight the answer to each of your questions.

7. After you write your questions, compare them to those of one of your classmates.

    A. Did you and your partner have the same questions? _____

    B. Did you write questions on the same information? _____

    C. Did your partner do a better job phrasing the questions? _____

    D. How many questions did you write for the material? _____

8. Exchange papers with your partner. Have your partner turn your paper over so the material is not visible. Using your partner's questions, quiz your partner on the information. Then have your partner quiz you using your questions.

9. How did you do? _____ How did your partner do? _____

10. How many questions were you able to answer? _____

11. How many times did you have to practice answering the questions until you got them all right? _____

12. Do you think that developing recall questions in the margin of your own course notes will help you learn the information? Why or why not?

    _____

    _____

    _____

Figure 3.8 ● Notes on Piaget Lecture

9/17

Piaget – Intellectual Development

Development of perception

    knowledge of infants limited in 1960s

    believed no visual or hearing ability

    difficult to test

    now know infants do have percep abilities at birth

    prenatally can hear

Vision

    visual acuity poor at birth 20/600

    see at 20 ft what we see 600 ft away

    1 mo   20/150 = someone w glasses

    12 mo   20/20

    abilities improve as does abil to use them

    newborns have a fixed focus – 9″

    same distance as mom to baby's eyes when being fed

    eye muscles weak

    lack coordination = normal

Abilities at birth

    can see

    follow a bright light

    have preferences

    peep board experiment

        exper infant in seat

        2 panels w objects on each

        watch infant's pupils

        see preferred obj in infant's eye

    computer experiment

        now use TV camera connected to computer

WORKSHOP 3-4   What Would You Do?

In this workshop, you'll have a chance to consider a case study and make suggestions that Kellie could use to improve the quality of her lecture notes.

Kellie is a first-year Education major and plans to teach fourth grade when she graduates. When Kellie began to prepare for her first exam in Sociology, she pulled out her notes and began to read through them. She was surprised at how few notes she took for the first two chapters. Her notes were a mess and more of the page was covered in doodles than actual information. Kellie tried to pay attention in class, but the material seemed so boring to her that it was hard to stay focused. She copied everything the instructor wrote on the board and she did try to write down all of the definitions, but some were just too long and she couldn't remember all of the words. She was happy to see that her notes for the most recent chapter made more sense and she could remember the material better. That chapter had more to do with families and she thought some of the material might be useful to her as a teacher.

1. What mistakes did Kellie make when taking notes in class?

2. Why were her more recent notes better and more memorable than those for the first two chapters?

3. What should Kellie do differently in class so that she has a more accurate and complete set of notes to use for her next exam?

_____

_____

_____

_____

_____

_____

_____

_____

_____

_____

_____

_____

_____

Now think about the notes you took in one of your classes.

4. Look back at the notes you took from the first week of the course and compare them to the most recent set of notes you took. Are there any differences in your notes? What are they? Why do you think some of your notes are not as accurate and complete as others? What would you do (or plan to do) differently now?

_____

_____

_____

_____

_____

_____

_____

_____

_____

_____

_____

_____

_____

Taking Charge of Your Life Workshop

Building Relationships

You should be able to rely on the relationships in your life as a source of support. With the various demands of college, you cannot afford to be involved in relationships that drain you. How healthy are your relationships—with parents, friends, a significant other? Think about the positive and negative characteristics you bring to relationships as well as the state of your current relationships as you take the following self-assessment.

? **Where Are You Now?**

Take a few minutes to answer *yes* or *no* to the following questions.

	YES	NO
1. Are your relationships mostly positive and supportive?	_____	_____
2. Do you sometimes withhold your thoughts and opinions in your relationships?	_____	_____
3. Do you repeat mistakes from past relationships?	_____	_____
4. Are you aware of the positive characteristics of relationships, and do your relationships reflect those characteristics?	_____	_____
5. Do you sometimes get involved in relationships that are draining and unsupportive?	_____	_____
6. Do you trust the people with whom you have relationships?	_____	_____
7. Do you believe that healthy relationships require work?	_____	_____
8. Do you have the power to change the other person in a relationship?	_____	_____
9. Is it normal for relationships to change over time?	_____	_____
10. Does your "baggage" interfere with your relationships?	_____	_____
Total Points		_____

Give yourself one point for each *yes* answer you gave to questions 1, 4, 6, 7, and 9 and one point for each *no* answer you gave to questions 2, 3, 5, 8, and 10. Now total your points. A low score indicates that you could benefit from learning more about healthy relationships and integrating those aspects into your life. A high score indicates that your relationships are mostly positive and you understand the components of a healthy relationship.

Are You Relationship-Ready?

In order to develop healthy relationships with others, you need to be aware of your own strengths and weaknesses and what you "bring" to relationships. Your ability to contribute positively to a relationship is closely linked with your sense of self-worth. You may need to spend some time working on yourself so that you can improve your relationships with others. Consider the following tips to help you in that process.

- **Assess your own well-being at this stage in your life.** Do you respect yourself and act accordingly? Are you comfortable with who you are and the decisions you make? Think about your past relationships. Do you bring your own "baggage" to relationships? Are you able to communicate your feelings and opinions? Do you feel secure? There is great value in doing some introspection so that you understand how past relationships have affected you and your thoughts and feelings. Having this understanding will allow you to approach your future relationships in a healthier way.

- **Figure out what you want and what you don't want in a relationship.** So what is it that you have learned from past relationships—the good and the bad? And what is best for you right now? What behaviors are completely unacceptable to you in a friend or a significant other? Are you willing to take a stance—even if that means leaving the relationship—if the behavior continues? Clarifying personal preferences and principles now helps to strengthen your resolve to maintain healthy relationships in the future.

- **Examine your priorities.** It's no secret that college students usually juggle a great deal of responsibilities. Think about what is most important to you right now and what role your relationships should play in supporting your goals. You cannot afford to be involved in relationships that drain and distract you from the task at hand. All students can benefit from asking the question, "Is now a good time for me to be in a relationship?" College life demands a lot of you, and you often may not have the time and energy to devote to some relationships. When it comes to a romantic relationship, you may feel that you do want to be in a committed relationship or you might want to "play the field" (in a positive, healthy way, of course). The point is to do some introspection to get a grasp on how you truly feel—and make decisions accordingly.

Healthy versus Unhealthy Relationships

For better or worse, we all grow up with our own interpretation of the role that we should play in relationships as well as what we can expect from others. Relationships should be uplifting and positive, but the unfortunate reality is that students often find themselves involved in quite the opposite circumstances. Whether you are experiencing conflict with a roommate, clashing with parents, or struggling in a long-distance relationship, the impact can be significant. When a relationship is more a source of tension and stress than of support and joy, you should seriously consider changing your situation. Evaluate the relationship: Is the other person willing to work with you to make improvements, or do you face a lot of resistance? Trying to preserve a relationship that is unhealthy is hard on both people—and can make the situation go from bad to worse.

Sadly, estimates range from 960,000 incidents of violence against a current or former spouse, boyfriend, or girlfriend per year[1] to three million women who are physically abused by their husbands or boyfriends per year.[2] If you are being harmed—emotionally or physically—you need to remove yourself from the relationship as soon as possible. Seek assistance from a support person to help you through the process.

The following guidelines will not only help you build healthy relationships, but also avoid harmful relationships.

Get Down to Basics

We take for granted that relationships should develop naturally. You need to re-member that, for better or worse, each of us grew up observing the relationships of our relatives. You may not have had the opportunity to witness or be a part of a truly positive relationship. The good news is that you are at a stage in life when you are able to choose the people with whom you form relationships as well as your role in those relationships. Keep in mind that the following components are non-negotiable in healthy relationships:

- **Respect.** We may not always agree with loved ones' viewpoints, but we must honor their right to hold and express their ideas. In addition, a solid sense of self-respect facilitates the process of respecting others.

- **Honesty.** At a minimum, you deserve to know the truth and your partner de-serves to hear the truth from you. From mutual honesty stems trust—another essential building block to healthy relationships.

- **Communication.** For some people, articulating needs and desires can be very difficult. However, openly talking through emotions and conflicts that arise can prevent misunderstanding, hurt, and resentment. The more you practice open and honest communication, the easier the process becomes.

- **Support.** Everyone deserves to be in relationships that are positive and healthy. You should help nurture the growth and development of the other person—and he or she should do the same for you. If you are diminished or controlled in any way in a relationship, it is time to move on.

Work on the Basics

Even the healthiest of relationships require work on a consistent basis. Because we are human and are continually changing (and hopefully growing), so too should our relationships be evolving. For example, the relationship you have with a parent is not (and should not be) the same as when you were 15. You can see how problems arise when one person does not allow the relationship to change despite obvious shifts in circumstances. The bottom line is that relationships really are works in progress. No one can expect that "honeymoon phase" of a romantic relationship to last forever, and even the closest of friends can disagree from time to time. If the relationship is worth it to both people, stay committed to working on it.

---

[1] U.S. Department of Justice, *Violence by Intimates: Analysis of Data on Crimes by Current or Former Spouses, Boyfriends, and Girlfriends*, March 1998.
[2] The Commonwealth Fund, *Health Concerns Across a Woman's Lifespan: 1998 Survey of Women's Health*, May 1999.

You Can't Change the Other Person

Too often, we enter into relationships expecting that the other person is going to change—that the bad habit or opposing viewpoint will shift over time or with our influence. Each of us would do well to realize that we do not have the power to change the other person—we can only change our perception. Maybe that bad habit isn't a big deal after all, or it's overshadowed by an array of positive characteristics. On the other hand, maybe that habit contributes to your unhappiness or the unhealthiness of the relationship. Do not expect the other person to change just because you want him or her to—the question then becomes, what are you willing to live with?

Relationships can (and should) be one of the great joys in life and are worth the hard work that is sometimes required. It is up to you to evaluate the status of your current relationships and make wise decisions accordingly. It is also up to you to seek people to share your life who are supportive and positive. Don't settle for situations that do not maximize your happiness and well-being—and remember you have the power to choose and shape your relationships.

 RESOURCES

- University of Chicago's Student Counseling & Resource Service hosts a virtual pamphlet collection on all aspects of relationships—from building healthy ones to coping with breaking up and resolving conflicts. Visit the site at **counseling.uchicago.edu/resources/virtualpamphlets/relationships.shtml**

- Need to do some work on yourself? Check out Pamela B. Brewer's book, *Relationships in Progress: A Pocket Guide to Creating a Healthy Relationship With Yourself and For Yourself* (Twenty-Six By Two Publishing/CLPS Inc, 1997).

What Do You Do Now?

Building Relationships Scenario

Kevin is a sophomore living on campus, and his girlfriend is a first-year student at a university 3 hours away. Lately, the couple has been arguing a lot, mostly over the phone. Kevin feels as though his girlfriend is paranoid and possessive when he talks about hanging out with his friends at school.

1. If you were Kevin, what would you do?

_____

_____

_____

_____

_____

_____

_____

_____

Now think about your own life and the positive and negative qualities you bring to your relationships.

2. List those qualities in the space that follows.

Positive Qualities:

_____

_____

_____

_____

_____

_____

_____

Negative Qualities:

_____

_____

_____

_____

_____

_____

_____

3. List one thing you need to change. How is it interfering in your relationships? What can you do to make sure you make the change?

_____

_____

_____

_____

_____

_____

_____

_____

_____

4. Now evaluate the two most prominent relationships in your life. On a scale of 1 to 10, with 1 being very unhealthy and 10 being very healthy, rate the health status of your relationships.

Relationship with _____   ***Scale from 1 to 10:*** _____

Relationship with _____   ***Scale from 1 to 10:*** _____

5. Describe your relationship with one of the people you listed in question 4. Explain your rationale for assigning the rating you listed in question 4.

_____

_____

_____

_____

_____

_____

_____

_____

_____

_____

_____

_____

_____

_____

_____

_____

_____

_____

_____

_____

_____

_____

_____

6. How do you plan to improve your relationship with the person you described in question 5? List three actions you can take to improve your relationship.

a. _____

_____

_____

b. _____

_____

_____

c. _____

_____

_____

Improving Your Learning and Memory

CHAPTER 4

In this chapter you will learn more about:

- How you learn and remember
- How rehearsal strategies help you learn
- How elaboration strategies help you remember
- How organizational strategies aid learning and memory
- How self-testing strategies monitor learning and memory

? **Where Are You Now?**

Take a few minutes to answer *yes* or *no* to the following questions.

		YES	NO
1.	Do you often know the answer to a question but find that you can't think of it?	_____	_____
2.	Do you organize or group information to help you remember it?	_____	_____
3.	After you study, do you go back and test yourself to monitor your learning?	_____	_____
4.	Do you make up rhymes or words to help you remember some information?	_____	_____
5.	Do you space your practice when reviewing information?	_____	_____
6.	Do you try to memorize all the information that you need to know for an exam?	_____	_____
7.	Do you often find that you get confused by closely related information?	_____	_____
8.	Do you often forget a lot of the information that you studied by the time you take the test?	_____	_____
9.	Do you recall exam answers after you leave the room?	_____	_____
10.	Do you try to learn and remember information just by making up a rhyme, word, or other memory aid?	_____	_____
	Total Points	_____	

Give yourself 1 point for each *yes* answer to questions 2, 3, 4, and 5, and 1 point for each *no* answer to questions 1, 6, 7, 8, 9, and 10. Now total up your points. A low score indicates that you need to improve your memory skills. A high score indicates that you are already using many good memory strategies.

Why Do You Need a Good Memory?

To be successful on college quizzes and exams, you need a good memory. There is so much information to learn for most college exams that just reading over the material won't work. Similarly, you have to learn information to the point that you can explain it or even apply it to new situations; you can't just memorize information for college exams. You may have already found that most college instructors don't use questions on exams that require you to simply recognize the correct answer. Many questions are rephrased so that you have to recall the correct answer from memory and then compare that answer to those listed in multiple-choice and matching tests to find the correct alternative. To answer completion, short-answer, and essay questions, you must be able to recall the information from memory with few if any clues. In this chapter you'll learn how information is both stored in memory and how it is retrieved. You'll also learn a number of strategies that you can use to improve your memory—strategies that help you store information in such a way that you'll be able to find it during an exam.

How You Learn and Remember

How do you know the answers to exam questions? Why do you forget some of the information that you study? Why do you recall the answer to a question 5 minutes after the exam is over that you couldn't answer during the exam? To answer these questions, you need to learn about how memory works.

Learning information. We learn by processing information into *long-term memory* (LTM). To store information in memory, you have to pay attention to it, make it meaningful, and work on it to move it into LTM. Figure 4.1, which was adapted from a model developed by Bourne, Dominowski, Loftus, and Healy,[1] shows the three types of memory (represented as boxes) and the memory processes (represented as arrows).

● *Sensory Registers.* Stimuli constantly bombard our sensory registers, but we are able to be selective about what we want to learn by paying attention to some of the stimuli and ignoring others. To learn anything we must encode it—we must pay attention to it and interpret it in a meaningful way. If you're sitting in class and thinking about something other than what the instructor is saying, you'll never be able to learn and remember the class material. In the same way, if you're reading your textbook at the same time you're holding a conversation with your roommate, you probably won't remember what you read. Even if you do pay attention to (focus on) what you're hearing or reading, you still won't learn it if you don't understand it. Some students assume that if they read the material several times they will be able to remember it. Have you read something in one of your textbooks recently that you simply didn't understand? I remember reading essays for my Philosophy class that made no sense to me. I really didn't understand them until my professor explained them in class. Have you ever had that experience? Did you ever go to a restaurant and see some of the dishes on the menu written in a language you didn't understand? Did you read a poem or story that made no sense to you because it was written about something you'd never heard of? If you can't make something meaningful, you can't learn or remember it.

● *Short-Term Memory.* We work on information in *short-term memory* (STM) to place it into LTM in such a way that it can be retrieved later. To store information so that you can find it for an exam, for example, you need to practice the material,

Figure 4.1 ● Information Processing Model

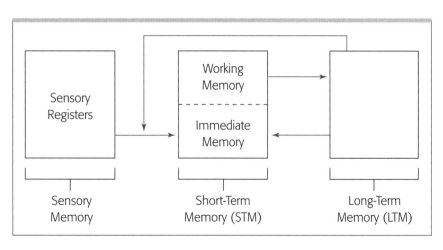

[1] L. E. Bourne, R. L. Dominowski, E. F. Loftus, and A. F. Healy, *Cognitive Processes*, 2nd ed. (Englewood Cliffs, NJ: Prentice Hall, 1986).

organize it, and add cues (hooks or tags to help you find it in memory) to it. Many of the study strategies that you'll learn in this chapter and in the remainder of the text are used to store information in memory. Although it is critical to make information meaningful, just doing that doesn't move it into LTM. You have to work on the material in your STM to move it into LTM. However, you can only hold on to information for about 20 to 30 seconds in STM unless you rehearse it or process it in some way. If you don't work on the material and move it into LTM, you won't remember it. Many students think that reading over the material a few times will get it into memory. As you'll see later in this chapter, that works only for very simple tasks. In college, you have so much material to learn and much of it is very complex. You can't just memorize information anymore; you have to understand it and know how it is connected to the other material you are learning. This requires working on the material in more active ways.

● *Long-Term Memory.* Once material has been processed in working memory, it can be moved into LTM. Long-term memory has an almost unlimited capacity. In fact, the more we learn, the more capacity for learning we seem to have. Building long-term memories seems to provide a structure for adding new memories. One of the reasons for that is that we rely on our LTM to encode new information. You couldn't identify a cloud shaped like an elephant if you didn't already have prior knowledge of an elephant in your LTM. Long-term memory is vast and may be compared to a huge warehouse full of filing cabinets. Information (memories) is placed in specific folders, in specific sections, in specific drawers, in specific file cabinets, in specific sections of the warehouse. Unless the information is organized, labeled, and placed in the correct file, it can easily be lost. By using the strategies presented in the next part of this chapter, you'll be able to store information in a more organized way in your LTM.

Remembering. We remember by retrieving information from LTM. Retrieval involves getting information back out of memory. In order to retrieve information for an exam, you have to find it somewhere in your LTM. Although retrieval often seems to occur instantaneously, it does involve a process of identifying a cue that triggers your memory and opens the correct file, in the correct drawer, in the correct filing cabinet in your memory. To retrieve an answer for an exam question, you often are able to use a cue found in the question. For example, if you had a question about which of the three types of memory involved working on information to store it, you could use the word "working" as your cue. You just read that we work on information to store it in LTM in the working memory. You may recall that working memory is part of STM. However, that doesn't always work. You may find that the cue you used to store the information in LTM is not in the question or even in any of the answers of a multiple-choice question. If the material isn't carefully classified, labeled, and placed in the correct file with multiple cues, it can be easily lost or require more time and effort to retrieve. According to Kenneth Higbee, "remembering is hard work, and memory techniques do not necessarily make it easy, they just make it more effective."[2]

Forgetting. To be successful in college you need to use active learning strategies that help you store information and retrieve it. Once you learn something, it remains in your LTM almost indefinitely. However, we all forget things. Why do you remember some information but forget other information? Why can you remember

[2]Kenneth L. Higbee, *Your Memory: How It Works and How to Improve It* (New York, Marlowe & Company, 1996), p. 5.

the answer to a question when you practice it, but have difficulty remembering it during the exam? There are a number of memory problems that lead to forgetting.

● *Never really learned it.* As you read earlier, many students think that reading over material a few times will ensure their memory of it for the exam. However, just reading over information doesn't guarantee that you will get information into LTM. In fact, just reading over information isn't very effective in storing information at all.

● *Cramming.* When you cram for a test, you try to learn all of the information during one long study session. This often leads to practicing the information only one or two times. Although you may move some of the information into memory, you probably won't have time to store it in an organized way. You may find that during the exam, you remember having studied the information but can't locate it in LTM within the time constraints of the exam.

● *Not understanding the information.* Even if you practice information seven or eight times, you can't learn it if you don't really understand it. You may have some visual memory of some of the information and would be able to recognize it on the exam if the professor worded the answer exactly as it appeared in your text or notes, but you won't be able to identify the answer if it's phrased differently.

● *Stored with too few cues.* Another problem that leads to forgetting is storing information with too few cues. If you don't use a variety of strategies when studying, you may only store the information with one or two cues. If the professor doesn't include the exact cue (key word or phrase) in his or her question or answer, you may not be able to locate the information in your LTM. Although you stored it, you won't be able to find it.

● *Interference.* Studying closely related information often leads to interference. You reach into your LTM storehouse and pull out one piece of information instead of the other. In order to reduce interference, you need to clearly separate closely related information. You can do that by creating separate cues and self-testing to be sure that you know the difference between the two similar terms or concepts.

Using active strategies can improve your memory. If you use a variety of active study strategies, you'll be able to store and remember information more effectively. In the next section of this chapter, you'll be introduced to *rehearsal, elaboration, organizational,* and *self-testing* strategies. In future chapters, you'll learn more about using these strategies, but for now, you'll see how each of these types of strategies can help you learn and remember more of your course material.

Use Rehearsal Strategies to Store Information

What are rehearsal strategies? Rehearsal strategies involve repetition of the information you want to learn. Have you ever participated in a recital? Have you performed in a concert or play or been on a sports team? You probably had to learn a new song to play or sing, a new part for a play, or even a new play for a game. Think about how many times you practiced the musical piece, the lines for your part, or the new play. Did you only practice once? Did you practice ten or more times? Did you find that the more you practiced the more effectively you could perform? Many students don't realize that a quiz or an exam is a recital, too. You can't practice the material only one or two times and expect to be able to perform well on the exam. All learning strategies involve rehearsal of some type, but there are two different types of rehearsal strategies.

● *Low-level rehearsal strategies.* Reading over material a few times, saying it over and over again, or even copying it or writing it several times are examples of low-level rehearsal strategies. They work well for very simple tasks, such as recalling a short list of things. However, they don't work well for college-level learning because you don't change the material in any way to rehearse it. You simply are memorizing the information in the same form that it originally appeared.

● *High-level rehearsal strategies.* High-level rehearsal strategies incorporate many of the elaboration, organizational, and self-testing strategies that you'll learn about in the remainder of this chapter and throughout this text. High-level rehearsal strategies make you work on the material to store it—you must change the material in some way or create and practice cues that are outside of the material. Many of the active learning strategies that you read about in Chapter 1 involve high-level rehearsal. Taking notes, generating questions, making maps and charts, and preparing study sheets are a few of the high-level rehearsal strategies that you may already be using.

Why do they work? Each time you practice the material, you make the memory of it stronger because you continue to put the information into the same file in your LTM. All of these strategies help you learn information and store it in LTM in an organized way—in a way that will help you find it again during an exam. In most cases, as you'll see, you also either add additional cues to the material or practice using those cues to retrieve the material from LTM. In a recent study, students who used the high-level rehearsal strategies learned and remembered the information better than those students who used the low-level rehearsal strategies. Those who generated questions or took notes outperformed students who simply read or copied the material on the same test.[3]

Use Elaboration Strategies to Build Cues for Retrieval

What are elaboration strategies? Elaboration strategies involve forming connections and expanding on the material. Many of the high-level rehearsal strategies that you just read about involve elaboration. Writing questions in the margin, taking notes, making study sheets, and even explaining the material out loud are all examples of elaboration strategies that help you form more cues. Another form of elaboration involves creating mnemonics (memory aids) to help you retrieve information that is stored in LTM. You'll learn some strategies for using mnemonics in this chapter and will have many opportunities to practice the other elaboration strategies in later chapters in this text.

Types of elaboration strategies. There are many strategies that involve elaborating on the material, but some of the more commonly used strategies are briefly described below. Many of these strategies are familiar to you already and others will be described in more detail in later chapters.

● *Writing questions in the margin.* When you write questions in the margin of your text or notes, you're adding additional cues (the key words in the question) to the material to be learned. The questions provide you with cues to trigger your memory for the information. During an exam, you may find the same cue in the question or in one of the possible answers. Cues help you open the correct file in your LTM

---

[3]D. Van Blerkom, M. Van Blerkom, and S. Bertsch, "Study Strategies and the Generation Effect," *Journal of College Reading and Learning* 37 (1) (2006): 7–18.

storehouse and allow you to access the information you need to answer the question. In Chapter 3, you had an opportunity to practice writing questions in the margin of a set of lecture notes and then to use those questions to prompt your memory. Did you find that the questions worked well in triggering your memory for the correct answers? In Chapter 6, you'll have a chance to practice writing questions in the margin of your text.

● *Taking notes.* When you take notes or explain the material out loud, you're putting the information into your own words, adding additional cues, and/or creating connections that were not originally there. You'll discover in Chapter 7 that note taking also allows you to show how information presented in one section of the text is related to material presented later in the same chapter or in other chapters. Similarly, you can show how information from the text is connected to information presented in lecture. You can also elaborate on text and lecture material by adding your own examples for some of the information that is presented. Finally, note taking is a powerful elaboration strategy because you can also make connections between the new information that you want to learn and your own prior knowledge of the subject. By connecting the new material to old, already-learned material, you make it easier to learn and remember.

● *Making study sheets.* You'll learn how to make study sheets in Chapter 8. Study sheets provide you with layers of cues to aid your memory and retrieval of the information. Study sheets are one-page compilations of all of the important information on one specific topic. Because each study sheet has its own topic, you need only recall the topic of the study sheet that you made to recall the main points or headings on it; they then serve as cues to help you remember the details.

● *Using mnemonic devices.* Mnemonic devices or memory aids help you build cues to increase your ability to recall information that is already stored in LTM. They serve as cues for retrieval. You have probably created visual images, rhymes, or even songs to help you recall material you had to learn. There are many types of mnemonic devices that can help you recall information, but two of the most useful are *acronyms* and *acrostics*.

Acronyms. Acronyms are words made up of the first letters of other words. They can be real words such as HOMES (standing for the five Great Lakes) and ROSE (standing for the four types of learning and memory strategies described in this chapter) or nonsense words such as PAIM (standing for the four kinds of fossils: Petrified, Actual Remains, Imprint, or Molds and Casts). Acronyms can help you remember lists of things that you studied. Look at the examples of acronyms that Kwan, Heather, and Cheri created to remember information for their exams (Figure 4.2). Use the following five steps to create and practice your own acronyms. You'll have an opportunity to practice these steps in Workshops 4-2 and 4-3.

Five Steps to Creating Acronyms

1. List the information you need to learn in meaningful phrases.
2. Circle or underline a keyword in each meaningful phrase.
3. Write down the first letter of each keyword.
4. Rearrange the letters to form a memorable acronym.
5. Practice the association from the acronym to the keyword and then from the keyword to the meaningful phrase.

Figure 4.2 ● Student Examples of Acronyms

Swinburne's and Aquinas's Views

Swinburne—SWOMP		Aquinas—ICON	
S	simultaneously	I	immutable
W	within time	C	continuum
O	own actions	O	omniscient
M	mutable	N	not in time
P	personable		

Kwan's Acronyms

FASCISM

1. Authoritarian governments
2. Masses are incapable of governing themselves (democratically)
3. State terrorism is used
4. Hierarchically structured organic society
5. Elites govern

A M S H E = SHAME

Heather's Acronym

Four Stages of Food Processing

1. Ingestion—eating
2. Digestion—breaking down food
3. Absorption—cells absorb nutrients
4. Elimination—undigested wastes removed

I D A E = IDEA (extra association: Eating is a good IDEA)

Cheri's Acronym

Acrostics. Acrostics are phrases or sentences that are made up of words beginning with the first letters of other words. "Every Good Boy Does Fine" is an acrostic commonly used to remember the names of the lines in music class. Acrostics can be funny, outrageous, or personal (related to your own life). In any case, because you need to use acrostics to recall the information you want to remember, you need to make them memorable, too. Acrostics provide you with cues to recall the information that you learned for your exam. They can be short or long so they work for simple or more complex information. Many students find that they are very helpful for recalling main and/or supporting points for essay answers. You create acrostics in the same way as acronyms; the only difference is that you don't rearrange the letters and you change the first letter of each of the keywords into other words in a phrase or sentence. Take a look at the examples of acrostics that Terri and Todd created to remember information for their exams (Figure 4.3). You'll have an opportunity to practice creating and using acrostics in Workshops 4-2 and 4-3.

Figure 4.3 ● Student
Examples of Acrostics

Four Classes of Heterotrophic Organisms

Carnivores—animal eaters

Herbivores—plant eaters

Omnivores—animal and plant eaters

Decomposers—eat decaying organisms

"Can Henry Omit Dents"

Terri's Acrostic

Five Building Blocks of Structure

1. Job design
2. Departmentalization
3. Coordinating mechanisms
4. Span of management
5. Delegation

"Jeff is depressed about coming to see David"

Todd's Acrostic

Why do they work? When you use elaboration strategies, you make connections between the new material that you are trying to learn and old (previously learned) material that you already have stored in your LTM. By connecting the new material to previously learned material, you provide yourself with a ready-made filing system for storing and locating the new material. Elaboration strategies such as mnemonics can also help you retrieve information from your LTM. According to Kenneth Higbee, "A mnemonic system may help you in at least three ways when you are trying to find items in your memory: (1) It will give you a place to start your search, a way to locate the first item. (2) It will give you a way of proceeding systematically from one item to the next. (3) It will let you know when your recall is finished, when you have reached the last item."[4]

Use Organizational Strategies to Aid Learning and Memory

What are organizational strategies? Organizational strategies help you organize or restructure information to show how it's related. Listing or grouping information is effective for simple tasks, but you need to use high-level organizational strategies like taking notes, mapping, charting, or making study sheets to learn other material for your exams. Organizational strategies help you see how the information is connected. The more organized information is when we put it into LTM, the easier it is to get it back out.

Types of organizational strategies. There are many ways to organize text and lecture material. You can take notes in written, mapping, or charting formats. In Chapter 3, you learned about restructuring lecture information when editing

---

[4]K. Higbee, *Your Memory: How It Works and How to Improve It* (Englewood Cliffs, NJ: Prentice Hall, 1977), p. 78.

your notes. You'll learn more about taking notes to organize text information in Chapter 7. Note taking helps you see how main points and supporting details are related and charting allows you to see similarities and differences among things to be learned. In Chapter 8, you'll learn how to create study sheets to both elaborate on and organize the information from both text and lecture on individual topics. The workshops in Chapters 7 and 8 provide you with opportunities to practice organizing information to make it more memorable.

Why do they work? Organizational strategies are effective for helping students learn and remember information for several reasons. First, the more organized information is, the easier it is to learn and remember. Have you ever tried to learn a set of lecture notes that contained information in a jumbled form? For example, it would be much more difficult to learn the details about ancient Greece and ancient Rome if the information was scrambled together than if it was separated into two columns or two sections in your notes. When you organize information, you can pull together bits and pieces of material that may be scattered throughout a chapter or in your notes so that all of the material related to one topic is together. Second, in the process of organizing information, as you'll see in Chapter 7, you create more cues in the form of headings, subheadings, and related details. In the case of maps and charts especially, you also create location cues and color cues. Learning information with multiple cues helps you locate the information more easily in LTM. By using organizational strategies to learn information, you actually create new ways of remembering it.

Use Self-Testing Strategies to Monitor Learning and Memory

What are self-testing strategies? Self-testing strategies allow you to keep tabs on your learning. When you quiz yourself on the material, you can find out what you do know and what you still don't know. There are many types of self-tests. You can recite the answers to questions that you write in the margin of your text and lecture notes. You can recite or write the definitions to the technical terminology or other identifying terms you need to know. You can cover the details in your notes and recite them using only the heading as a cue. You can take end-of-chapter tests, online tests, or answer sample questions provided by the professor. Some students who work in groups discuss the material and then ask each other questions on the information. Finally, you can actually write your own exam questions using the same format (multiple-choice, true/false, and so on) as the questions you'll have on the test.

Why do they work? When you quiz yourself on the material, you're actually practicing retrieval. Instead of simply practicing the material to store it in LTM, self-testing allows you to practice using a variety of cues to retrieve the information from memory. What do you really have to do on a test? Do you have to learn information? No, you have to retrieve it. Many students don't realize that by self-testing they are replicating what they will have to do on the exam itself. Self-testing strategies help you monitor three things:

- Do you know the answer to the question?
- Do the cues that you developed work—do they help you find the answer to the question?
- Do the study strategies that you used work—did you get the information into LTM?

WORKSHOP 4-1 Evaluate Your Memory Strategies

In this workshop, you'll have a chance to evaluate your memory strategies. Write the names of the fifty states in the space below, putting the first one you recall in the box marked number 1 and the next in the box marked number 2 and so on. Write as many as you can recall in 2 minutes. Feel free to use abbreviations. Then answer the questions below.

1. Alambama	11. Indiana	21. Vermont	31. Maryland	41.
2. Alaska	12. Iowa	22. NH	32. Wisconin	42.
3. Arizona	13. Illinois	23. North Carolina	33. Nevada	43.
4. Arkansas	14. Missippi	24. South Carolina	34.	44.
5. California	15. Massach	25. Oregon	35.	45.
6. colorado	16. Missouri	26. North Dakota	36.	46.
7. Delaware	17. Michigan	27. South Dakota	37.	47.
8. Florida	18. Maine	28. Wyoming	38.	48.
9. Georgia	19. conneticut	29. Oklahoma	39.	49.
10. Hawaii	20. Rhode Island	30. Texas	40.	50.

1. What were the first six states that you wrote?

1. Alabama   2. Alaska   3. Arizona
4. Arkansas   5. California   6. Colorado

2. What memory strategies did you use to recall them? Check all that apply.

- ☐ List states geographically
- ☑ List states in alphabetical order
- ☑ List your state and surrounding states
- ☐ Other _____
- ☑ List states you have visited
- ☐ List states of your relatives
- ☐ Other _____
- ☐ Other _____

3. What were the last six states that you wrote?

1. _____   2. _____   3. _____

4. _____   5. _____   6. _____

4. What memory strategies did you use to recall those states?

_____

_____

_____

_____

_____

_____

5. How did you learn the fifty states?

_____

_____

_____

_____

_____

_____

6. Did you use the same strategies to recall them as you did to learn them? If not, why not?

_____

_____

_____

_____

_____

_____

7. What strategies do you use now to learn and recall course information?

_____

_____

_____

_____

_____

_____

_____

_____

_____

WORKSHOP 4-2 Practice Memory Strategies

In this workshop, you'll have a chance to practice using acronyms and acrostics to aid your memory of text information.

1. Look at the list of strategies for improving your listening skills that you read about in Chapter 3. Each strategy has been shortened to a meaningful phrase. Compare each one to the actual strategy listed in Chapter 3.

   1. Read the chapter before the lecture.   Red
   2. Review your last set of notes.   Roses
   3. Decide that you want to listen.   Drew
   4. Focus your attention physically.   People
   5. Focus your attention mentally.   Loving
   6. Listen with an open mind.   Monkeys
   7. Take notes.   Not
   8. Hold yourself accountable.   Antelope

2. Circle or underline the following key words in each of the meaningful phrases: chapter, review, decide, physically, mentally, open mind, notes, and accountable.

3. Write the first letter of each key word or phrase next to it in the right margin.

4. Rearrange the letters to form an acronym. Create a second one if you wish.

   _____

   _____

   _____

   _____

5. Use each of the first letters to form an acrostic. Pretend that your instructor told you that you needed to know the information in order.

   _____

   _____

   _____

6. Practice the connection of the acronym (or acrostic) back to the key words and then practice connecting the key words to each meaningful phrase. How many times did you practice?

   _____

   _____

   _____

7. Write the acronym that you developed in the space below without looking back at your paper.

   _____

8. Now use the acronym to try to recall the eight strategies. Without looking back, list as many as you can in the space below.

   1. _____
   2. _____
   3. _____
   4. _____
   5. _____
   6. _____
   7. _____
   8. _____

9. How many did you get right? _____

   _____

10. Check the list and write down the ones you missed in the space below.

    _____

    _____

    _____

    _____

11. How many times did you practice before trying to write the list? _____

    _____

12. What would you do differently the next time you needed to use an acronym or acrostic to help you learn and remember course information?

    _____

    _____

    _____

    _____

    _____

    _____

    _____

    _____

WORKSHOP 4-3   Develop Mnemonics to Aid Recall

In this workshop, you'll have an opportunity to practice creating acronyms and acrostics to help you remember course information. You may also find that you create other memory aids (associations, visual images, or even rhymes) to recall the material at the same time. Circle or underline key words and then write the first letters in the margin.

1. Create mnemonics to help you recall the five causes of wasted time.

Inability to set or stick to priorities   *People*

Inability to say no   *Never*

Inability to delegate responsibility   *Drive*

Inability to throw things away   *Two*

Inability to accept anything less than perfection[5]   *Automobiles*

ACRONYM:

_____

ACROSTIC:

_____

_____

_____

2. Create mnemonics to help you recall the seven characteristics of nonverbal communication.

Nonverbal communication is symbolic

Nonverbal communication is rule guided

Nonverbal communication may be intentional or unintentional

Nonverbal communication reflects culture

Nonverbal communication is perceived to be more believable

Nonverbal communication is multichanneled

Nonverbal communication is continuous[6]

ACRONYM:

_____

ACROSTIC:

_____

_____

_____

[5]Wayne Weiten and Margaret Lloyd, *Psychology Applied to Modern Life*, 7th ed. (Belmont, CA: Wadsworth, 2003), pp. 108–109.

[6]Julia T. Wood, *Interpersonal Communication*, 4th ed. (Belmont, CA: Wadsworth, 2004), pp. 130–131.

3. Create mnemonics to recall the seven factors that determine the effects of oil on ocean ecosystems.

     Type of oil   T

     Amount of oil released   A

     Distance of release from the shore   D

     Time of year   T

     Weather conditions   W

     Average water temperature   T

     Ocean currents[7]   O

ACRONYM:

_____

ACROSTIC:

_____

_____

_____

4. Make a list of the information you need to learn for one of your classes. Then create an acronym and acrostic.

_____

_____

_____

_____

_____

_____

_____

_____

_____

_____

_____

ACRONYM:

_____

ACROSTIC:

_____

_____

_____

[7]G. Tyler Miller, Jr., *Living in the Environment*, 13th ed. (Pacific Grove, CA: Brooks/Cole, 2004), p. 501.

WORKSHOP 4-4   What Would You Do?

In this workshop, you'll have a chance to consider a case study and make suggestions that Angela could use to improve her memory of course information.

Angela is a first-year Psychology major. After failing her second exam in Introductory Psychology, Angela's professor referred her to the Tutoring Center on campus. Angela didn't really want to go for help, but she felt so frustrated that she figured she'd give it a try. *Why not*, she thought, *nothing else has worked.* After her first exam, she decided she needed to study more, so she read the three chapters in her text twice this time and read over her notes three times. She even made flash cards for all of the bold-faced terms (her friend said that helped her a lot). When she explained all of that to the Tutorial Coordinator, Ms. Jones, she expected her to be impressed. Instead, Ms. Jones asked her the topic of one of the chapters. Angela told her the first chapter was about motivation. Ms. Jones then asked her to explain everything she knew about motivation in her own words. Angela began rattling off some of the definitions but was unable to explain anything more than that.

1. Why couldn't Angela explain the information from the chapter on motivation?

   _____

   _____

   _____

   _____

   _____

   _____

   _____

   _____

   _____

   _____

2. Why couldn't Angela remember the information for her exam? What mistakes did she make when studying that led to her memory problems?

   _____

   _____

   _____

   _____

   _____

   _____

   _____

   _____

3. What should Angela do differently to prepare for her next exam?

_____

_____

_____

_____

_____

_____

_____

_____

_____

_____

_____

_____

_____

Now think about a time when you really couldn't remember the information you had studied.

4. How did you prepare? What memory strategies did you use? Were you able to recall the information during the exam? What do you think you will do differently to prepare for your next exam?

_____

_____

_____

_____

_____

_____

_____

_____

_____

_____

_____

_____

_____

_____

_____

_____

Taking Charge of Your Life Workshop

Working Collaboratively

Do you avoid working in a group as much as possible? If so, you may not realize the many advantages that group work brings. Not only do you gain valuable skills through group experiences that you can apply to a future career, you also can get more immediate, positive results by collaborating that you may not get by working alone.

? Where Are You Now?

Take a few minutes to answer *yes* or *no* to the following questions.

	YES	NO
1. Do you understand the benefits of working within groups?	____	____
2. Do you participate in study groups to learn course material?	____	____
3. Do you avoid group work as much as possible?	____	____
4. Do you lack the ability to be assertive in a group setting?	____	____
5. Are you patient with other group members even when they don't share your perspective?	____	____
6. Are there times when you slack off in the group, knowing that other group members will take care of the work?	____	____
7. Are you a member of a student organization that works together on common projects?	____	____
8. Do you believe that group work can help you in a future job?	____	____
9. Do you schedule classes that you know incorporate group work?	____	____
10. Do you feel that group work is a negative part of college life?	____	____
Total Points		____

Give yourself one point for each *yes* answer you gave to questions 1, 2, 4, 5, and 9 and one point for each *no* answer you gave to questions 3, 6, 7, 8, and 10. Now total your points. A low score indicates that you could benefit from learning more about the benefits and steps involved in collaborative learning. A high score indicates that you are aware of the advantages of working in a group.

In high school, did you belong to a sports team, participate in a theater production, or become involved in a group project for a class? Have you had an opportunity at college to work within a group setting? If so, you may already be aware of some of the advantages and challenges of group work. College presents numerous opportunities to work in collaboration with fellow students, and you can benefit greatly from these experiences. Understanding the payoff of learning to work effectively within a group will serve you both during your time at college and after graduation.

Discover a Variety of Opportunities for Collaborative Work

Academic Projects

How do you feel when your professor announces that you will form a group with your peers and work collaboratively? Increasingly, college instructors are building group work into their curricula.[1] The assignments could focus on problem-solving, debating, developing a presentation or paper, and so on. The group is expected to work outside of class, perhaps on multiple occasions, and develop the project. In addition, many college instructors will also group students to work on an in-class activity that enhances a particular topic. This technique creates an opportunity for students to approach the material in a more hands-on fashion and to exchange and apply classmate viewpoints in a common effort.

Student Organizations

One of the greatest aspects of college life is the myriad opportunities for students to join groups that represent diverse interests and purposes. Inherent in each of these organizations is the necessity to exist and work together as a group. Just by joining a Greek organization, a club, student government, or an intramural team, you share a common purpose with other members. Whether that purpose is to win games or raise money for a charity, you must form relationships and collaborate so that the group meets its goal.

Study Groups

Forming groups to enhance performance in a particular course is a great strategy for academic success. Group studying can be a very effective learning tool, as participants share their particular knowledge base and perspectives—not to mention the fact that each student brings to the table his or her own set of notes and study materials. The group setting increases the odds that you will hit upon information that will appear on the test. In addition, studying within a group context allows you to test your learning in a variety of ways because each person will approach the material from a different angle. You also will verbalize and explain the information to one another, which helps make the material more meaningful and easier to store in long-term memory. The more varied approaches to studying that you

---

[1]Gamson, Z. F. "Collaborative learning comes of age." In S. Kadel & J.A. Keenhner (eds.), *Collaborative learning: A sourcebook for higher education* (Vol. 2, pp. 5–17). (University Park, PA: National Center for Postsecondary Teaching, Learning, and Assessment, The Pennsylvania State University, 1994).

use, the more likely you are to be successful. The following strategies can be helpful when developing study groups so that you and your fellow group members can make the most of your collaboration.

- **Start early in the semester.** Identify fellow students whom you think will make good group members, noting who comes to class prepared. You could also ask your instructor to make an announcement for anyone interested in forming a study group. The key is to form the group within the first couple of weeks so that you can benefit from the collaboration early in the semester.

- **Be ready to work.** At your first meeting, set a regular meeting time and discuss the group's expectations of one another, including the idea that everyone should make a contribution in the group. Agree that each member should do his or her best to be prompt for meetings and to come prepared.

- **Be efficient.** Maximize the use of each member's time. Reserve more social conversations for the conclusion of the meeting, after your work is done and when each person can choose whether or not to stay to chat. Decide in advance how long you will meet and set an agenda of what you will accomplish so that you stay on task.

Tips for Collaborative Learning

As you can see, the opportunities for collaboration proliferate in college. Now, take a few moments to consider your own comfort level and skills when it comes to group work. It would seem that people who are naturally more extroverted would have an easier time working in a group—this may or may not be the case. An outgoing student may have more difficulty listening to the viewpoints of others. Conversely, a more shy student may have a hard time voicing her opinions. Like all skills, becoming an effective collaborator requires practice. In the meantime, here are some tips that can help you successfully navigate group work.

- **Be assertive.** Whether you have a grade riding on the group project or not, stating your opinions and making a contribution are essential to having a good group experience. If someone is dominating the project, try to find an ally within the group and stick together. Firmly and politely stick to your ground if it is important to you.

- **Be patient.** While being assertive is important, you don't want to come across as the dominating member of the group. Patience can truly be a virtue when it comes to group work. Remind yourself that everyone can make a contribution—even if he or she works at a slower pace or has a different viewpoint. Try to remember that another member may feel just as strongly as you do about his or her opinion. Try to listen without judging—this is truly a skill that can benefit you in all areas of life.

- **Do your part.** Groups don't work when someone decides not to do his or her part. Volunteer to do your share and then follow through. Show up to all group meetings. Your fellow group members really do rely on you. Too many students think that someone else will do the work if they don't. Remember that instructors are likely checking up on the contribution level of each group member, and even if they aren't, maintaining your integrity now is good practice for your post-grad career.

The Benefits of Working Collaboratively

So we know that working collaboratively is definitely a skill that you will need to acquire. The work, however, can certainly pay off. Research indicates that group work promotes positive attitudes about learning, academic achievement, and persistence in college.[2] For some incentive, let's explore some of the direct benefits of being an experienced and effective collaborator.

Most Jobs Require Collaboration of Some Kind

Depending on the career that you choose, group work can take on a variety of forms. Some of you will choose a career, such as advertising or engineering, that requires you to work on common projects with co-workers. Many occupations also require you to join committees to work on a project, issue, or event. If you have varied experience collaborating with others, you will make yourself more marketable as a prospective employee.

You Build Important Skills

It would take too long to review all of the ways that group work builds skills, so let's focus on a few. First of all, you learn to communicate more effectively. A student with a more reserved, introverted personality must make his or her positions and perspectives known to the group, and group work presents the opportunity to practice this skill. And for that student who is more outgoing and extroverted, he or she must learn to be patient and listen to others in the group, which are also very important skills. In addition, developing and giving an oral presentation in a group setting helps put some students at ease and builds confidence for future solo presentations. As stated previously, each opportunity to work collaboratively prepares you for the next time.

You Work on "Real World" Issues

In their research focusing on what college students can learn from group projects, Colbeck, Campbell, and Bjorklund note that students benefit from working on what they refer to as "real world projects." The students used the term to describe problems faced in their future careers that have many possible solutions. The focus is more on the problem-solving practice than on a predetermined "right answer."[3] These "real world" opportunities may also be found in extracurricular activities, with group members using practical skills to work toward a goal. For example, an organization that hosts an event for the campus community must rely on members to plan, promote, and implement all details associated with the project. Future employers look favorably on students with this kind of experience.

You Grow as an Individual

We have alluded to that fact that groups can certainly present difficult challenges. Learning to be patient, dealing with difficult people, and taking a stand when necessary are all skills that will benefit you not only in the classroom and in the work

---

[2]Springer, L., Stanne, M. E., & Donovan, S. "Effects of small-group learning on undergraduates in science, mathematics, engineering, and technology: A meta-analysis." Paper presented at the annual meeting of the Association for the Study of Higher Education, Albuquerque, NM, November 1997.

[3]Colbeck, C., Campbell, S. & Bjorklund, S. (2000). "Grouping in the dark: What college students learn from group projects." *The Journal of Higher Education*, 71, 60–83.

force, but in any life circumstance. Also, figuring out that the world is much bigger than you are, with people who have a variety of viewpoints and perspectives, can help you grow and develop. This sense of interdependence—the idea that we are all in this together despite our differences—can help you work through many of life's challenges. It is also possible that you will develop meaningful relationships with fellow group members. The bond that is formed when working on a common goal can be very strong and friendships can form.

What Do You Do Now?

Working Collaboratively

Brad is taking a sociology course that covers a large amount of content in a short period of time. He would like to put together a study group that meets regularly to keep up with the material.

1. What characteristics should he look for in prospective group members?

_____

_____

_____

_____

_____

_____

_____

2. What standards should the group have?

_____

_____

_____

_____

_____

_____

_____

Think about a time in the past that you worked collaboratively with others.

3. What was the nature and purpose of your group?

_____

_____

_____

_____

_____

_____

4. Did the group work well together or not?

_____

_____

_____

_____

_____

_____

5. What were the positives and negatives of working in that group?

_____

_____

_____

_____

_____

_____

6. To what extent did you meet your goal?

_____

_____

_____

_____

_____

_____

7. What should the group have done differently to be more successful?

_____

_____

_____

_____

_____

_____

8. What will you do differently the next time you work in a group?

_____

_____

_____

_____

_____

_____

Reading Your Textbook

CHAPTER 5

In this chapter you will learn more about:

- Why you need a reading/study system
- How to use the P2R reading/study system
- How to use the SQ3R reading/study system
- How to use the S-RUN-R reading/study system

? Where Are You Now?

Take a few minutes to answer *yes* or *no* to the following questions.

	YES	NO
1. Do you highlight or mark your textbook as you read?	_____	_____
2. Do you use a reading/study system when you read text material?	_____	_____
3. Do you preview a chapter before you begin to read it?	_____	_____
4. Do you usually try to read an entire chapter once you start?	_____	_____
5. Do you think about the material as you read your textbook?	_____	_____
6. Do you tend to read your text chapters again before the exam?	_____	_____
7. Do you generally pause at the end of each paragraph or page to think about what you have read?	_____	_____
8. Do you use different strategies to read more difficult text assignments?	_____	_____
9. Do you often forget what you have read when you complete a reading assignment?	_____	_____
10. Do you quiz yourself on the material after you read your assignment?	_____	_____
Total Points	_____	

Give yourself 1 point for each *yes* answer to questions 1, 2, 3, 5, 7, 8, and 10, and 1 point for each *no* answer to questions 4, 6, and 9. Now total up your points. A low score indicates that you need some help in text reading. A high score indicates that you are already using many good text-reading strategies.

Become an Active Reader

Reading college textbooks is a different kind of reading from the reading you did in high school because college texts are different from high school texts. The chapters are longer and contain a wealth of new technical terminology. They don't just seem harder to read and understand—they are. If you use a reading/study system to read your text material, you will become an active reader. You'll understand more of the material and remember more of it. Although there are many reading/study systems, you should find that the P2R, SQ3R, or S-RUN-R reading/study systems will help you improve your comprehension when reading and prepare your text for later review. You'll have an opportunity to try out each of the reading/study systems in the workshops at the end of the chapter so you can see which one(s) works best for each of your texts.

Why You Need to Use a Reading/Study System

College textbooks are different. College texts are more "idea dense" than most high school texts; that is, they contain many more facts and ideas per page. You also may have noticed that your text chapters are much longer—a fifty-page chapter is typical, and some students report that they have sixty-, seventy-, eighty-, and even ninety-page chapters. You may have also noticed that the print is often smaller, that there are fewer pictures, and that the material tends to be a bit dry. There are many factors that make your texts more difficult to read and understand. College texts are also more difficult to read because they contain material that you've never heard of before—you lack background on the information, which makes it harder to understand. College texts also contain new, specialized, and technical terminology. You probably are reading words that are unfamiliar to you—you may have difficulty pronouncing some of them and probably don't know the meanings of many of the others. Your texts contain more long sentences, averaging thirty words or more (some contain fifty words or more). This is a problem because by the time you read the end of the sentence, you may not remember the beginning. As you learned in the last chapter, you can only hold information in short-term memory for 20 to 30 seconds. If you stumble over a few words, go back to reread, or simply read slowly; long sentences can put a strain on your short-term memory capacity.

To become an active reader. Reading can be a passive activity. You can look at all of the words on a page of text and not remember having read them. Has this ever happened to you? Although you know you read the words, you could have been daydreaming or thinking about something else. You need to use a reading/study system to keep you actively engaged as you read your text. By highlighting in a thoughtful way, by taking notes, or by writing questions about the material in the margin of the text, you can read more actively.

To monitor your comprehension. As you read your textbook, you should be aware not only of what you are reading but also of whether you understand what you are reading. You need to pause frequently to reflect on what you have read and check to make sure you understand the material. You can monitor your comprehension by stopping every so often (at the end of a paragraph, headed section, or page) and asking yourself what you just read and whether you understood it. When you do have a problem with comprehension—when comprehension breaks down—you need do something to correct the problem. You may have to go back and reread a portion of the material. You may need to look up the definition of unfamiliar vocabulary words or new technical terms to gain a better understanding of the material. When you're reading material that's totally new to you, you may find that reading similar information written at a lower reading level (perhaps in the summary of the chapter or from material you find on the Internet) may help you build background on the material. Many of the steps in the three reading/study systems described in the remainder of the chapter contain other strategies for monitoring and improving your comprehension.

To prepare your text for later review. Each of the reading/study systems presented helps you prepare your text material for later review. In college you don't have time to reread all of your text chapters again before an exam, and you wouldn't benefit much from rereading anyway. As you read your text, you want to identify the important information that you'll need to learn for an exam (or to participate in a discussion, write a paper, or complete a project) and condense that material to a more manageable size. In Chapter 6, you'll learn more about how to mark your text to identify the important information and condense the material. You'll also learn strategies for organizing your text material in Chapter 7. When you organize information, you can learn it and remember it more easily. Each of the reading/study systems has steps built in to accomplish those goals.

The P2R Reading/Study System

What is P2R? The P2R reading/study system is designed for easy to average text material. Use P2R on the entire chapter or on ten-page chunks. It's a simple system and doesn't add a lot of time to your reading. However, as you'll see below, it provides you with a mechanism for increasing your understanding and memory of what you read.

What are the steps in P2R? There are three steps to P2R: preview the chapter, read actively, and review the material.

● *Preview the chapter.* Previewing takes only 2 to 5 minutes, but actually reduces the total time it takes to read the chapter. To preview, read the title of the chapter; read the introduction; as you quickly turn the pages of the chapter, read the headings and subheadings; glance at graphics and pictures; and finally, read the summary.

● *Read actively.* The second step in the P2R system is to read actively—to do something while you read. Most students tend to highlight the text or take notes as they read. You may also find it helpful to annotate the text by making notes or summarizing information in the margin. In Chapter 6, you'll also learn how to write questions in the margin of the text as you highlight each paragraph, section, or ten-page chunk. If your text is easy to understand, you may find that highlighting the material is sufficient. If you find that you understand the material better by taking notes or generating questions, then do that, too. There are many ways of being actively involved when reading, and you can decide which ones work for you.

● *Review.* The final step in P2R is to review. You may decide to do a review after each ten-page chunk, after completing the chapter, or both. There are many review strategies you can use. You could take notes if you highlighted as you read, you could write questions in your text or notes to review, or if you already wrote your questions, you could review by reciting the answers. Answering end-of-chapter questions, doing activities, reciting information using headings as cues, and taking online quizzes are some other ways of reviewing the information in the chapter. If you read your chapter in chunks (ten, fifteen, or twenty pages at one time), you could use one review strategy at the end of each chunk (that's a good time to generate questions in the margin) and then another one to review at the end (recite the answers to your questions). You can use one review strategy or several; that's up to you—try all of them, though, to see which ones work best for you.

Why does it work? There are many advantages to the P2R reading/study system.

● *Builds background.* Previewing gives you an overview of what the chapter is about, but it also helps to build some background on topics that may not be familiar to you. The preview can also remind you of information that you already know and it can help you access your long-term memory and "make accessible" information related to the new topics that you will be reading about. That can help you understand the material more easily.

● *Increases comprehension.* Even a 2- to 5-minute preview can help you understand your text better. A number of research studies have found that previewing can increase comprehension 10 to 20 percent. By using an active strategy to read the chapter, you also can improve your comprehension. The more involved you are with the material, the better you will understand it. When you highlight, you have to actually think about the material—you have to decide what's important and what isn't. Finally, using active strategies as you read increases your concentration. In order to highlight in a thoughtful manner (you'll learn more about that in the next chapter), take notes, or generate questions on the material, you need to pay attention to it and focus on the information.

● *Increases interest and motivation.* Although you may originally have felt the chapter would be uninteresting and rather boring, you might find during the preview that there are some topics that do seem interesting. When you are more interested in the material, you'll be more motivated to read and pay attention to the material. Using an active strategy can also increase your interest in and motivation toward the task. If you aren't very interested in the material but like taking notes, for example, knowing that you will be taking notes can increase your interest in reading the assignment.

● *Prepares your text for later review.* As you highlight or take notes, you're preparing your text for later review. You're identifying the important information and condensing it so that you can study more effectively for your exams. When you create word cards as you read or generate questions in the margin of the text or in the margin of the notes you take, you are preparing study aids in the form of self-tests that you can use to prepare for exams.

● *Monitors your learning.* Reviewing the material after reading gives you an opportunity to reinforce the important information and monitor your comprehension and memory of it. As you read, you often focus on only one piece of information at a time; however, as you review you can see how the information in the chapter is connected. Reviewing the material after reading also provides you with opportunities to test your understanding and memory. If you can recite the answers to your questions, answer end-of-chapter questions, or take online tests, you'll know that you understand and have learned the material.

The SQ3R Reading/Study System

What is SQ3R? SQ3R, developed by Francis Robinson in 1941, is one of the most widely taught reading/study systems.[1] You may have learned to use SQ3R in upper elementary school, junior high, or even high school. SQ3R is an acronym for Survey, Question, Read, Recite, and Review. Instead of going through the steps one time as

---

[1] F. Robinson, *Effective Study*, 4th ed. (New York: Harper & Row, 1970), pp. 32–36. SQ3R material adapted from Robinson's original text.

you did for P2R, SQ3R is done on every headed section in your text. This difference makes SQ3R a more time-consuming system, so save it for your more difficult textbooks.

What are the steps in SQ3R? There are five basic steps used in SQ3R: survey the chapter, turn the heading into a question, read to find the answer, recite the answer, and review the answer.

● *Survey.* Go through the chapter quickly, glance at the headings, and then read the final paragraph of the chapter in order to get a general idea of what it's about.

● *Question.* Before you read the first headed section, turn the heading into a question in your mind. You don't need to write it down. How would you change the heading "Sensory Adaptation" into a question? One of the most typical questions (though not necessarily the best) is "What is sensory adaptation?" Formulating a question for each heading forces you to think about what you're about to read.

● *Read.* Read the headed section next to find the answer to your question. Looking for the answer helps you stay actively involved as you read.

● *Recite.* At the end of each headed section, recite the answer to your question in your own words, without looking at the text.

● *Review.* After reading the chapter, go back and look at each heading, recall the question you formulated, and try to answer it again.

Adapting SQ3R. Although SQ3R is very effective in helping students gain a better understanding of their reading assignments, it was not originally designed for college textbooks. Because of that, it has a few drawbacks. You can make SQ3R a more appropriate system for college texts by making the following changes.

● *Formulate broad questions.* As you look at each heading, formulate a broad question that will help you look for all of the important information as you read, instead of just one answer to one specific question. If you only read to find the answer to the question, "What is sensory adaptation?," you would have focused only on the definition and omitted all of the other important information. Using questions such as, "What's important about sensory adaptation?" or "What do I need to know about sensory adaptation?" will focus your reading on all the important information.

● *Highlight the answer to your question.* Instead of simply reading to find the answer to your question, highlight each point. That way you will have a record of the important information when you're ready to study for exams. If you don't like to highlight, you could write your question in the margin across from the heading and then write the answers in the margin below (do this in the text or on notebook paper if your text has narrow margins).

● *Recite using the headings as cues.* When you finish reading each section, stop and cover the material you highlighted or noted and recite the material using the headings as cues.

● *Review.* Go back at the end of the chapter and write questions about the details in the headed sections, recite the answers to your questions, answer end-of-chapter questions, or take online tests. Instead of simply repeating the same answers that you gave before, try to make connections within the material or focus on specific points that you'll need to know for an exam.

Why does it work? SQ3R is a very effective reading/study system for a number of reasons.

● *Repetition.* First, SQ3R provides you with a great deal of repetition of the material. You get at least three repetitions of each of the main points as you focus your reading to answer your question, recite the answer to your question, and review the answer again. If you adapt SQ3R as suggested here, you'll get even more repetition in the process of using some of the active strategies that were described.

● *Small chunks of material.* Second, SQ3R allows you to deal with very small units of material at one time. You may have already discovered that reading ten pages of text is more effective than reading the whole chapter at one time (helps you stay motivated, focused, interested, and leads to better comprehension and memory of the material). Working on one headed section at a time works even better for more difficult material. You'll understand the information in that section before moving on to the next section.

● *Monitors comprehension.* Finally, SQ3R has a built-in comprehension monitoring system. Not being able to find the answer to your question, put the information in your own words, make notes about the material or highlight it (in the adapted format) is a signal that either you weren't paying attention as you read or you simply didn't understand what you read.

The S-RUN-R Reading/Study System

What is S-RUN-R? The SQ3R reading/study system has been adapted by many reading and study skills educators. S-RUN was designed by Nancy Bailey because her students were reluctant to use SQ3R.[2] The S-RUN-R reading/study system combines Bailey's system with a review step to better meet the needs of college students. Because you focus on one headed section at a time, S-RUN-R should be used on more difficult text material.

What are the steps in S-RUN-R? There are five basic steps to S-RUN-R: survey, read, underline, note take, and review.

● *Survey.* Survey the entire chapter by reading the title, introduction, headings, and summary (glance at pictures, charts, and graphs).

● *Read.* Instead of formulating a question about the heading, copy the heading on note paper next to the margin. Then read the headed section as you would any other text material.

● *Underline.* After you finish reading each paragraph, think about what was important in the paragraph and underline (highlight) the important information. Highlighting, as you'll see in the next chapter, is a better method of marking, so feel free to make the change.

● *Note take.* As soon as you finish highlighting the headed section, stop and turn back to your notebook paper. Now take notes on the information you marked.

---

[2] Nancy Bailey, "S-RUN: Beyond SQ3R," *Journal of Reading* 32 (1988): 170. S-RUN-R material adapted from Bailey's original text.

Don't just copy what you highlighted; take notes in your own words as much as possible. Continue jotting down each heading, reading, underlining or highlighting the important information, and taking notes for each remaining headed section.

● *Review.* When you've completed the entire chapter, review to reinforce the important information. You can recite the details using each heading in your notes as a cue. You can do end-of-chapter questions, create recall questions in the margin of your text or notes (you'll learn more about how to do that in the next chapter), or do online quizzes or tests.

Why does it work? S-RUN-R provides you with many of the same benefits as SQ3R. It allows you to read the material in smaller chunks, helps monitor comprehension, and provides you with a great deal of repetition. Unlike SQ3R, S-RUN-R helps you focus on all of the important information in the section rather than just one answer to one question. S-RUN-R also increases comprehension, condenses the material, and prepares the text for later review.

● *Identifies all of the important information.* S-RUN-R is designed to help you identify all of the important information in the headed section rather than one answer to one specific question.

● *Increases repetition.* You actually get more repetition on the important information with S-RUN-R than any of the other reading/study systems. You gain a little information during your survey, another repetition as you read the paragraph, another chance to read the material as you highlight it (your eyes do follow your marker, don't they?), another repetition when you go back and read your highlighting before taking notes, another repetition as you write the material in your notes, and at least one more as you review the material. If you then create questions and practice answering them, you'll have at least three more. That's up to nine repetitions on the material.

● *Increases comprehension.* S-RUN-R also dramatically increases comprehension. Working on the material in small chunks gives you an opportunity to understand each concept well before moving on to the next section in the text. You'll also increase your comprehension because you're writing the notes in your own words. Finally, S-RUN-R makes you think about what you are reading. You can't highlight effectively, take notes, write questions, and actively review the material without thinking about what the text material means.

● *Condenses the text for later review.* In the process of highlighting the text and taking notes, you're identifying the important information that you'll have to review for an exam and condensing the material for study. Without highlighting or note-taking, you would have to reread the entire chapter again before your exam, which is not a very effective way to use your study time, as you'll learn in Chapter 8. With a good set of notes to review, you can spend your study time learning the material, rather than trying to repeat the process of identifying what you need to learn.

WORKSHOP 5-1 **Evaluate Your Reading Strategies**

In this workshop, you'll have a chance to evaluate your current text-reading strategies. Rank the difficulty level of the text material using this scale: 1 = very easy, 2 = fairly easy, 3 = average, 4 = somewhat difficult, 5 = very difficult. Rate your understanding and memory of the material using the following scale: 1 = none, 2 = a little, 3 = some, 4 = most, 5 = all.

Part I: Read the text excerpt, "Features of Communication" (Figure 5.1), and then answer the following questions.

1. How difficult was the text material?   1   2   3   4   5

2. How much of the material did you understand?   1   2   3   4   5

3. How much of the material can you remember?   1   2   3   4   5

4. What problems did you have reading the text material?

_____

_____

_____

_____

_____

_____

5. What strategies did you use when reading the text material?

_____

_____

_____

_____

_____

_____

6. What strategies do you think would help you read similar material in the future?

_____

_____

_____

_____

_____

_____

_____

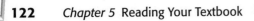

Part II: Read the text excerpt, "Extratropical Cyclones" (Figure 5.2), and then answer the following questions.

1. How difficult was the text material?   1   2   3   4   5

2. How much of the material did you understand?   1   2   3   4   5

3. How much of the material can you remember?   1   2   3   4   5

4. What made this text material more difficult to read than the material in the first excerpt?

_____

_____

_____

_____

_____

_____

5. What problems did you have reading the text material?

_____

_____

_____

_____

_____

_____

6. What strategies did you use when reading the text material?

_____

_____

_____

_____

_____

_____

7. What strategies do you think would help you read similar material in the future?

_____

_____

_____

_____

_____

Figure 5.1 ● Excerpt from a Communications Text

Features of Communication

The definition of communication has four important facets. We'll discuss each of them.

Process   Communication is a **process,** which means that it is ongoing and always in motion. It's hard to tell when communication starts and stops because what happened before we talk with someone may influence our interaction, and what occurs in a particular encounter may affect the future. That communication is a process means it is always in motion, moving forward and changing continuously. We cannot freeze communication at any one moment.

Systemic   Communication takes place within **systems.** A system consists of interrelated parts that affect one another. In family communication, for instance, each family member is part of the system. In addition, the physical environment and the time of day are elements of the system that affect inter-action. People interact differently in a living room than they do on a beach, and we may be more alert at certain times of day than others. The history of a system also affects communication. If a family has a history of listening sensitively and working out problems constructively, when someone says, "There's something we need to talk about," the others are unlikely to become defensive. On the other hand, if the family has a record of nasty conflicts and bickering, the same comment might arouse strong defensiveness. A lingering kiss might be an appropriate way to show affection in a private setting, but the same action would raise eyebrows in an office.

Communication is also affected by the larger systems within which it takes place. For example, different cultures have distinct understandings of appropriate verbal and nonverbal behaviors. Many Asian cultures place a high value on saving face, so Asians try not to cause personal embarrassment to others by disagreeing overtly. It would be inappropriate to perceive people from Asian cultures as passive if they don't assert themselves in the same ways that many Westerners do. Arab cultures consider it normal to be nearer to one another when talking than most Westerners find comfortable. And in Bulgaria, head nods mean "no" rather than "yes" (Munter, 1993). Therefore, to interpret communication we have to consider the systems in which it takes place. In Chapter 7 we'll discuss different communication practices in diverse cultural contexts.

Symbolic   Communication is symbolic. It relies on **symbols,** which are abstract, arbitrary, and ambiguous representations of other things. We might symbolize love by giving a ring, saying "I love you," or closely embracing the other person. A promotion might be symbolized by a new title and a larger office. Later in this chapter and also in Chapter 4 we'll have more to say about symbols. For now, just remember that human communication involves interaction with and through symbols.

From *Communication Mosaics: An Introduction to the Field of Communication,* 3rd edition by WOOD. 2004. Reprinted with permission of Wadsworth, a division of Thomson Learning: www.thomsonrights.com Fax: 800-730-2215.

Figure 5.2 ● Excerpt from an Oceanography Text

Extratropical Cyclones

Extratropical cyclones form at the boundary between each hemisphere's polar cell and its Ferrel cell—the **polar front.** These great storms occur mainly in the winter hemisphere when temperature and density differences across the polar front are most pronounced. Remember, the cold wind poleward of the front is generally moving from the east; the warmer air equatorward of the front is generally moving from the west (see again Figure 7.9). The smooth flow of winds past each other at the front may be interrupted by zones of alternating high and low atmospheric pressure that bend the front into a series of waves. Because of the difference in wind direction in the air masses north and south of the polar front, the wave shape will enlarge, and a twist will form along the front. The different densities of the air masses prevent easy mixing, so the cold, dense air mass will slide beneath the warmer, lighter one. Formation of this twist in the Northern Hemisphere, as seen from above, is shown in Figure 7.13. The twisting mass of air becomes an extratropical cyclone.

The twist that generates an extratropical cyclone circulates to the left in the Northern Hemisphere, seemingly in opposition to the Coriolis effect. The reasons for this paradox become clear, however, when we consider the wind directions and the nature of interruption of the air flow between the cells. (In fact, the leftward motion of the cyclone *is* Coriolis-driven because the large-scale air flow pattern at the *edges* of the cells is generated in part by the Coriolis effect.) Wind speed increases as the storm "wraps up" in much the same way that a spinning skater increases rotation speed by pulling in his or her arms close to the body. Air rushing toward the center of the spinning storm rises to form a low-pressure zone at the center. Extratropical cyclones are embedded in the westerly winds and thus move eastward. They are typically 1,000 to 2,500 kilometers (620 to 1,600 miles) in diameter and last from two to five days. Figure 7.14 provides a beautiful example. The wind and precipitation associated with these fronts are sometimes referred to as **frontal storms.**

North America's most violent extratropical cyclones are the **nor'easters** (northeasters) that sweep the Eastern Seaboard in winter. The name indicates the direction from which the storm's most powerful winds approach. About 30 times a year, nor'easters moving along the mid-Atlantic and New England coasts generate wind and waves with enough force to erode beaches and offshore barrier islands, disrupt communication and shipping schedules, damage shore and harbor installations, and break power lines. About every hundred years a nor'easter devastates coastal settlements. Inspite of a long history of destruction, people continue to build on unstable exposed coasts (Figure 7.15).

WORKSHOP 5-2 **Use S-RUN-R to Increase Comprehension**

In this workshop, you'll have a chance to practice using the S-RUN-R reading/study system. Use the text excerpt, "The Renaissance" (Figure 5.3), and follow the steps listed below. You will need your own notebook paper to complete this workshop.

1. Survey the text material to build some background.

2. Read the first heading and copy it next to the margin on notebook paper.

3. Then read the first paragraph and think about what you would want to study for an exam.

4. Highlight the important information in the paragraph and then read the next paragraph and so on until you complete the headed section.

5. At the end of the first headed section, go back and reread the information that you highlighted and take notes, using your own words as much as possible.

6. Continue to read the text material, repeating steps 2 through 5 for each headed section.

7. Review the information by creating recall questions in the margin of your notes. Underline or highlight the answers to each of your questions.

8. Practice the information by covering the information in your notes and answering the questions that you wrote.

9. Compare your highlighting and your text notes with those of one of your classmates. Look at the content and the organization. What differences do you see?

_____

_____

_____

_____

_____

_____

_____

_____

_____

_____

_____

_____

10. Compare your questions with those of one of your classmates. Do your classmate's questions provide good coverage of the important information in the excerpt? Why or why not?

_____

_____

_____

_____

_____

11. What changes would you suggest your classmate make the next time he or she writes questions?

_____

_____

_____

_____

_____

12. Did you find the S-RUN-R reading/study system helpful in reading and understanding the text material? Why or why not?

_____

_____

_____

_____

_____

13. Did you find the S-RUN-R reading/study system helpful in remembering the text material? Why or why not?

_____

_____

_____

_____

_____

14. Would you use S-RUN-R for any of your own textbook reading assignments? Why or why not?

_____

_____

_____

_____

_____

Figure 5.3 ● Excerpt from a History Textbook

 THE RENAISSANCE

People who lived in Italy between 1350 and 1550 or so believed that they had witnessed a rebirth of classical antiquity—the world of the Greeks and Romans. To them, this marked a new age, which historians later called the Renaissance (French for "rebirth") and viewed as a distinct period of European history, which began in Italy and then spread to the rest of Europe.

Renaissance Italy was largely an urban society. The city-states became the centers of Italian political, economic, and social life. Within this new urban society, a secular spirit emerged as increasing wealth created new possibilities for the enjoyment of worldly things.

The Renaissance was also an age of recovery from the disasters of the fourteenth century, including the Black Death, political disorder, and economic recession. In pursuing that recovery, Italian intellectuals became intensely interested in the glories of their own past, the Greco-Roman culture of antiquity.

A new view of human beings emerged as people in the Italian Renaissance began to emphasize individual ability. The fifteenth-century Florentine architect Leon Battista Alberti expressed the new philosophy succinctly: "Men can do all things if they will."[1] This high regard for human worth and for individual potentiality gave rise to a new social ideal of the well-rounded personality or "universal person" (*l'uomo universale*) who was capable of achievements in many areas of life.

RENAISSANCE SOCIETY

After the severe economic reversals and social upheavals of the fourteenth century, the European economy gradually recovered as manufacturing and trade increased in volume. The Italians and especially the Venetians expanded their wealthy commercial empire, rivaled only by the increasingly powerful Hanseatic League, a commercial and military alliance of north German coastal towns. Not until the sixteenth century, when overseas discoveries gave new importance to the states facing the Atlantic, did the Italian city-states begin to suffer from the competitive advantages of the more powerful national territorial states.

In the Middle Ages, society was divided into three estates: the clergy, or first estate, whose preeminence was grounded in the belief that people should be guided to spiritual ends; the nobility, or second estate, whose privileges rested on the principle that nobles provided security and justice for society; and the peasants and inhabitants of the towns and cities, the third estate.

Although this social order continued into the Renaissance, some changes also became evident.

The Nobility

Throughout much of Europe, the landholding nobles faced declining real incomes during most of the fourteenth and fifteenth centuries. Many members of the old nobility survived, however, and new blood also infused its ranks. By 1500, the nobles, old and new, who constituted between 2 and 3 percent of the population in most countries, managed to dominate society, as they had done in the Middle Ages, holding important political posts and serving as advisers to the king.

By 1500, certain ideals came to be expected of the noble, or aristocrat. These were best expressed in *The Book of the Courtier*, by the Italian Baldassare Castiglione (1478–1529). Castiglione described the three fundamental attributes of the perfect courtier. First, nobles are born, not made, and they should exhibit impeccable character, grace, and talents. Second, the perfect noble must participate in military and bodily exercises, because the principal profession of a courtier was arms; however, unlike the medieval knight, who was primarily concerned with military skill, the Renaissance noble must also seek a classical education and adorn his life with the arts. Third, the noble was expected to follow a certain standard of conduct. Nobles should not hide their accomplishments but show them with grace. The aim of the perfect noble was to serve his prince in an effective and honest way.

Peasants and Townspeople

Except in the heavily urban areas of northern Italy and Flanders, peasants made up the overwhelming mass of the third estate—they constituted 85 to 90 percent of the total European population. Serfdom decreased as the manorial system continued its decline. Increasingly, the labor dues owed by a peasant to his lord were converted into rents paid in money. By 1500, especially in western Europe, more and more peasants were becoming legally free.

The remainder of the third estate were inhabitants of towns and cities, originally merchants and artisans. But by the fifteenth century, the Renaissance town or city had become more complex. At the top of urban society were the patricians, whose wealth from capitalistic enterprises in trade, industry, and banking enabled them to dominate their urban communities economically, socially, and politically. Below them were the petty burghers—the

Figure 5.3 ● *Continued*

shop-keepers, artisans, guild masters, and guildsmen—who were largely concerned with providing goods and services for local consumption. Below these two groups were the propertyless workers earning pitiful wages and the unemployed, living squalid and miserable lives. These poor city-dwellers constituted 30 to 40 percent of the urban population.

Family and Marriage in Renaissance Italy

The family bond was a source of great security in the urban world of Renaissance Italy. To maintain the family, parents carefully arranged marriages, often to strengthen business or family ties. Details were worked out well in advance, sometimes when children were only two or three, and reinforced by a legally binding marriage contract. The important aspect of the contract was the size of the dowry, a sum of money presented by the wife's family to the husband upon marriage.

The father-husband was the center of the Italian family. He gave it his name, managed all finances (his wife had no share in his wealth), and made the crucial decisions that determined his children's lives. A father's authority over his children was absolute until he died or formally freed his children. In Renaissance Italy, children did not become adults on reaching a certain age; adulthood came only when the father went before a judge and formally emancipated them. The age of emancipation varied from early teens to late twenties.

The wife managed the household, a position that gave women a certain degree of autonomy in their daily lives. Most wives, however, also knew that their primary function was to bear children. Upper-class wives were frequently pregnant; Alessandra Strozzi of Florence, for example, who had been married at the age of sixteen, bore eight children in ten years. For women in the Renaissance, childbirth was a fearful occasion. Not only was it painful, but it could be deadly; possibly as many as one woman in ten died in childbirth.

From *World History: Volume II: Since 1400*, 4th edition by DUIKER/SPIELVOGEL. 2004. Reprinted with permission of Wadsworth, a division of Thomson Learning: www.thomsonrights.com Fax: 800-730-2215.

WORKSHOP 5-3 Select the Right Reading/Study System

In this workshop, you'll have an opportunity to practice using each of the three reading/study systems with your own text information. You'll need to bring your own textbooks with you to complete this workshop.

1. Select a chapter in one of your texts that you haven't read before. Begin reading the chapter by using the P2R reading/study system (read two or three pages) and then proceed to use more complex systems (S-RUN-R and SQ3R) if you find that you don't understand the material or have difficulty remembering what you read.

2. Complete the chart below. In each of the boxes put a checkmark to indicate the reading/study system that provided you with good understanding of the material, good memory of the material, and ease at identifying the important information.

Text:

Reading/study system	P2R	SQ3R	S-RUN-R
Good understanding of the material			
Good memory of the material			
Ease in identifying important information			

3. Select a chapter in another text and follow the same process listed in number 1.

4. Complete the chart below. In each of the boxes put a checkmark to indicate the reading/study system that provided you with good understanding of the material, good memory of the material, and ease at identifying the important information.

Text:

Reading/study system	P2R	SQ3R	S-RUN-R
Good understanding of the material			
Good memory of the material			
Ease in identifying important information			

5. Select a chapter in another text and follow the same process listed in number 1.

6. Complete the chart below. In each of the boxes put a checkmark to indicate the reading/study system that provided you with good understanding of the material, good memory of the material, and ease at identifying the important information.

Text:

Reading/study system	P2R	SQ3R	S-RUN-R
Good understanding of the material			
Good memory of the material			
Ease in identifying important information			

7. What changes did you notice in your level of comprehension when using each of the reading/study systems?

_____

_____

_____

_____

_____

_____

8. What adaptations, if any, would you make to make one or more of the reading/study systems work for you?

_____

_____

_____

_____

_____

_____

9. Which reading/study system do you plan to use for each of your texts?

Course Text	**System Preferred**
_____	_____
_____	_____
_____	_____

WORKSHOP 5-4   What Would You Do?

In this workshop, you'll have a chance to consider a case study and make suggestions that Matt could use when reading his college texts.

Matt is undecided about a major, so he is taking a number of introductory courses this term. He is enrolled in Western Civilization, Public Speaking, Psychology, College Algebra, and Composition. Matt has a lot of reading to do each week, but he is having a hard time getting motivated to read some of his texts and is frustrated because he can't remember very much of what he has read after he closes the book. Matt uses different strategies for each text. He generally skims the chapters for his Public Speaking text because the class really focuses on speeches, not on tests. He hates reading his Western Civ text because the chapters are so long and most are really boring. He generally reads and highlights one chapter during a study session from 8 to 11 P.M. Matt likes his Psychology text and is thinking about becoming a Psychology major. He wants an A in the course so he takes notes as he reads. So far, he's gotten Cs on both of his exams and isn't sure what he should do differently. For Composition class, Matt is expected to read a variety of novels and poetry. He isn't sure what the professor is looking for, so he has no clue about what to highlight as he reads. Most of the time, he can follow the plot line, but he doesn't understand the underlying themes the other students talk about in class.

1. Why is Matt having difficulty reading and understanding his textbooks?

_____

_____

_____

_____

_____

_____

_____

2. What mistakes is Matt making when reading his texts?

_____

_____

_____

_____

_____

_____

_____

_____

3. What should Matt do differently when reading each of his texts?

_____

_____

_____

_____

_____

_____

_____

_____

_____

_____

_____

_____

_____

_____

_____

Now think about a time when you had difficulty understanding or remembering the information in your textbooks.

4. Which textbooks were difficult to read and understand? What strategies did you originally use? Why do you think that they were not effective? What would you do differently?

_____

_____

_____

_____

_____

_____

_____

_____

_____

_____

_____

_____

_____

_____

_____

_____

Taking Charge of Your Life Workshop

Celebrating Diversity

College presents a unique opportunity to interact with and learn about people who have different backgrounds and life experiences. As students meet and learn about one another, they expand their views of the world and of themselves. How open are you to this opportunity? Answer the following questions to assess your current perspective on diversity issues.

? Where Are You Now?

Take a few minutes to answer *yes* or *no* to the following questions.

	YES	NO
1. Do you tend to make an effort to overcome your feelings when your comfort zone is challenged by a person who is different from you?	_____	_____
2. Do you avoid new situations or people who are different from you?	_____	_____
3. Do you take full advantage of opportunities to build connections with students who are different from you (through classes, clubs, events, and so on)?	_____	_____
4. Are you aware of any prejudices that you hold?	_____	_____
5. Have you made judgments about others based on external characteristics?	_____	_____
6. Do you understand how you have come to hold your personal beliefs?	_____	_____
7. Do you challenge your own prejudices through talking to others, reading, or seeking out information from some other source?	_____	_____
8. Have you laughed at or remained silent during a joke or other remark that perpetuates a stereotype?	_____	_____
9. Do you know why your generation is considered more inclusive than previous generations?	_____	_____
10. Do you believe that there is no need for you to overcome your prejudices?	_____	_____
Total Points		_____

Give yourself one point for each *yes* answer you gave to questions 1, 3, 4, 6, 7, and 9 and one point for each *no* answer you gave to questions 2, 5, 8, and 10. Now total your points. A low score indicates that you could benefit from assessing your views on diversity and doing some work to overcome prejudices. A high score indicates that you probably have a positive perspective on diversity issues and that you actively work to overcome prejudices.

Each of us has a unique perspective and therefore has something valuable to offer the world and one another. However, there may be times when you feel uncomfortable or intimidated when faced with a person or a situation that is different—when your comfort zone is challenged. This reaction is natural; however, the ability to overcome these feelings and connect with others is critical to becoming a well-adjusted, mature individual. Evaluate your own willingness to become more aware and inclusive as you consider the following information.

Embrace the Diversity on Your Campus

You probably came to college realizing that you would meet other students who are different from you. Were you prepared for the variety and extent of differences you have encountered? Differences abound, in terms of appearance, preference, race, ethnicity, culture, religion, economic background, and more! In addition, the college environment is designed to encourage and foster connections with other students, faculty, and staff. Take advantage of the unique environment that college offers—you may not have the same opportunity again.

What Are Your Own Barriers?

If you hesitate at the idea of interacting with someone who is different from you, you will benefit from asking yourself why. Is it because you naturally are a shy person, or are the reasons more complicated? Let's face it: Each of us carries around preconceptions about others belonging to different groups—about the way they act, their beliefs, and so on. We often allow these preconceptions to morph into judgments, and suddenly we have reached a verdict about someone without knowing the person at all. We must work hard at times in order to overcome prejudices, but the results are well worth the effort.

What Do You Have to Lose?

Holding on to negative feelings not only hurts the group of people affected but also limits your own ability to take advantage of life's possibilities. Do you really want to lead your life burdened by negativity and misunderstanding? Ask yourself how you have arrived at these feelings. It is true that some students grow up hearing negative messages about certain groups of people and now solidly hold these beliefs. But another exciting aspect of college is the freedom for students to think critically and develop personal beliefs and ideas. You also might want to ask yourself, "What do I have to lose by extending myself to someone who is different?" It should become clear that you won't benefit in any way by holding on to the negative belief and that you actually have much to gain—your own growth and development and perhaps a new relationship.

The Bad News

Unfortunately, too many people are unwilling to work to overcome their prejudices, and at times those beliefs transform into behaviors such as discrimination or even hate crimes. As much as our society has made strides reducing prejudice and discrimination, the Department of Justice reports that in 2004, over 7,600 criminal incidents occurred, motivated by a bias against race, religion, disability, ethnicity, or sexual orientation.[1] It is likely that this figure is a low estimate of the number of hate crimes that actually occur because so few victims report crimes to police. This sad reality reminds us that we have a long way to go in building a truly inclusive world.

The Good News

You are a member of the Millennial Generation, which is credited with being the world's first generation to think of itself as global.[2] The computer, through countless Internet sites and pathways of communication, has enabled you to connect with and learn about people on the other side of the globe. In addition, the Millennial Generation recognizes the value of collaborating together, ignoring superficial differences to accomplish a common goal.[3] Future employers will most certainly value this skill. How can this quality benefit you in your own career?

Hopefully you are convinced that overcoming personal prejudices is a good idea—for a lot of reasons. As mentioned, some of us have carried around our beliefs since childhood. Shifting your thought patterns may require some time, patience, and energy. The following tips can help you in this process.

- **Think Critically.** First, take an honest inventory of your own thoughts and beliefs. What prejudices do you hold and why do you hold them? If you can trace the source of your belief, you might find that it isn't very credible. Challenge your belief by gathering evidence that refutes it. What knowledge have you already acquired and what experiences have you had that challenge your belief? Seek opportunities to squash your prejudices and build more positive thought patterns. Join a club, attend a lecture, take a class—the point is to take action.

- **Appreciate Differences.** Wouldn't it be a rather boring world if everyone looked the same and shared the same opinions? Our differences are what make us unique, and we should value what we can learn from one another. Our nation is founded on the principles of equality and embracing differences—values that make us a strong society.

- **Don't Be a Bystander.** Have you ever laughed at a joke made at the expense of someone else? Or perhaps you remained quiet despite not finding humor in the remark. Each time we laugh or even remain silent, we perpetuate the stereotype. When you find the courage to speak up and express your disagreement, not only do you improve upon and strengthen your beliefs, you also challenge somebody else to question his or her own misperception.

- **Take Classes and Attend Events.** College offers you wonderful opportunities to broaden your view of the world. Attend social events, sample ethnic foods, and experience international films, music, or poetry readings. Search your course catalog for literature, political science, anthropology, or history of another culture. Take a foreign language or study abroad. Each opportunity will allow you to learn more about our global society—and a chance to learn more about yourself.

---

[1] *Hate Crime Statistics.* United States Department of Justice, 2004.
[2] Howe, Neil and William Strauss. *Millennials Rising: The Next Great Generation.* New York: Vintage Books, 2000.
[3] *Ibid.*

- **Look for Common Ground.** When you allow yourself to put aside differences, you are able to appreciate the common denominator among all of us—we are human. We share the same basic needs, and we all experience great happiness and great sadness from time to time. At times, we share similar goals and experiences. When you feel divided by differences with someone else, it can be reassuring and powerful to remember that we are all bonded by the human experience.

 RESOURCES

- Check out Ball State University's Diversity Resource Web at **www.bsu.edu/ students/cpsc/diversity/divresources/**. The site contains information and links on general diversity issues as well as information for specific populations.
- Visit Security on Campus, Inc.'s student site at **www.securityoncampus.org/ students/index.html**, which offers campus crime information for students.

What Do You Do Now?

Celebrating Diversity Scenario

Jack is a first-year student who grew up in a small town. He recognizes that he is uncomfortable interacting with students of different races and sexual preferences.

1. List five specific actions Jack can take to overcome his discomfort.

1. _____
2. _____
3. _____
4. _____
5. _____

Now think about your own beliefs, how you interact with others, and your willingness to interact with and learn about people who have different cultures, backgrounds, and preferences.

2. List three of your own limitations and three specific actions you can take to overcome your limitations.

Limitations:

1. _____
2. _____
3. _____

Action Steps:

1. _____
2. _____
3. _____

Marking Your Textbook

CHAPTER 6

In this chapter you will learn more about:

- Why you need to mark your textbook
- How to mark your text
- What to mark
- How to write questions in the margin
- How to review your text marking

? **Where Are You Now?**

Take a few minutes to answer *yes* or *no* to the following questions.

	YES	NO
1. Do you highlight or mark your textbook as you read?	_____	_____
2. Do you find that you often get to the end of a page and have no idea what you just read?	_____	_____
3. Do you begin to highlight or underline an important point before you finish the sentence?	_____	_____
4. Do you evaluate your text marking after an exam?	_____	_____
5. Does your marking make sense when you read it again before the exam?	_____	_____
6. Do you rehighlight or remark your text when you review for an exam?	_____	_____
7. Do you mark the headings and subheadings in your text?	_____	_____
8. Do you make notes in the margin when you read your text?	_____	_____
9. Do you tend to mark key words rather than phrases or entire sentences?	_____	_____
10. Do you ever reread the unmarked sections of your text before an exam?	_____	_____
Total Points		_____

Give yourself 1 point for each *yes* answer to questions 1, 4, 5, 6, 7, and 8, and 1 point for each *no* answer to questions 2, 3, 9, and 10. Now total up your points. A low score indicates that you need some help in text marking. A high score indicates that you are already using many good text-marking strategies.

What Is Text Marking?

How would you define text marking? Most students answer that question as highlighting or underlining words or sentences. Although you can mark a text by simply highlighting (or underlining) words or sentences, there is more to marking than that. When you mark a text, you are essentially identifying the important information and condensing it for later review. In the process, you should gain a better understanding of what you are reading and learn some of the information. In many ways, text marking is similar to taking lecture notes. You identify the topic under discussion (generally contained in the heading or subheadings of the text) and then jot down the details. In lecture, you are writing those details and, as you'll see later in the chapter, you can actually do the same thing as you read your text. You can highlight the important information and/or you can take notes as you read. In this chapter you'll learn more about how to highlight, how to annotate the text (write summary notes in the margin), and how to predict and write exam questions in the margin of the text.

Why Mark?

Promotes active reading. Do you get to the end of the page and realize that you have no idea what you just read? Have you ever found that you highlighted everything on the page? Some students read their textbooks passively—they don't really pay attention to or think about what they are reading. Has this ever happened to you? Marking your textbook helps you become an active reader. Marking also helps you focus your concentration as you read. When you know that you're going to highlight the important information in your text, you have a purpose for reading— your purpose is to locate and mark the important information. Marking also keeps you alert; you're constantly making decisions about what's important and what isn't. You need to think about what you're reading in order to decide what's important enough to mark.

Condenses the material. Marking your text also helps you condense the material for later review. If you take the time to identify the important information and mark it as you read your text chapters, you won't have to waste precious study time going back to read those chapters again before the exam. If you don't mark your text as you read, you may find that you won't have time to go back and study the text material before your exam. Relying only on lecture notes will cost you points you should have earned on the exam.

Improves comprehension. Marking your text can also improve your comprehension of the material. Mindless marking (dragging a highlighter across the page without thinking about the material) will not help your comprehension. To improve your comprehension, you need to mark in a thoughtful manner. You'll learn more about how to do that later in this chapter. You benefit from thoughtful marking in several ways:

- You get a second reading of the important information as your eyes follow your marker across the words.
- You make the material more meaningful when you annotate your text by writing summary statements in the margin.
- You interpret and reinforce important information when you generate questions in the margin of your text.

How to Mark Your Text

Read the paragraph before marking. Have you ever watched other students mark their texts? Some of them start highlighting before they even finish reading the first sentence. Do you? If you highlight as you read, you'll probably mark a lot of information that you don't really need. After all, you can't really decide what's important until you read at least a sentence—one complete thought. In fact, you'll find that if you read the entire paragraph before you begin to mark, you'll be able to make a better judgment about what's important and what to mark. If you're used to marking as you read, wait until you read the entire sentence before marking anything. Once you're comfortable doing that, read two sentences before going back to mark. Continue adding more sentences until you can read to the end of the paragraph before you begin to mark your text. You'll have better comprehension and condense the material even more.

Highlight, don't underline. Highlighting is actually better than underlining. Do a little experiment. Take a pen or pencil and underline this sentence. What did you see? Most students report seeing the tip of the pen or the line. Some see the blank space below the words. You don't really see the words because you're probably trying to keep the line straight and keep from drawing the line through the words. Now take your highlighter and highlight this sentence. What did you see? Hopefully, you saw the words as you marked them. One of the greatest advantages of highlighting is getting a second reading of the important information. When you first read a sentence, you don't know what's important in it until you finish reading it. However, after you have read the entire sentence, you are better able to determine whether there was something important in it. As you highlight the sentence, you are actually paying more attention to the important information. In many ways, this is similar to what happens when you're watching a football (or other game) on television. After something important happens, you get to see it again during the instant replay. Do you pay even closer attention to the instant replay? I know I do. The second reading that you get during marking is like an instant replay of the material.

Mark meaningful phrases. The best marker is the student who can mark all of the important information in the fewest words. That means that you need to mark the important information within the sentence and not the whole sentence. Have you ever finished reading a sentence in your text and found yourself thinking, "Oh, there's something important in there." Instead of marking the entire sentence, you need to learn to ask yourself *where* the important information is located. You need to learn to mark meaningful phrases—combinations of words or actual phrases that contain the important piece of information. You might find that the important information occurs in the first part of the sentence, the middle, or at the end. You may also find that by linking or connecting together key words, you can form your own meaningful phrase (see Figure 6.1). Marking the meaningful phrases will both increase your comprehension because you're forced to think about the material you plan to mark and help you further condense the material in your text. You'll have an opportunity to evaluate your own marking techniques in Workshop 6-1.

Annotate your text. You can annotate your text by writing summary notes in the margin. Annotating the text can help increase your level of interaction with the text. When you summarize information in the margin, you have to think about what it means and put it in your own words. This increases your understanding of the material. You may find that jotting down the main point at the beginning of a headed section helps you focus your reading. Then as you read the material, you can make brief notes about the details that support that point. Take a look at the marginal notes that were included with Figure 6.1. You'll have an opportunity to practice annotating the text in Workshop 6-2.

Write questions in the margin. By writing questions about the important information in the margin of the text, you can dramatically increase your comprehension and memory of the material. After reading and highlighting a paragraph, headed section, or ten-page chunk of the chapter, go back and take another look at the material that you marked. Put your finger on something that you think you'll need to know for your quiz or exam and make up a question about the material. You can use some of the information that you highlighted in the question and another part of the highlighted material as the answer. After writing the question in the

Figure 6.1 ● Example of Highlighted Text with Marginal Notes

WHY ARE THE OCEANS IMPORTANT?

Earth = "Ocean"	As landlubbers, we tend to think of Earth in terms of land, but Earth is largely a water planet. A more accurate name for the planet would be Ocean, because salt-water oceans cover more than 71 percent of its surface.
"O" → survival of all life	The oceans play key roles in the survival of virtually all life on Earth. Because of their size and currents, the oceans mix and
1. dilute waste	dilute many human-produced wastes flowing or dumped into them to less harmful or even harmless levels, as long as they
2. regulate climate	are not overloaded. Oceans also play a major role in regulating Earth's climate by distributing solar heat through ocean currents and by evaporation as part of the global hydrologic cycle. They also participate in other important nutrient cycles.
3. regulate temp	By serving as a gigantic reservoir for carbon dioxide, oceans help regulate the temperature of the troposphere. Oceans
4. habitat ≈ 250,000 species	provide habitats for about 250,000 species of marine plants and animals, which are food for many organisms, including human beings. They also supply us with iron, sand, gravel, phosphates, magnesium, oil, natural gas, and many other
5. source of nat. resources	valuable resources.

margin of your text, underline the answer. Figure 6.2 demonstrates the steps to follow when writing questions in the margin. You'll learn more about how to predict test questions and write them in the margin in Workshop 6-3.

What to Mark

Mark headings. The headings and subheadings in your text are important and should be highlighted. They contain the most important information in the text because they identify the topic to which all of the information within the section relates. If you don't mark the headings, you may not review that material again as you study for your exam. The headings in your text serve the same purpose as the headings in your lecture notes. Would your lecture notes make sense if you didn't include the headings?

Mark main ideas. The main idea statements in your text are also important. Many students don't mark the main idea statements because they don't contain a specific fact, statistic, or definition. In fact, they are general statements about the topic and tend not to include "buzzwords" or even boldface words. However, they are important because they contain the main points about the topic that the author is making. Professors expect students to understand the information that they are studying—they expect students to understand the main ideas presented in the text, not just to memorize the details. Generally, you can find the main idea statements in either the first sentence (topic sentence) or in the last sentence (concluding sentence). Occasionally, you'll find that the main idea is not directly stated and must be inferred from the details.

Figure 6.2 ● Example of Predicted Questions

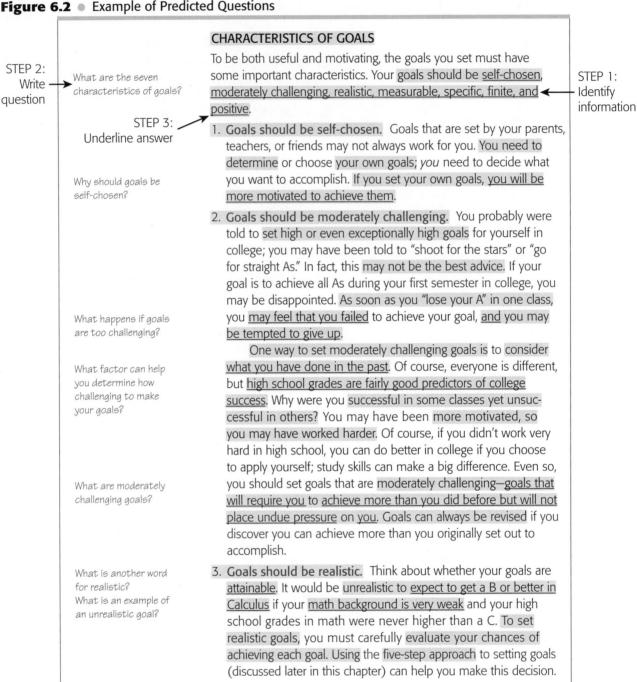

Mark supporting details. Once you identify the main ideas and mark them, it's fairly easy to identify and mark the supporting details. As you read, look for information that backs up or supports the main points that were made. Supporting details can be facts, statistics, examples, definitions, reasons, causes, effects, and so on. Any information that further explains or defends the main ideas can be described as supporting details. Typically, you'll find the supporting details within the sentences in the headed section. Some details are also included in the margin of the text, in text boxes, in the graphic displays, and in the figure legend below photos and graphic displays. You'll have a chance to practice marking all of the important information in Workshop 6-2.

Figure 6.3 ● Samples of Text Marking

Sample 1: Marking Too Little

The largest and most magnificent of all the pyramids was built under King Khufu. Constructed at Giza around 2540 B.C.E., this famous Great Pyramid covers thirteen acres, measures 756 feet at each side of its base, and stands 481 feet high. Its four sides are almost precisely oriented to the four points of the compass. The interior included a grand gallery to the burial chamber, which was built of granite with a lidless sarcophagus for the pharaoh's body. The Great Pyramid still stands as a visible symbol of the power of the Egyptian kings and the spiritual conviction that underlay Egyptian society. No pyramid built later ever matched its size or splendor.

Sample 2: Marking Too Selectively

The largest and most magnificent of all the pyramids was built under King Khufu. Constructed at Giza around 2540 B.C.E., this famous Great Pyramid covers thirteen acres, measures 756 feet at each side of its base, and stands 481 feet high. Its four sides are almost precisely oriented to the four points of the compass. The interior included a grand gallery to the burial chamber, which was built of granite with a lidless sarcophagus for the pharaoh's body. The Great Pyramid still stands as a visible symbol of the power of the Egyptian kings and the spiritual conviction that underlay Egyptian society. No pyramid built later ever matched its size or splendor.

Sample 3: Marking Meaningful Phrases

The largest and most magnificent of all the pyramids was built under King Khufu. Constructed at Giza around 2540 B.C.E., this famous Great Pyramid covers thirteen acres, measures 756 feet at each side of its base, and stands 481 feet high. Its four sides are almost precisely oriented to the four points of the compass. The interior included a grand gallery to the burial chamber, which was built of granite with a lidless sarcophagus for the pharaoh's body. The Great Pyramid still stands as a visible symbol of the power of the Egyptian kings and the spiritual conviction that underlay Egyptian society. No pyramid built later ever matched its size or splendor.

From *World History: Volume 1: to 1400*, 4th edition by DUIKER/SPIELVOGEL. 2004. Reprinted with permission of Wadsworth, a division of Thomson Learning: www.thomsonrights.com Fax: 800-730-2215.

Be sure to mark all of the supporting details. If you are too selective and mark only one or two of the details, you won't study and learn all of the information for your exam (see Figure 6.3). Have you ever studied for an exam but earned a low grade? Did you ever go back and check your textbook to see if you even marked the information that was included on the exam? Even though you studied, you may not have studied all of the information that you needed, resulting in your poor test performance. Your poor performance on the exam may have been a direct result of marking too little or marking too selectively.

How to Review Your Text Marking

Remark your text. One of the most common ways to review text material is to reread the highlighted information. However, as you know, passively reading the material without doing something will lead to little learning. To get more actively involved, you can remark your text. As you review the material for an exam, read the information that you highlighted and think about what you still may need to learn for your exam. Some of the material may be "old hat" by that time and you won't need to keep working on it. You can remark your text by using a different colored marker, by underlining (if you haven't used underlining to indicate the answers to questions in the margin), or by putting brackets around material you want to review again. By marking again, you are forcing yourself to make decisions about the material—forcing yourself to think about what you're reading.

Take notes. Another good way to review your text material is to take notes on the highlighted material. You could annotate the text by noting the main points in the margin and then listing the details using summary notes in the margin directly across from each of the points. You could also move outside the text and take notes on notebook paper, on index cards, or on a computer. You'll learn more about how to take notes in Chapter 7. For now, though, simply write the heading next to the margin (or at the top of an index card) and then indent slightly on the next line and begin making notes on the important information. Write in meaningful phrases and use your own words as much as possible.

Recite from the headings. We also learn by reciting information. Cover the highlighted information in your text with a piece of paper or your hand and use the heading as a cue to trigger your memory. Then recite as many of the details about that heading as you can recall. Uncover the material and take another look at the highlighted information to check your memory. Although you're reading the material again to review, you're also reading with a purpose—you are checking to see which information you were able to recall and which information you missed or recited incorrectly. By reciting the material from memory, you're practicing connecting the information to the heading and are thereby creating a cue to use during the exam. In the process of reciting you'll probably find that you do put a lot of the information in your own words—you won't just recite it word for word. This active review also helps you better understand and learn the material.

Recite the answers to your questions. Reciting the information using the headings helps you learn the information in a global or connected way. However, you still need to learn some information in an isolated way—you need to know specific answers to specific questions. To learn all of the fine details within the text, you need to practice answering your questions in the margin. Cover the text material and read your first question. Recite the answer to the question from memory and then slide your hand or paper down to check the answer. If you get it right, move on to the next question. If you miss it, do it again. Continue practicing the answers to your questions until you can get them all right. Here again you are probably answering the questions using your own words, adding meaning and cues to the material.

WORKSHOP 6-1 · Evaluate Your Text-Marking Strategies

In this workshop, you'll have a chance to evaluate your text-marking strategies. Read the text excerpt on stress (Figure 6.4) and highlight the important information. Use a highlighter for this activity. Then answer the questions on the next page.

Figure 6.4 ● Text Excerpt on Stress

THE NATURE OF STRESS

The word *stress* has been used in different ways by different theorists. We'll define **stress as any circumstances that threaten or are perceived to threaten one's well-being and that thereby tax one's coping abilities.** The threat may be to immediate physical safety, long-range security, self-esteem, reputation, peace of mind, or many other things that one values. Stress is a complex concept, so let's explore a little further.

Stress as an Everyday Event

The word *stress* tends to spark images of overwhelming, traumatic crises. People may think of tornadoes, hurricanes, floods, and earthquakes. Undeniably, major disasters of this sort are extremely stressful events. Studies conducted in the aftermath of natural disasters typically find elevated rates of psychological problems and physical illness in the communities affected by these disasters (Brende, 2000; Raphael & Dobson, 2000). However, these unusual events are only a small part of what constitutes stress. Many everyday events, such as waiting in line, having car trouble, shopping for Christmas presents, misplacing your checkbook, and staring at bills you can't pay are also stressful. Researchers have found that everyday problems and the minor nuisances of life are also important forms of stress (Kohn, Lafreniere, & Gurevich, 1991). Of course, major and minor stressors are not entirely independent. A major stressful event, such as going through a divorce, can trigger a cascade of minor stressors, such as looking for an attorney, changing bank accounts, taking on new house hold responsibilities, and so forth (Pillow, Zautra, & Sandler, 1996).

You might guess that minor stresses would produce minor effects, but that isn't necessarily true. Richard Lazarus and his colleagues, who developed a scale to measure everyday hassles, have shown that routine hassles may have significant harmful effects on mental and physical health (Delongis, Folkman, & Lazarus, 1988). Why would minor hassles be related to mental health? The answer isn't entirely clear yet, but it may be because of the *cumulative* nature of stress (Seta, Seta, & Wang, 1991). Stress adds up. Routine stresses at home, at school, and at work might be fairly benign individually, but collectively they could create great strain.

Appraisal: Stress Lies in the Eye of the Beholder

The experience of feeling stressed depends on what events one notices and how one chooses to appraise or interpret them (Lazarus, 1999). Events that are stressful for one person may be routine for another. For example, many people find flying in an airplane somewhat stressful, but frequent fliers may not be bothered at all. Some people enjoy the excitement of going out on a date with someone new; others find the uncertainty terrifying.

Often, people aren't very objective in their appraisals of potentially stressful events. A study of hospitalized patients awaiting surgery showed only a slight correlation between the objective seriousness of a person's upcoming surgery and the amount of fear experienced by the patients (Janis, 1958). Clearly, some people are more prone than others to feel threatened by life's difficulties. A number of studies have shown that anxious, neurotic people report more stress than others (Watson, David, & Suls, 1999), as do people who are relatively unhappy (Seidlitz & Diener, 1993). Thus, stress lies in the eye (actually, the mind) of the beholder. People's appraisals of stressful events are highly subjective.

From *Psychology: Themes and Variations* (Brief, Paperbound edition with Concept Chart and InfoTrac), 6th edition by WEITEN. 2005. Reprinted with permission of Wadsworth, a division of Thomson Learning: www.thomsonrights.com Fax 800-730-2215.

1. Did you read to the end of the paragraph before marking the text? _____

2. Did marking the text improve your understanding of the material? _____

3. Go back and read the highlighted information. Does it make sense? _____

4. Compare your marking to that of your instructor. Use a different colored marker to replicate the information marked by your instructor.

   a. Did you highlight too much? _____ Too little? _____ The correct information? _____

   b. Did you mark all of the important information that your instructor had marked? Explain.

   _____
   _____
   _____
   _____
   _____

   c. Did you mark more information than your instructor? Explain.

   _____
   _____
   _____
   _____
   _____

   d. Did you mark meaningful phrases or did you mark whole sentences? Explain.

   _____
   _____
   _____
   _____
   _____

   e. What changes would you make the next time you mark your text?

   _____
   _____
   _____
   _____
   _____
   _____

WORKSHOP 6-2 Practice Marking Your Text

In this workshop, you'll have a chance to evaluate your text-marking strategies that you learned in this chapter. Be sure to read to the end of the paragraph before marking, think about what's important, and then mark meaningful phrases. Use the text excerpt, "Political Theories and the Media" (Figure 6.5), and follow the steps listed below.

1. Read the first paragraph and highlight the important information.

2. Compare your marking to that of your instructor. How did your marking compare?

_____

_____

_____

_____

_____

3. Read the headed section, "The Soviet Theory," highlight the important information, and annotate the text by adding marginal notes.

4. Compare your marking to that of one of your classmates. How did your marking compare? Did you include the same information in your marginal notes?

_____

_____

_____

_____

_____

_____

5. Compare your marking to that of your instructor. How did your marking compare? Did you include the same information in your marginal notes?

_____

_____

_____

_____

_____

_____

6. Read the headed section, "The Authoritarian Theory," highlight the important information, and annotate the text.

7. Compare your marking to that of one of your classmates. How did your marking compare?

_____

_____

_____

_____

_____

8. Compare your marking to that of your instructor. How did your marking compare?

_____

_____

_____

_____

_____

9. Continue reading the remainder of the excerpt, highlight the important information, and annotate the text.

10. Compare your marking to that of one of your classmates. How did your marking compare?

_____

_____

_____

_____

_____

11. Compare your marking to that of your instructor. How did your marking compare?

_____

_____

_____

_____

_____

12. What changes did you make in the way you mark your text material?

_____

_____

_____

_____

_____

Figure 6.5 ● Text Excerpt on Political Theories and the Media

▶ POLITICAL THEORIES AND THE MEDIA

No institution as sizable and influential as the mass media can escape involvement with government and politics. The media are not only channels for the transmission of political information and debate, but also significant players with a direct stake in government's attitude toward free speech and dissent. Remember that *the way a country's political system is organized affects the way the media within that country operate*. Media systems can be divided broadly into those systems that allow dissent and those that do not.

To categorize the political organization of media systems, scholars often begin with the 1956 book *Four Theories of the Press*, by Fred S. Siebert, Theodore Peterson and Wilbur Schramm. These four theories, which originally were used to describe the political systems under which media operated in different countries, were (1) the Soviet theory, (2) the authoritarian theory, (3) the libertarian theory and (4) the social responsibility theory. A fifth description, the more modern *developmental theory*, updates the original categories.

The Soviet Theory Historically in the Soviet Union (which dissolved in 1991 into several independent nations and states), the government owned and operated the mass media. All media employees were government employees, expected to serve the government's interests.

Top media executives also served as leaders in the Communist party. Even when the press controls loosened in the 1980s, the mass media were part of the government's policy. Government control came *before* the media published or broadcast; people who controlled the media could exercise *prior restraint*. They could review copy and look at programs before they appeared.

This description of the Soviet press system was conceived before the events of the 1990s challenged the basic assumptions of Soviet government. Many Eastern bloc countries, such as Romania, Slovakia and the Czech Republic that once operated under Soviet influence, based their media systems on the communist model. Today, the media systems in these countries are in transition.

The Authoritarian Theory Media that operate under the authoritarian theory can be either publicly or privately owned. This concept of the press developed in Europe after Gutenberg. Until the 1850s, presses in Europe were privately owned, and the aristocracy (which governed the countries) wanted some sort of control over what was printed about them. The aristocracy had the financial and political power necessary to make the rules about what would be printed.

Their first idea was to license everyone who owned a press so the license could be revoked if someone published something unfavorable about the government. The British crown licensed the first colonial newspapers in America. Licensing wasn't very successful in the United States, however, because many people who owned presses didn't apply for licenses.

The next authoritarian attempt to control the press was to review material after it was published. A printer who was discovered publishing material that strongly challenged the government could be heavily fined or even put to death.

Today, many governments still maintain this type of rigid control over the media. Most monarchies, for example, operate in an authoritarian tradition, which tolerates very little dissent. Media systems that serve at the government's pleasure and with the government's approval are common.

(continued)

Figure 6.5 ● *Continued*

The Libertarian Theory   The concept of a libertarian press evolved from the idea that people who are given all the information on an issue will be able to discern what is true and what is false and will make good choices. This is an idea embraced by the writers of the U.S. Constitution and by other democratic governments.

This theory assumes, of course, that the media's main goal is to convey the truth and that the media will not cave in to outside pressures, such as from advertisers or corporate owners. This theory also assumes that people with opposing viewpoints will be heard—that the media will present all points of view, in what is commonly called the free marketplace of ideas.

The First Amendment to the U.S. Constitution concisely advocates the idea of freedom of the press. Theoretically, America today operates under the libertarian theory, although this ideal has been challenged often by changes in the media industries since the Constitution was adopted.

The Social Responsibility Theory   This theory accepts the concept of a libertarian press but prescribes what the media should do. Someone who believes in the social responsibility theory believes that members of the press will do their jobs well only if periodically reminded about their duties.

This theory grew out of the 1947 Hutchins Commission Report on the Free and Responsible Press. The commission listed five goals for the press, including the need for truthful and complete reporting of all sides of an issue. The commission concluded that the American press' privileged position in the Constitution means that the press must always work to be responsible to society.

If the media fail to meet their responsibilities to society, the social responsibility theory holds that the government should encourage the media to comply. In this way the libertarian and the social responsibility theories differ. The libertarian theory assumes the media will work well without government interference; the social responsibility theory advocates government oversight for media that don't act in society's best interest.

The Developmental Theory   A fifth description for media systems that can be added to describe today's media has been called the developmental or Third World theory. Under this system, named for the developing nations where it is most often found, the media *can* be privately owned, but usually are owned by the government.

The media are used to promote the country's social and economic goals and to direct a sense of national purpose. For example, a developmental media system might be used to promote birth control or to encourage children to attend school. The media become an outlet for some types of government propaganda, then, but in the name of economic and social progress for the country.

Although the theory that best describes the American media is the libertarian theory, throughout their history the American media have struggled with both authoritarian and social responsibility debates: Should the press be free to print secret government documents, for example? What responsibility do the networks have to provide worthwhile programming to their audiences? The media, the government and the public continually modify and adjust their interpretations of how the media should operate.

From *Media/Impact: An Introduction to Mass Media*, 7th edition by BIAGI. 2005. Reprinted with permission of Wadsworth, a division of Thomson Learning: www.thomsonrights.com Fax 800-730-2215.

WORKSHOP 6-3 Learn to Write Questions in the Margin

In this workshop, you'll learn to predict possible test questions and write them in the margin of your text. First, look at the steps for writing questions in the margin listed below. Your instructor will then lead you through a practice session using the text excerpt, "Supply" (Figure 6.6), and provide you with feedback on the questions that you write. Then mark the text material, "Desert Biomes" (Figure 6.7), and write questions in the margin and underline the answers.

1. Read and highlight the important information in the text.

2. Stop at the end of a paragraph, headed section, or after a ten-page chunk to generate questions about the information.

3. Reread what you highlighted and put your finger on some piece of information that you need to learn for a quiz or exam.

4. Write a question about it directly across from the information you highlighted.

5. Generate questions from major headings, smaller headings, and within the text material.

   - Write small so you can write many questions.
   - Write horizontally, not diagonally.
   - Don't write yes/no or true/false questions.
   - Use words like *who, what, why,* and *how* to start your questions.
   - Use a 3-inch strip of paper to simulate your margin if your text doesn't have a wide margin. Then insert the paper into the text (mark the page number on the paper).

6. Use part of the material that you highlighted in the question and part of it as the answer.

7. Underline the answer to each of the questions. Don't underline everything you highlighted; just underline the actual answer to the question.

8. You can write one question in red, for example, and the next in blue and then underline the answers in the same color as the question. Continue alternating colors to separate your questions and answers.

9. You could also number each question and then put the corresponding number just above the answers (^{①}answer, ^{②}answer), as a superscript.

10. Study by covering the text material and answering the questions out loud or in writing.

11. Check the answer to each question to be sure you were correct before going on to the next question.

12. Continue to practice answering the questions until you get them all right.

Figure 6.6 ● Text Excerpt on Supply

SUPPLY

We now turn to the other side of the market and examine the behavior of sellers. The **quantity supplied** of any good or service is the amount that sellers are willing and able to sell. Once again, to focus our thinking, let's consider the market for ice cream and look at the factors that determine the quantity supplied.

What Determines the Quantity an Individual Supplies?

Imagine that you are running Student Sweets, a company that produces and sells ice cream. What determines the quantity of ice cream you are willing to produce and offer for sale? Here are some possible answers.

Price The price of ice cream is one determinant of the quantity supplied. When the price of ice cream is high, selling ice cream is profitable, and so the quantity supplied is large. As a seller of ice cream, you work long hours, buy many ice-cream machines, and hire many workers. By contrast, when the price of ice cream is low, your business is less profitable, and so you will produce less ice cream. At an even lower price, you may choose to go out of business altogether, and your quantity supplied falls to zero.

Because the quantity supplied rises as the price rises and falls as the price falls, we say that the quantity supplied is *positively related* to the price of the good. This relationship between price and quantity supplied is called the **law of supply:** Other things equal, when the price of a good rises, the quantity supplied of the good also rises.

Input Prices To produce its output of ice cream, Student Sweets uses various inputs: cream, sugar, flavoring, ice-cream machines, the buildings in which the ice cream is made, and the labor of workers to mix the ingredients and operate the machines. When the price of one or more of these inputs rises, producing ice cream is less profitable, and your firm supplies less ice cream. If input prices rise substantially, you might shut down your firm and supply no ice cream at all. Thus, the supply of a good is negatively related to the price of the inputs used to make the good.

Technology The technology for turning inputs into ice cream is yet another determinant of supply. The invention of the mechanized ice-cream machine, for example, reduced the amount of labor necessary to make ice cream. By reducing firms' costs, the advance in technology raised the supply of ice cream.

Expectations The amount of ice cream you supply today may depend on your expectations of the future. For example, if you expect the price of ice cream to rise in the future, you will put some of your current production into storage and supply less to the market today.

Figure 6.7 ● Text Excerpt on Desert Biomes

DESERT BIOMES

What Are the Major Types of Deserts?   A **desert** is an area where evaporation exceeds precipitation. Precipitation is typically less than 25 centimeters (10 inches) a year and is often scattered unevenly throughout the year. Deserts have sparse, widely spaced, mostly low vegetation, with the density of plants determined primarily by the frequency and amount of precipitation.

Deserts cover about 30% of the earth's land, and are situated mainly between tropical and subtropical regions north and south of the equator, at about 30° north and 30° south latitude (Figure 7-11). In these areas, air that has lost its moisture over the tropics falls back toward the earth (Figure 7-6). The largest deserts are in the interiors of continents, far from moist sea air and moisture-bearing winds. Other, more local deserts form on the downwind sides of mountain ranges because of the rain shadow effect (Figure 7-10).

The baking sun warms the ground in the desert during the day. At night, however, most of this heat quickly escapes because desert soils (Figure 5-16) have little vegetation and moisture and the skies are usually clear. This explains why in a desert you may roast during the day but shiver at night.

Low rainfall combined with different average temperatures creates tropical, temperate, and cold deserts (Figures 7-12 and 7-14). In *tropical deserts*, such as the southern Sahara (Arabic for "the desert") in Africa, temperatures are usually high year-round. Average annual rainfall is less than 2 centimeters (0.8 inch), and rain typically falls during only one or two months of the year, if at all (Figure 7-14, left). Chile's Atacama tropical desert has had no measurable precipitation in over 28 years. These driest places on earth typically have few plants and a hard, windblown surface strewn with rocks and some sand.

Daytime temperatures in *temperate deserts* art hot in summer and cool in winter, and these deserts have more precipitation than tropical deserts (Figure 7-14, center). Examples are the Mojave, Sonoran, and Chihuahuan deserts, which occupy much of the American southwest and northern and western Mexico. The vegetation is sparse, consisting mostly of widely dispersed, drought-resistant shrubs and cacti or other succulents. Animals are adapted to the lack of water and temperature variations (Figure 7-15). In *cold deserts*, such as the Gobi Desert in China, winters are cold and summers are warm or hot; precipitation is low (Figure 7-14, right).

In the semiarid zones between deserts and grasslands, we find *semidesert*. This biome is dominated by thorn trees and shrubs adapted to long dry spells followed by brief, sometimes heavy rains.

From *Living in the Environment*, 13th edition by MILLER. 2004. Reprinted with permission of Brooks/Cole, a division of Thomson Learning: www.thomsonrights.com Fax 800-730-2215.

WORKSHOP 6-4 **What Would You Do?**

In this workshop, you'll have a chance to consider a case study and make suggestions that Keisha could use when marking her college texts.

Keisha is an Art major and enjoys exploring her creativity and using color when marking her texts. She came up with a system for marking that makes it fun and interesting. Keisha reads to the end of a sentence and then decides what type of information is presented. She uses a pink highlighter to mark all of the headings and subheadings in her text, green for the main idea statements, yellow for details, blue for definitions, and orange for examples. Although this system does take some additional time, Keisha feels that the extra time and effort she is putting into her reading will pay off when exam time rolls around. In class, though, she is frustrated when she doesn't remember the material well enough to participate in the class discussion. She has talked about this to one of her classmates and found that she spent three times as much time reading the chapter as her friend who was actively involved in the discussion. Keisha was shocked when she got her first quiz back and only earned a D on it. She thought she had done better.

1. Why is Keisha having difficulty remembering what she has read?

_____

_____

_____

_____

_____

_____

_____

_____

2. Why might Keisha's marking system cause her to have lower comprehension and memory of the material?

_____

_____

_____

_____

_____

_____

_____

_____

_____

3. What changes should Keisha make when marking her text?

_____

_____

_____

_____

_____

_____

_____

_____

_____

_____

_____

_____

_____

_____

_____

Now think about a time when you had difficulty understanding or remembering the information in your textbooks.

4. How did you mark your text? Why do you think some of your marking methods could have interfered with your comprehension and memory of the material? What do you plan to do differently?

_____

_____

_____

_____

_____

_____

_____

_____

_____

_____

_____

_____

_____

_____

Taking Charge of Your Life Workshop

Making Wise Decisions

As a college student, you not only face important academic choices but also difficult personal decisions. Trying to figure out what is best for you—and then doing
it—can seem like a monumental task when faced with so many different demands.
Take the following assessment to clarify what you know and how you feel about
your decisions regarding alcohol, tobacco, and sex.

? Where Are You Now?

Take a few minutes to answer *yes* or *no* to the following questions.

		YES	NO
1.	Do you make decisions that harm your health and well-being?	___	___
2.	Do you make decisions based upon your values system?	___	___
3.	Do you tend to believe that most students consume alcohol heavily?	___	___
4.	Do you know the rate at which the average student metabolizes alcohol?	___	___
5.	Do you watch out for your friends?	___	___
6.	Do you use drugs or tobacco products?	___	___
7.	Do you know the abstinence rate for college students?	___	___
8.	Do you know the current risks associated with being sexually active?	___	___
9.	Do you sometimes mix alcohol and sex?	___	___
10.	Are you proactive about your sexual health?	___	___

Total Points _____

Give yourself one point for each *yes* answer you gave to questions 2, 4, 5, 7, 8, and 10 and one
point for each *no* answer you gave to questions 1, 3, 6, and 9. Now total your points. A low score
indicates that you could benefit from making healthier decisions and/or improving your awareness
of current alcohol, tobacco, and sexuality issues. A high score indicates you are aware of the risks
associated with alcohol, tobacco use, and being sexually active, and your choices in these areas are
mostly positive.

The first step in the decision-making process should be an honest evaluation of your values. Your personal beliefs are likely to change and develop throughout your college career. Your values should guide your decisions, but unfortunately, this process does not always occur. It is worthwhile to do a values check every once in a while to remind yourself what you stand for and what you believe in. Then, consider whether or not your decisions are consistent with your values. Ask yourself if your behavior reflects what you want for yourself and who you want to be.

Let's face it—we all have regrets. Each of us wishes we could take back one or more moments in our lives. Because we are human, we tend to make errors in judgment or just throw caution to the wind and do something—just because we want to—not necessarily because it's in our best interest. This tendency is particularly true when we are talking about alcohol and other drug use among college students. You might be thinking: *What is the big deal anyway?* Consider the following ideas and your current decision-making process regarding alcohol.

Substance Abuse: Really a Rite of Passage?

Many prospective college students entertain notions of the movies *Animal House* and *Old School* as they anticipate what college will be like. Sure, you might come across that scene from time to time on any given campus, but it certainly isn't the widespread norm that the infamous movies depict. Some students seem to think that they should take on the role of the partier—because that's what it means to be a true college student. The reality, however, is that few students can actually continue consistent substance use and do well academically. In fact, several studies reveal an association between grade averages and levels of alcohol consumption, with higher use associated with lower GPAs and lower use with higher GPAs.[1]

The True Picture

The National College Health Assessment (NCHA) is administered on college campuses across the country every year. The NCHA indicates that students tend to misperceive the rates of fellow students' substance use, actually believing that their peers drink more than they really do.[2] The media exacerbates this misperception by featuring stories on students who die from alcohol poisoning or the rare alcohol-related riot on campus, while not mentioning the vast majority of college students who make good decisions most of the time. The danger can occur when students who hold these misperceptions decide to drink excessively because they think that "everyone is doing it." In other words, they shift their behavior to mimic the false norm. The bottom line is that college students tend to keep their substance use under control, and just having that knowledge can help you make healthy decisions.

---

[1] Perkins, W. "Surveying the Damage: A Review of Research on Consequences of Alcohol Misuse in College Populations." *Journal of Studies on Alcohol.* Supplement 14: 91–139, 2002.
[2] American College Health Association. American College Health Association-National College Health Assessment (ACHA-NCHA) Web Summary. Updated April 2006. Available at www.acha.org/projects_programs/ncha_sampledata.cfm.2006.

When Enough Is Enough

While many of you do choose to abstain from alcohol, others are making the decision to drink. The important thing to keep in mind is that the more pleasurable effects of alcohol actually occur at lower dosages. For example, you may feel more sociable and upbeat after a drink or two. The more you drink, the more likely you will experience negative effects, such as impaired judgment and motor skills and nausea. At higher blood alcohol contents (BACs), students are also more likely to experience consequences like getting into arguments and fights, making poor sexual decisions, and choosing to drive under the influence. In addition, the body can metabolize just one standard drink per hour. Exceeding that rate leads to problems. In other words, if you choose to drink, keep it at a low rate to avoid the negative "stuff."

Thought You Knew the Differences between Men and Women?

Women simply cannot, and should not, attempt to keep up with males when it comes to drinking. For various reasons, including hormonal, body fat, and weight discrepancies, women do not metabolize alcohol as efficiently—or as quickly—as men. This information is important not only for women to consider but also for guys to keep in mind with regard to their female friends and girlfriends.

What Are Friends For?

As mentioned earlier, each of us makes a bad decision every once in a while. In these instances, friends do one another a great service by trying to make sure nothing bad happens—which could mean volunteering to be the designated driver, not leaving a friend behind at a party, or intervening when a friend is about to do something you know he or she will later regret. Friends can go a long way to keep one another safe.

Avoid the Tobacco Trap

Do you or someone you care about smoke cigarettes or use smokeless tobacco? As you may well know, nicotine is enormously addictive—and many students either start smoking or increase use while in college. Some students tend to light up when socializing, while others use tobacco as a stress reliever. Some even smoke to suppress their appetites. Each of these factors (and still others) adds to the challenge of quitting, but doing so now rather than waiting until after college has many benefits: You avoid developing a heavier habit. You reduce (and perhaps eliminate) significant health risks. You save tons of money . . . and so on.

Sexuality: Making the Right Choice

In terms of sexual decision-making, you must consider several factors when choosing whether or not to have sex. It surprises some students to discover that more than a quarter of the student population actually chooses to abstain, and that another 50 percent of students have only had one sexual partner in the past year.[3] If you are choosing to be sexually active, consider the following guidelines.

---

[3] American College Health Association. American College Health Association-National College Health Assessment (ACHA-NCHA) Web Summary. Updated April 2006. Available at www.acha.org/projects_programs/ncha_sampledata.cfm.2006.

Respect Yourself and Your Partner

Reflect on your values and make decisions that won't compromise your health and well-being. Next, make sure you communicate your intentions. Too many people enter into a sexual relationship without really knowing what the experience does (or doesn't) mean. For example, one person might be thinking, "This is great. We can have a good time tonight and may not see each other again." At the same time, the other person might think, "This is great. He (or she) must really like me—this relationship is going somewhere." You can see how misunderstandings and hurt feelings result.

Get Checked Out

You owe it to yourself and your future partner to know where you stand in terms of your sexual health. Women age 18 and older should have an annual gynecological exam, whether or not they are sexually active. At that time, women can be screened for a variety of sexually transmitted infections (STIs) and discuss birth control options. For males, it may require a bit of extra effort to seek out STI screening—but it is worth it. Many STIs go undetected because the individual does not experience any symptoms. Untreated bacterial infections like chlamydia and gonorrhea can lead to serious health risks, including infertility. Bacterial STIs are usually easily treated and cured. On the other hand, viruses such as herpes and HPV are infections that one can carry for a lifetime. However, treatment and prevention strategies can dramatically reduce outbreaks, and you are much better off knowing your health status. If you are sexually active, you should get an STI screening once a year. Check out the services at your campus health center—most are prepared to deal with the specific issues of college students.

Use Condom Sense

You must weigh the risks associated with sex as you make your decision. Of course, abstinence is 100-percent effective in preventing STIs and pregnancy. If you are choosing to be sexually active, however, using condoms consistently and correctly is essential. Unfortunately, as one report indicates, only 43 percent of students report always using condoms during sexual intercourse, and 24 percent report never using condoms.[4] Even people who are well aware of the risks of STIs and unplanned pregnancy are choosing not to use condoms. Now, more than ever, the health risks are simply too severe not to. And in order to prevent pregnancy, you should discuss options with your partner and health care provider to decide upon a method that works best for you.

Reduce Regrets

You must decide, based upon your values and where you are in your life, if being sexually active or using alcohol, tobacco, or drugs is a good idea. Weigh all the evidence and make a good decision *for you* and then stick to that decision. Do not allow your friends, the "heat of the moment," or anything else to interfere with

---

[4] M. Eisenberg, "Differences in Sexual Risk Behaviors Between College Students With Same-Sex and Opposite-Sex Experience: Results from a National Survey." *Archives of Sexual Behavior*, 30: 575–89, 2001.

your decision. After all, making decisions is fairly easy—sticking to them is the real challenge. And as we said at the start, each of us makes mistakes from time to time. As cliché as it sounds, the key is to learn from the mistake and take steps to avoid repeating it. That is a true sign of strength and maturity.

 RESOURCES

- Visit the Higher Ed Center's website at **www.edc.org/hec/students/**, a comprehensive site geared to college student alcohol use, which offers treatment resources, a myths-and-misconceptions quiz, resources for class assignments, and much more.

- **www.smartersex.org** is another great site geared to college students. You can pick up the latest information on abstinence, STIs, contraception, and healthy relationships—you can even submit a question to their resident "sexpert"!

What Do You Do Now?

Making Wise Decisions Scenario

Jill is beginning her second semester in college. Her GPA is low, primarily because of too much partying. She would like to make some changes and improve her GPA, but she isn't sure what to do.

1. List five specific actions she can take to help her cause.

1. _____
2. _____
3. _____
4. _____
5. _____

Now think about your own life.

2. Have you recently made a decision that compromised your health and well-being? First, write out the negative choice you made and then list your values pertaining to this issue (what you truly want for yourself). Finally, list the positive choice you want to make and come up with a few strategies to help make it happen.

Negative Choice: _____

_____

_____

_____

_____

_____

_____

Values Regarding This Issue: _____

_____

_____

_____

_____

_____

_____

_____

_____

_____

Positive Choice: _____

_____

_____

_____

_____

_____

_____

_____

_____

_____

_____

_____

Strategies: _____

_____

_____

_____

_____

_____

_____

_____

_____

_____

_____

_____

_____

_____

_____

Organizing Text Information

CHAPTER 7

In this chapter you will learn more about:

- Why you need to organize text information
- How to take written text notes
- How to map information
- How to chart information

? Where Are You Now?

Take a few minutes to answer *yes* or *no* to the following questions.

	YES	NO
1. Do you take notes on textbook material after you've highlighted the chapter or section?	_____	_____
2. Do you ever get confused about which details refer to which topic?	_____	_____
3. Do you ever have fifteen or twenty details listed under one heading in your notes?	_____	_____
4. Do you evaluate your text notes after an exam?	_____	_____
5. Do you usually copy information from the text in the same wording that the author used in the book?	_____	_____
6. Do you recite your text notes when you review for an exam?	_____	_____
7. Do you create concept maps when you take notes on the textbook material?	_____	_____
8. Are your text notes a good summary of the text material?	_____	_____
9. Do you tend to write down only key words when you take notes?	_____	_____
10. Do you create headings and/or subheadings in your notes to better organize the information?	_____	_____
Total Points		_____

Give yourself 1 point for each *yes* answer to questions 1, 4, 6, 7, and 8, and 1 point for each *no* answer to questions 2, 3, 5, 9, and 10. Now total up your points. A low score indicates that you need some help in taking notes on text material. A high score indicates that you are already using many good note-taking strategies.

Take Text Notes to Organize Text Material

In the last chapter you learned how to mark your text. Although highlighting the text and/or making marginal notes works well for some material, it doesn't work for all text material. Some texts have narrow margins, double columns, or poorly organized information. In those cases, you may find that taking notes during or after reading will help you organize the material and understand it better. You don't have to take notes on all of your texts. Highlighting probably will work well for some of the texts you read. Taking notes as you read the chapter will take more time, so save it for your more difficult texts or for those that lack organization. You may also find that you like taking notes—that it improves your understanding of the material. You can take notes as you read the chapter or after you've read and highlighted it.

Why You Need to Organize Text Information

To improve your memory. In Chapter 4, you learned that it's easier to learn and remember information when it's well organized. You've probably discovered that a lot of your text material is not as well organized as you'd like it to be. Although taking text notes is more time consuming than highlighting or underlining, it has many advantages. When you take notes on the text information, you have an opportunity to change it—to act on it. You can condense the material, organize it, put it in your own words, and add other information to it. Research studies have found that taking notes on difficult text material is helpful because you're forced to organize the information in a way that makes sense to you. That helps you understand the material you're reading, learn it, and recall it during quizzes and exams.

To group details under appropriate subheadings. Take a look at some of your own textbooks. Are there any long selections of material with only a single heading? Are they a page long, two pages long? Even though it's only about a page long, the text excerpt in Figure 7.1 is a good example. Take a few minutes and read through it. You may have noticed that there are no subheadings in this section to separate and organize all of the information about asteroids. Without subheadings, you might find yourself confused by the information presented in the section. All of the details seem to blur together. Can you recall the specific characteristics of each type of asteroid? Can you even remember the different shapes of asteroids? Do you know which example goes with which shape? Although highlighting the information would help you condense it, you can't reorganize the details with a marker. Subheadings help you divide the information in a headed section into smaller chunks, which are much easier to recall than long lists of details. What subheadings could this author have included that would have better organized the material? Take another look at the section and ask yourself what common information is provided about asteroids. In Workshop 7-1, you'll have an opportunity to organize this information by taking written notes.

To separate details by creating new headings or subheadings. Did you recently read a chapter that included details on the same topic spread across a number of headed sections? Would you find it confusing to read more about asteroids five pages later when you were reading a section on meteorites? You could easily confuse the details on asteroids with the details on meteorites. Many textbook authors refer back to earlier topics in later headed sections to make comparisons or show contrasts. Although this may help you better understand the similarities and differences between the topics, it can lead to confusion because the heading doesn't serve well as a cue for the details that refer to the other topic. In Workshop 7-2, you'll have a chance to see how taking written text notes will help you separate and organize text material.

To create graphic displays. Some text material is easier to remember when it's organized into graphic displays. Many authors include charts, graphs, and concept maps of one form or another to help students see how information is organized. You've probably seen them in your science, history, and economics texts, just to name a few. Have you found that they make the material easier to learn and remember? As you probably have noticed, not all of the text material has been organized for you. You have to create your own concept maps and charts to better organize the other material. If you're a visual or kinesthetic learner, you'll find that

Figure 7.1 ● Text Excerpt on Properties of Asteroids

Properties of Asteroids Asteroids are too small to be resolved by Earth-based telescopes, so we see no details of their shape or composition. Yet astronomers have learned a surprising amount about these little worlds, and spacecraft are giving us a few close-ups.

From the infrared radiation emitted by asteroids, astronomers can calculate their sizes. Ceres, the largest, is about 30 percent the diameter of our moon, and Pallas, next largest, is only 15 percent the diameter of the moon. Most are much smaller.

Because the brightness of the typical asteroid varies over periods of hours, astronomers concluded that most asteroids are not spherical. As their irregular shapes rotate, they reflect varying amounts of sunlight and their brightness varies. Presumably, most are irregularly shaped worlds with too little gravity to pull themselves into a spherical form.

Recent observations have confirmed that asteroids are irregular in shape. The Galileo spacecraft on its way to Jupiter passed through the asteroid belt twice as it looped through the inner solar system. By very careful planning, controllers directed Galileo to pass only 16,000 km from the asteroid Gaspra in late 1990. Galileo found the asteroid an oblong world 20 by 12 by 11 km covered by a layer of shattered rock soil about a meter deep and marked by numerous craters (see, Figure 16-11). Again in August 1993, Galileo passed only 3500 km from the asteroid Ida and returned photos of an irregularly shaped, cratered world 52 km long (Figure 19-6a). In fact, the photos reveal that Ida is orbited by a 1.5-km diameter moon, apparently the product of an ancient collision.

Earth-based radar confirms the irregular shape of asteroids. Asteroid Castalia (Figure 19-6b) was imaged repeatedly at 9-minute intervals as it passed near Earth, and the radar images clearly show a dumbbell shape tumbling through space. The asteroid Toutatis (Figure 19-6c) has also been imaged by radar, and it appears to be two objects 4 and 2.5 km in diameter held together by their weak gravity like two peanuts. Some experts now suspect that many asteroids are binary objects, two bodies that collided and are now loosely bonded together.

Not all asteroids lie in the asteroid belt. Spacewatch, a program searching for small asteroids passing near Earth, has found about 100 times more near-Earth asteroids than astronomers had expected. Limited to objects smaller than 100 meters in diameter, the study suggests that as many as 50 such asteroids pass within the moon's orbit each day. The danger of impacts by such objects is small but significant, and this has even led to a hearing before Congress (The Threat of Large Earth-Orbit-Crossing Asteroids, March 24, 1993). The actual danger seems small, and astronomers are more interested in the origin of these bodies. The best guess is that they are fragments from the main asteroid belt.

The color and spectra of asteroids help us understand their composition. From their bright, reddish colors astronomers classify some asteroids, including Gaspra, as S types (Figure 19-7). They may be silicates mixed with metals, or they may resemble chondrites. C-type asteroids are very dark—about as bright as a lump of coal. They appear to be carbonaceous. M-type asteroids, bright but not red, appear to be mostly iron-nickel alloys. S types are common in the inner belt, and C types are common in the outer belt. That distribution is a clue to the origin of asteroids.

From *Horizons, Exploring the Universe* (with the Sky CD-ROM, AceAstronomy and Virtual Astronomy Labs) 9th edition by SEEDS. 2006. Reprinted with permission of Brooks/Cole, a division of Thomson Learning: www.thomsonrights.com Fax 800-730-2215.

creating graphic displays of the information helps you see how the information is organized and connected. When you create maps and charts, you are reformatting the information, creating an organizational structure that you understand. In Workshop 7-3, you'll learn to create maps and charts to organize and separate closely related details. You'll find that when you do create your own organizational system for the text material, you'll be able to learn and remember it better.

How to Take Written Notes

Read and highlight first. Before you begin to take notes on text material, you should read through the material and highlight the important information. If the text is fairly well organized, you may be able to take notes at the end of each headed section. If not, you may need to read several headed sections ahead before beginning to make your notes. You need to get a broader look at the material so that you can restructure it, if necessary, by creating your own headings, adding subheadings, moving details under the appropriate headings or subheadings, and so on. If you're reading a difficult text, taking notes after you read each paragraph or headed section will help you better understand the material. If you're reading a text that is not as difficult, you could wait to take your text notes after reading and marking the chapter as a way of reviewing the material.

Select a format for written notes. Most students use the same method for taking written notes that they use for taking lecture notes. You can organize text information effectively by using either the outline style (either formal or informal) or by taking modified-block notes. Both of these formats lend themselves to organizing the information in a way that makes it easy to learn and remember.

● *Outline the information.* If you like formal outlining (with Roman numerals, letters, and numbers), use it to take your text notes. Formal outlines encourage you to organize information in a hierarchical (top down) method. You have headings, subheadings, details, details that support those details, and so on. You can also use informal outlining by simply indenting the information for each subordinate point instead of labeling each with numbers and letters. The organizational structure is exactly the same. Be sure to use your own words as much as possible (but don't change the technical terms used in the text, as they will be used on tests, too). Write meaningful phrases as shown in Figure 7.2 so that the material makes sense to you when you go back to study for exams.

● *Take modified-block notes.* Many students like using modified-block notes because they are easy to do and still provide an excellent system of organization. Although you typically only write down headings and then related details when taking lecture notes, you should be able to generate subheadings to better organize the details when taking text notes. An example of text notes in modified-block format is shown in Figure 7.3. The subheadings shown in these notes did not exist in the text material. They were created by the student who wrote the notes to better organize the information. Again, write the information in your own words when possible to make the material more meaningful.

Add recall questions to your notes. After taking written text notes, you should write questions in the margin about the important details within your notes. Make up as many questions as you can, putting each question directly across from its answer within the notes. Then either highlight or underline the answer to the question. You may want to alternate writing the questions and then underlining the answers using two different colored pens so that you can easily see which answer goes with which question. You can also number each of the questions and answers. Look at Figure 7.3, which also includes questions in the margin. Be sure to cover the text material and practice reciting the answers aloud until you know the information.

Figure 7.2 ● Sample Notes in Informal Outline Form

Benthic Communities

Rocky Intertidal Communities
    Intertidal zone
        land between highest and lowest marshes
        hundreds of species
    Problems living there
        wave shock — force of crashing waves
        temperature change
        ice grinding against shoreline
            higher altitudes
        intense sunlight
            in tropics
    Reasons for diversity
        large quantities of food available
            strong currents keep nutrients stirred
        large number of habitats available
            high, salty splash pools
            cool, dark crevices
            provide hiding places
                rest places
                attachment sites
                mating nooks
Sand Beach and Cobble Communities
    Three types
        Sand beaches
            forbidding place for small organisms

Mapping Information

Why map? Maps are visual displays of information. They provide you with a way of organizing text material in easy-to-remember pictures or diagrams. If you're a visual learner, you'll be able to actually picture your map during an exam and recall the information. If you're a kinesthetic learner, you'll be able to recall how you set up the map—you'll remember the location of the information, the headings and subheadings you created, and the details within each of the clusters. Mapping is also effective because you create so many cues to locate specific details in long-term memory. Both semantic webs and hierarchical maps are effective in helping you organize information and include enough detail to study for exams. Mapping is especially effective because you have to move outside of the author's organizational framework and create your own. Changing text information into graphical displays increases both your learning and retention of the material.

Figure 7.3 ● Modified-Block Notes with Recall Questions

	Types of Political Organizations
◐	**Band Societies**
What are the characteristics of band societies?	Characteristics
What is the occupation of bands?	• Least complex
How large are the groups?	• small, nomadic groups of food collectors
	• can range from 20 to several hundred
	• members share all belongings
How much role specialization is there?	• very little role specialization
What is egalitarian?	• egalitarian – few differences in status and wealth
How much political integration occurs?	Political Integration
	• have least – bands are independent
What is the political integration based on?	• based on kinship and marriage
What ties members of bands together?	• bound together by language and culture
◐	Leadership roles
What type of leadership occurs in bands?	• informal – no designated authority
Who serves as leader? Why?	• older men are leaders – respected for their wisdom and experience
Who makes decisions?	• decisions made by adult men
What are the powers of a head man?	• head man advises – has no power
What is an example of a band society?	Example !Kung of the Kalahari
What are the characteristics of tribal societies?	**Tribal Societies** Characteristics
What is their occupation?	• food producers
What are pops. like?	• populations – large, dense, sedentary

Hierarchical maps. Hierarchical maps provide you with a top-down organizational structure for the material. At the top of your map, you should write the major topic of the map. If you were mapping the information on asteroids, *Asteroids* would be the topic of your map. You would then move down the paper a little and write in all of the headings. These could be headings that were used in the text or they could be the headings that you create yourself. On the next level, you would write subheadings. Below each subheading, you would write the details. Wendy's hierarchical map in Figure 7.4 models these steps. You could color code each of the four clusters to help separate the information.

Semantic webs. Semantic webs are also an effective way to organize text information. To create a semantic web you need to put the core concept (or topic) or core question (the topic in question form) in the center of a piece of paper. You then

Figure 7.4 ● Wendy's Hierarchical Map

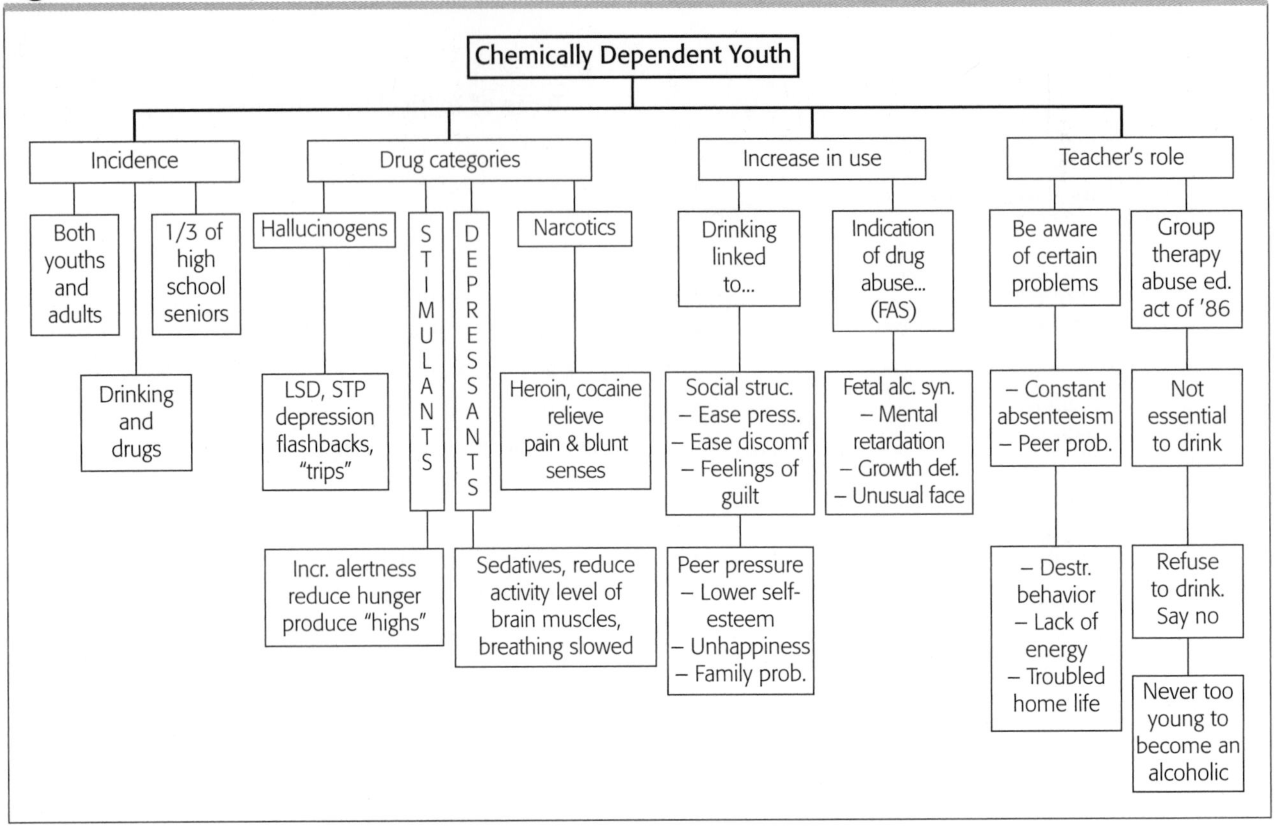

add web strands (headings) and strand supports (details). You can also add strand ties (words that show how some of the details are related) if you want. When dealing with college-level material, you need to include a lot of detail in order to put all of the information into your notes. Therefore, you will need to add more levels of strand supports. In the map shown in Figure 7.5, Christy created subheadings (you could call them second-level web strands) to divide and separate the details. She also included many different levels of strand supports to note all of the important information in the text.

Charting Information

What is a chart? A chart is a graphic display of information that shows the similarities of and differences between closely related information. You can only create charts when you have information that is similar—three types of notes, four types of rocks, four types of societies, for example. Creating charts helps you group and organize the details about similar topics, helping you see both their similarities and their differences. One of the advantages of creating a matrix, a chart with rows and columns, is that you must create categories (subheadings) to group or classify the details for each of the types (headings).

How to create a chart. To create a chart, you need to list the things being compared down the left side (or across the top) and then create categories across the top (or down the side). Look at Melissa's chart in Figure 7.6. Each of Piaget's stages

Figure 7.5 ● Christy's Semantic Web

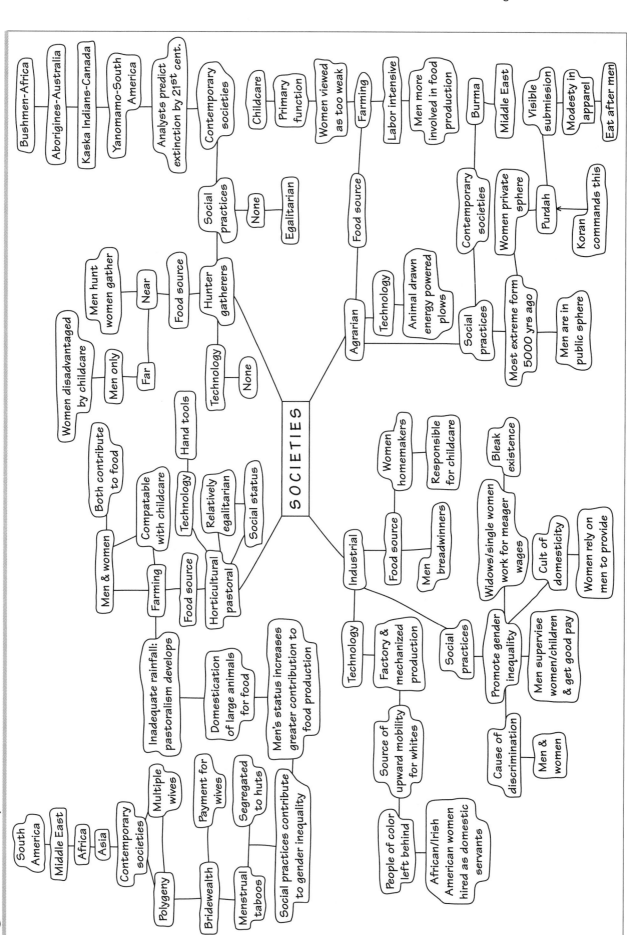

of development includes details about the age, definition, level of development, and key concept. These categories (subheadings) were not included in the text material, but the details about each were described. When you're reading about topics that are similar, you need to think about the type of information you're being given about each topic. Once you've established the categories, go back and fill in the details. You may find that you don't have details for each category in your chart. The author of the text may have omitted a detail about one or two of the topics but included others. As you complete Workshop 7-3, you'll have an opportunity to practice creating categories for your chart. One of the advantages of charting information is that you must create a system to organize the material. Learning to chart information, then, will help you learn to think about how to create subheadings to organize text material.

How to learn the material. Studying from a chart is actually very easy. You can do it many ways. Assuming you have the topics down the side, you could cover each row of details and then recite each detail about the sensorimotor period, for example, using the categories as cues. You could also recite the information for each category by covering the details in one column at a time and using the topics as your cues. In this case, you would recite the age for the sensorimotor, preoperational, concrete, and formal operations periods (the last two are not shown in the chart). Once you know the information by reciting it, you could take out a blank sheet of paper and reconstruct your chart from memory. Charts provide you with multiple levels of cues: topics, categories, details, and location cues.

Figure 7.6 ● Melissa's Chart

Overview of Piaget's Stage Theory				
Period	Age	Definition	Development	Key Concept or Flaw
Sensorimotor	birth to age 2	Ability to coordinate sensory inputs with motor actions	Symbolic thought Behavior dominated by innate reflexes	Key concept: Object permanence Recognizing that object continues to exist even when no longer visible
Preoperational	age 2 to age 7	Improve use of mental images Preoperational because of all the weaknesses	Development of symbolic thinking Not yet grasped concept of conservation: quantities remain constant regardless of shape or appearance	Key flaws: Centration: Focus on one part of problem Irreversibility: Inability to undo an action Egocentrism: Inability to share others' viewpoints Animism: Believe all things are living

WORKSHOP 7-1 Learn to Organize Text Information

In this workshop, you'll learn some new strategies for organizing text material. Read the text excerpt, "Properties of Asteroids" (refer back to Figure 7.1), and highlight the important information. Then answer the questions below.

1. Jot down four or five subheadings that you think could be used to organize this material.

_____   _____

_____   _____

_____   _____

_____   _____

2. Compare your list to that of one of your classmates. Did you have the same subheadings? _____ Which ones were different?

_____   _____

_____   _____

_____   _____

_____   _____

3. Compare your list to that of another of your classmates. Did you have the same subheadings? _____ Which ones were different?

_____   _____

_____   _____

_____   _____

_____   _____

4. Now that you've considered other ways of organizing this material, which subheadings do you think should be used?

_____   _____

_____   _____

_____   _____

_____   _____

5. Go back to the text excerpt. What similar information are you given about each of the asteroids? List some of the similar details below.

_____   _____

_____   _____

_____   _____

_____   _____

6. What categories would you form to describe each set of details?

   _____   _____
   _____   _____
   _____   _____
   _____   _____

7. Now list each of the category names and then group the details below each category.

   _____   _____

   _____   _____
   _____   _____
   _____   _____
   _____   _____
   _____   _____

   _____   _____

   _____   _____
   _____   _____
   _____   _____
   _____   _____
   _____   _____

8. Go back and compare your groups to those of your classmates. Make any necessary changes. What changes did you make?

   _____
   _____
   _____
   _____
   _____
   _____

9. Use the note pages on the following pages or use your own paper to take written notes on the text material using outline or modified-block notes. Use "Properties of Asteroids" as the heading and then use the category names you created as the subheadings. Add the details.

10. How closely do your notes match those of your instructor?

   _____
   _____
   _____
   _____
   _____

WORKSHOP 7-2　Practice Creating Headings and Subheadings

In this workshop, you'll have a chance to practice organizing text material by creating headings and/or subheadings in your notes. You'll need four different colored highlighters and notebook paper for this activity. Be sure to read to the end of the paragraph before marking, think about what's important, and then mark meaningful phrases. Use the text excerpt, "The Old and Middle Kingdoms" (Figure 7.7), and follow the steps listed below.

1. As you read the text excerpt, use one of your highlighters to mark all of the details related to the Early Dynastic Period, another color for the Old Kingdom, a third color for the Middle Kingdom, and a fourth color for information on the Intermediate Periods.

2. Did you find that you had to use the different colors across headed sections? _____ Why?

   _____

   _____

   _____

   _____

   _____

   _____

3. Did using multiple colors help you sort out the information and identify the details related to each period? _____

4. What new headings could you create to take notes on this material?

   _____

   _____

   _____

   _____

   _____

   _____

5. If you were to use the heading listed in the excerpt, what subheadings could you create to better organize the information?

   _____

   _____

   _____

   _____

   _____

   _____

6. Now jot down the details that relate to each of the subheadings listed below, separating them into two columns.

<table>
<tr><td align="center">**OLD KINGDOM**</td><td align="center">**MIDDLE KINGDOM**</td></tr>
</table>

_____   _____

_____   _____

_____   _____

_____   _____

_____   _____

_____   _____

_____   _____

_____   _____

_____   _____

_____   _____

_____   _____

_____   _____

_____   _____

_____   _____

7. Now take notes on the text material using your own note paper, separating the details that you highlighted.

8. Compare your notes to those of your instructor. How did your notes compare?

_____

_____

_____

_____

_____

_____

_____

_____

_____

_____

Figure 7.7 ● Text Excerpt on the Old and Middle Kingdoms

The Old and Middle Kingdoms

The basic framework for the study of Egyptian history was provided by Manetho, an Egyptian priest and historian who lived in the early third century B.C.E. He divided Egyptian history into thirty-one dynasties of kings. Based on Manetho and other king lists, modern historians have divided Egyptian history into three major periods, known as the Old Kingdom, the Middle Kingdom, and the New Kingdom. These were periods of long-term stability characterized by strong monarchical authority, competent bureaucracy, freedom from invasion, much construction of temples and pyramids, and considerable intellectual and cultural activity. But between the periods of stability were times of political chaos known as the Intermediate periods, which were characterized by weak political structures and rivalry for leadership, invasions, a decline in building activity, and a restructuring of society.

According to the Egyptians' own tradition, their land consisted initially of numerous populated areas ruled by tribal chieftains. Around 3100 B.C.E., the first Egyptian royal dynasty, under a king called Menes, united both Upper and Lower Egypt into a single kingdom. Henceforth, the king would be called "King of Upper and King of Lower Egypt," and the royal crown would be a double diadem, signifying the unification of all Egypt. Just as the Nile served to unite Upper and Lower Egypt physically, kingship served to unite the two areas politically.

The Old Kingdom encompassed the third through sixth dynasties of Egyptian kings, lasting from around 2700 to 2200 B.C.E. It was an age of prosperity and splendor, made visible in the construction of the greatest and largest pyramids in Egypt's history. The capital of the Old Kingdom was located at Memphis, south of the delta.

Kingship was a divine institution in ancient Egypt and formed part of a universal cosmic scheme. "What is the king of Upper and Lower Egypt? He is a god by whose dealings one lives, the father and mother of all men, alone by himself, without an equal."[4] In obeying their king, subjects helped to maintain the cosmic order. A breakdown in royal power could only mean that citizens were offending divinity and weakening the universal structure. Among the various titles of Egyptian kings, that of pharaoh (originally meaning "great house" or "palace") eventually came to be the most common.

Although they possessed absolute power, Egyptian kings were not supposed to rule arbitrarily, but according

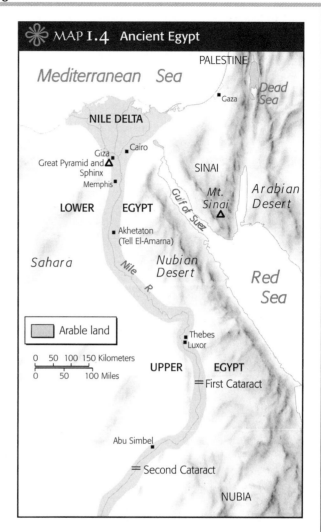

to set principles. The chief principle was called *Ma'at*, a spiritual precept that conveyed the ideas of truth and justice but especially right order and harmony. To ancient Egyptians, this fundamental order and harmony had existed throughout the universe since the beginning of time. Pharaohs were the divine instruments who maintained it and were themselves subject to it.

Despite the theory of divine order, the Old Kingdom eventually collapsed, ushering in a period of chaos. Finally, a new royal dynasty managed to pacify all Egypt and inaugurated the Middle Kingdom, a new period of stability lasting from c. 2050 to 1652 B.C.E. Egyptians later portrayed the Middle Kingdom as a golden age, a clear indication of its stability. Several factors contributed to its vitality. The nome structure was reorganized. The

(continued)

Figure 7.7 • *Continued*

boundaries of each nome were now settled precisely, and the obligations of the nomes to the state were clearly delineated. Nomarchs were confirmed as hereditary officeholders but with the understanding that their duties must be performed faithfully. These included the collection of taxes for the state and the recruitment of labor forces for royal projects, such as stone quarrying.

The Middle Kingdom was characterized by a new concern of the pharaohs for the people. In the Old Kingdom, the pharaoh had been viewed as an inaccessible god-king. Now he was portrayed as the shepherd of his people with the responsibility to build public works and provide for the public welfare. As one pharaoh expressed it: "He [a particular god] created me as one who should do that which he had done, and to carry out that which he commanded should be done. He appointed me herdsman of this land, for he knew who would keep it in order for him."[5]

Society and Economy in Ancient Egypt

Egyptian society had a simple structure in the Old and Middle Kingdoms; basically, it was organized along hierarchical lines with the god-king at the top. The king was surrounded by an upper class of nobles and priests who participated in the elaborate rituals of life that surrounded the pharaoh. This ruling class ran the government and managed its own landed estates, which provided much of its wealth.

Below the upper classes were merchants and artisans. Within Egypt, merchants engaged in an active trade up and down the Nile as well as in town and village markets. Some merchants also engaged in international trade; they were sent by the king to Crete and Syria, where they obtained wood and other products. Expeditions traveled into Nubia for ivory and down the Red Sea to Punt for incense and spices. Egyptian artisans exhibited unusually high standards of artisanship and physical beauty while producing an incredible variety of goods: stone dishes;

CHRONOLOGY

THE EGYPTIANS

Early Dynastic Period (Dynasties 1–2)	c. 3100–2700 B.C.E.
Old Kingdom (Dynasties 3–6)	c. 2700–2200 B.C.E.
First Intermediate Period (Dynasties 7–10)	c. 2200–2050 B.C.E.
Middle Kingdom (Dynasties 11–12)	c. 2050–1652 B.C.E.
Second Intermediate Period (Dynasties 13–17)	c. 1652–1567 B.C.E.
New Kingdom (Dynasties 18–20)	c. 1567–1085 B.C.E.
Post-Empire (Dynasties 21–31)	c. 1085–30 B.C.E.

beautifully painted boxes made of clay; wooden furniture; gold, silver, and copper tools and containers; paper and rope made of papyrus; and linen clothes.

By far the largest number of people in Egypt simply worked the land. In theory, the king owned all the land but granted out portions of it to his subjects. Large sections were in the possession of nobles and the temple complexes. Moreover, although free farmers who owned their own land had once existed, by the end of the Old Kingdom, this group had disappeared. Most of the lower classes were serfs, or common people bound to the land, who cultivated the estates. They paid taxes in the form of crops to the king, nobles, and priests, lived in small villages or towns, and provided military service and forced labor for building projects.

From *World History to 1500*, 3rd edition by DUIKER/SPIELVOGEL. 2001. Reprinted by permission of Wadsworth, a division of Thomson Learning: www.thomsonrights.com Fax 800-730-2215.

Note: In the fourth edition of the text, the authors created subheadings for the material.

WORKSHOP 7-3   Practice Mapping and Charting

In this workshop, you'll have an opportunity to practice organizing text material by mapping and charting. Read and highlight the text material, "Desert Biomes" (Figure 7.8). Then answer the following questions.

1. If you were going to create a chart to organize the information on Types of Deserts, what would you use as the headings for your chart? List them here.

   _____

   _____

   _____

   _____

2. What categories can you use to organize this information? Go back to the text material and look at the details that you marked. What similar information are you given about each type of desert? Write the categories in the space below.

   _____   _____

   _____   _____

   _____   _____

   _____   _____

3. Compare the headings (types of deserts) and subheadings (categories) that you wrote for your chart to those of one of your classmates. Did you have the same ones? If any were different, discuss them until you both reach a consensus. What changes did you make?

   _____

   _____

   _____

   _____

4. Compare the headings that you wrote to those of your course instructor and then write them down the left column of the chart in Figure 7.9. Then compare the categories for your chart or the subheadings and write them across the top of the chart in Figure 7.9.

5. Now fill in the details in each of the boxes within the chart. Go back and think about how you would take notes on the text information. Would you organize the material the same way? _____ Would you include the same subheadings? _____

6. Now that you've organized the information for your chart, work with a group of other students to develop a semantic web or hierarchical map for this material. Use unlined white paper to create your map.

7. Compare your map to that of your course instructor. What similarities or differences did you notice?

_____

_____

_____

_____

8. What changes would you make the next time you mapped text information?

_____

_____

_____

9. Finally, use your own paper to take written text notes on the text material using either outline or modified-block notes.

10. Did you use the same headings and subheadings that you created for your chart and map? _____ What changes did you make?

_____

_____

_____

11. Was it easier to take written notes once you figured out how to organize the material? Why or why not?

_____

_____

_____

_____

12. Compare your system of organization to that of your course instructor. Did you have the same headings? _____ Did you have the same subheadings? _____ Did you include all of the details?

_____

_____

_____

_____

13. What changes would you make in the written notes if you could go back and redo them?

_____

_____

_____

_____

Figure 7.8 ● Text Excerpt on Desert Biomes

 7-3 DESERT BIOMES

What Are the Major Types of Deserts? A desert is an area where evaporation exceeds precipitation. Precipitation is typically less than 25 centimeters (10 inches) a year and is often scattered unevenly throughout the year. Deserts have sparse, widely spaced, mostly low vegetation, with the density of plants determined primarily by the frequency and amount of precipitation.

Deserts cover about 30% of the earth's land, and are situated mainly between tropical and subtropical regions north and south of the equator, at about 30° north and 30° south latitude (Figure 7-11). In these areas, air that has lost its moisture over the tropics falls back toward the earth (Figure 7-6). The largest deserts are in the interiors of continents, far from moist sea air and moisture-bearing winds. Other, more local deserts form on the downwind sides of mountain ranges because of the rain shadow effect (Figure 7-10).

The baking sun warms the ground in the desert during the day. At night, however, most of this heat quickly escapes because desert soils (Figure 5-16) have little vegetation and moisture and the skies are usually clear. This explains why in a desert you may roast during the day but shiver at night.

Low rainfall combined with different average temperatures creates tropical, temperate, and cold deserts (Figures 7-12 and 7-14). In *tropical deserts*, such

as the southern Sahara (Arabic for "the desert") in Africa, temperatures are usually high year-round. Average annual rainfall is less than 2 centimeters (0.8 inch), and rain typically falls during only one or two months of the year, if at all (Figure 7-14, left). Chile's Atacama tropical desert has had no measurable precipitation in over 28 years. These driest places on earth typically have few plants and a hard, windblown surface strewn with rocks and some sand.

Daytime temperatures in *temperate deserts* are hot in summer and cool in winter, and these deserts have more precipitation than tropical deserts (Figure 7-14, center). Examples are the Mojave, Sonoran, and Chihuahuan deserts, which occupy much of the American southwest and northern and western Mexico. The vegetation is sparse, consisting mostly of widely dispersed, drought-resistant shrubs and cacti or other succulents. Animals are adapted to the lack of water and temperature variations (Figure 7-15). In *cold deserts*, such as the Gobi Desert in China, winters are cold and summers are warm or hot; precipitation is low (Figure 7-14, right).

In the semiarid zones between deserts and grass-lands, we find *semidesert*. This biome is dominated by thorn trees and shrubs adapted to long dry spells followed by brief, sometimes heavy rains.

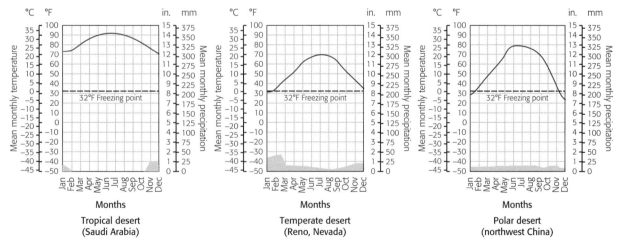

Tropical desert
(Saudi Arabia)

Temperate desert
(Reno, Nevada)

Polar desert
(northwest China)

Figure 7-14 Climate graphs showing typical variations in annual temperature and precipitation in tropical, temperate, and polar (cold) deserts.

(continued)

Figure 7.8 ● *Continued*

How Do Desert Plants and Animals Survive?

Adaptations for survival in the desert have two themes: "Beat the heat" and "Every drop of water counts." Desert stoneplants avoid predators by looking like stones, and their light coloration also reflects heat. Some desert plants are evergreens with wax-coated leaves (creosote bush) that minimize transpiration. Most desert perennials tend to have small leaves (coachman's whip) or no leaves (cacti), which helps them conserve water. Perennial shrubs such as mesquite and creosote plants grow deep roots to tap into groundwater, and they drop their leaves to survive in a dormant state during long dry spells.

Other perennials such as short (prickly pear; Figure 7-15) and tall (saguaro) cacti spread their shallow roots wide to quickly collect water after brief showers; they then store it in their spongy tissues. Most of these succulents are armed with sharp spines to discourage herbivores from feeding on their water-storing fleshy tissue. The spines also reduce overheating by reflecting some sunlight and by providing shade and insulation. Some desert plants, such as the creosote bush and sagebrush, also secrete toxins in the soil. This reduces competition for water and soil nutrients from nearby plants of other species.

Many desert plants are annual wildflowers and grasses that store much of their biomass in seeds during dry periods and remain inactive (sometimes for years) until they receive enough water to germinate. Shortly after a rain, in a frenzy of biological activity, the seeds germinate, grow, carpet the desert with a dazzling array of colorful flowers, produce new seed, and die—all in only a few weeks.

Other, less visible desert plants are mosses and lichens, which can tolerate extremely high temperatures, dry out completely, and become dormant until the next rain falls. In museums, some desert moss specimens have been known to recover and grow after 250 years without water.

If you visit a desert during the daytime you may see only a few lizards, a bird or two, and some insects. However deserts have a surprisingly large number of animal inhabitants that come out mostly in the cool of night. Most desert animals are small. They beat the heat and reduce water loss by evaporative cooling. They hide in cool burrows or rocky crevices by day and come out at night or in the early morning. Birds, ants, rodents, and other seed-eating herbivores are common, feeding on the multitudes of seeds produced by the desert's annual plants. Some deserts have a few large grazing animals such as gazelle and the endangered Arabian oryx.

Major carnivores in temperate North American deserts are coyotes, kit and gray foxes, and various species of snakes and owls that come out mainly at night to prey on the desert's many rodent species. The few daytime animals, such as fast-moving lizards and some snake species, are preyed upon mostly in the early morning and late afternoon by hawks and roadrunners.

Desert animals have physical adaptations for conserving water (Spotlight, right). Insects and reptiles have thick outer coverings to minimize water loss through evaporation. They also reduce water loss by having dry feces and by excreting a dried concentrate of urine. Some of the smallest desert animals, such as spiders and insects, get their water only from dew or from the food they eat. Some desert animals become dormant during periods of extreme heat or drought and are active only during the cooler months of the year. Arabian oryxes survive by licking the dew that accumulates at night on rocks and on one another's hair.

From *Living in the Environment*, 11th edition by MILLER. 2000. Reprinted with permission of Brooks/Cole, a division of Thomson Learning: www.thomsonrights.com Fax 800-730-2215.

DESERT BIOMES

Figure 7.9 ● Chart

WORKSHOP 7-4 What Would You Do?

In this workshop, you'll have a chance to consider a case study and make suggestions that Jon could use to better organize the information in his textbooks.

Jon is an Engineering major and does very well in his course work as long as it is lab-based. He likes hands-on activities and is especially good at design and drawing classes. His scores on the Learning Style Inventory indicated that he is a kinesthetic learner. He doesn't do as well in his general education classes. Although he takes notes in lecture, he often has difficulty recalling all of the details. When he reads his text assignments in Political Science and History, he can't seem to follow the authors' points. Just like his professors, the writers seem to jump from topic to topic and Jon is often too tired at 1:00 A.M. to follow their trains of thought. A friend suggested that he highlight his text assignments, but after trying that a couple of times, Jon gave up. He still found that on the exam he got confused about which details belonged with which topics. It all just seemed to run together. He liked working problems and drawing sketches of the projects he was working on much more. Those he could remember.

1. Why can Jon remember the material better for his Engineering classes than for his general education classes?

_____

_____

_____

_____

_____

_____

_____

_____

_____

_____

2. Why wasn't highlighting more helpful for Jon? What should he do instead?

_____

_____

_____

_____

_____

_____

_____

_____

3. Why would using different strategies be more effective for Jon?

_____

_____

_____

_____

_____

_____

_____

_____

_____

_____

_____

_____

Now think about a time when you read text material that was poorly organized. What did you do? Were you able to recall the information correctly on your quizzes and exams?

4. What material was confusing to you? Why? Did you try to organize the material in a different way? What strategies did you use? How effective were they? What do you plan to do differently?

_____

_____

_____

_____

_____

_____

_____

_____

_____

_____

_____

_____

_____

_____

Taking Charge of Your Life Workshop

Exploring Careers

Have you declared a major? If so, are you confident that your choice is a good fit for you? If not, are you taking steps to decide upon a suitable major? As we will discuss, it is absolutely essential for you to examine your career choices and do everything within your power to ensure that you are making the right choices. As you take the following self-assessment, think about the time and energy you have invested in this process.

? Where Are You Now?

Take a few minutes to answer *yes* or *no* to the following questions.

	YES	NO
1. Did you make your major/career choice based upon the wishes of someone else?	_____	_____
2. Since arriving at college, have you taken self-assessments to assess personal characteristics and preferences?	_____	_____
3. Is choosing a major that fits your interests and abilities of great importance to you?	_____	_____
4. Is your career choice inconsistent with your values?	_____	_____
5. Is your career choice inconsistent with your skills?	_____	_____
6. Is your career choice consistent with your interests?	_____	_____
7. Have you collected information about career choices through informational interviewing, job shadowing, or volunteering?	_____	_____
8. Have you taken classes that will help you make or reinforce your major selection?	_____	_____
9. Are you uninformed of the course requirements for your current major or one that you are interested in?	_____	_____
10. Have you visited your campus career services office?	_____	_____
Total Points		_____

Give yourself one point for each *yes* answer you gave to questions 2, 6, 7, 8, and 10 and one point for each *no* answer you gave to questions 1, 3, 4, 5, and 9. Now total your points. A low score indicates that you could benefit from taking more active steps in your career decision-making process. A high score indicates that you have taken steps to ensure that your major and career choices are a good fit for you.

The hectic life of a college student doesn't allow for a lot of quiet introspection, but taking some time to explore career options is well worth it. The process of career exploration should be ongoing and should include continuous self-evaluation. Some students simply don't do the work required to ensure that their major and career selections are right for them. Let's first discuss some common pitfalls of career decision-making that you'll want to avoid.

Whose Decision Is It Anyway?

Many students choose a major based upon the expectations of someone else—usually parents—who have dreamed of a certain occupation for their child since birth. Some of these students don't think critically about the career because the choice has already been made for them. Unfortunately, the dream turns out to be misguided because the student may not have the interest or aptitude for the job and finds out late in his or her college career. The bottom line is this: The career will be yours, so the choice absolutely must be your own.

Break Free of Tunnel Vision

Other students decide upon a certain career in high school and plow their way through college, never questioning their choice. However, most students find that the college years are an important time of personal growth and development. You will likely open your mind to new possibilities and change your opinions. You need to take these personal changes into account as you evaluate your major and career choices. Check in with yourself as you take different classes and have new experiences to make sure your choice is a good fit for you as you continue to evolve.

Don't Be Lazy—This Is Your Life We Are Talking About!

Still other students are simply too lazy to actively explore career options. They may be "busy" with the day-to-day responsibilities and social life of a college student. What could be more important than choosing the right major and career? After all, won't you be spending much of your post-graduate life on the job? It is in your best interest to do the minimal work required now to ensure a happy future. The point is that in terms of career exploration, it is essential that you are active—that you take the necessary initiative to progress through the exploration process. The following steps can serve as a guide as you navigate through that process.

1. **Self-Assessment.** This first step involves gathering information about yourself, and while some of you may have done some inventories in middle and high school, it is a good idea to do so again now that you're in college. Your campus career services office is a great resource, and the staff will be able to direct you to appropriate self-assessments. In fact, many colleges offer inventories online. The Myers-Briggs Type Indicator and the Strong Interest Inventory are two standard assessments that many college students take. Self-assessments can provide you with a set of results that include your personal characteristics as well as corresponding career options. In terms of personal introspection, you should assess the following components:

   • **Values and Interests.** Your values are your important beliefs, and choosing a career consistent with your belief system will contribute to job satisfaction. In addition, it should go without saying that one should choose a career consistent with interests, but too many students pursue a career for other reasons and end up disappointed because they are totally uninterested or dissatisfied with their jobs.

- **Skills/Aptitudes.** Being honest with yourself about personal strengths and weaknesses is critical to productive career planning. For example, if you need to take several higher-level math courses and math is your weakest area, you may need to reassess your major. After all, college coursework is the foundation for your future job. If you struggle now, you may struggle with future job responsibilities.

- **Priorities.** It is also essential to take into consideration what you want (and don't want) for yourself in your post-graduate life. What kind of work environment do you prefer? Will sitting behind a desk suit you, or do you prefer to be up and moving around? Is having a family important, and how will these plans fit with your career? How important is money, and will you make enough to support the lifestyle you desire? Where do you want to live, and is there a market in that region for your occupation? Too many students fall into the trap of believing that these questions don't need to be answered for a long time. The reality is that the time goes very quickly, and any plans you make now will help ensure your future happiness.

2. **Exploring Options.** Once you have an accurate profile of personal qualities that have been matched with appropriate majors and careers, it's time to gather information about the occupations. Too many students possess only a vague idea of the details of their career choice. Try to investigate prospective careers through as many of the following opportunities as possible. Your career services office can help guide you. Because your time may be limited during the semester, try to take advantage of breaks and summer vacation to get started on your search. Using one or all of the following strategies may be very helpful.

   - **Informational interview.** Most professionals enjoy talking about their jobs with interested students. To gain the most from an informational interview, come prepared with plenty of questions. You'll receive candid information on both the positive and negative aspects of the job—from someone who is speaking from experience.

   - **Job shadowing.** Observing a professional on the job provides you with keen insight into the day-to-day responsibilities of the job you are considering. You may discover something about the occupation that you had never realized, and this information is invaluable in making a decision about whether or not to enter a certain field. Shadowing multiple professionals in various settings will provide you with different perspectives.

   - **Volunteering.** Many people welcome the extra help you can give, and at the same time you pick up valuable experience and insight into the job. In addition, a future employer will value your initiative to gain experience without the incentive of income or credits.

   - **Internships.** Talk to one of your professors or your advisor about internship possibilities. Many majors have requirements regarding internships, and the coordinator can help you with the process as well as connect you with appropriate internship sites. Don't wait until your junior or senior year to look into internship or volunteer opportunities. Again, the practical experience on your resume is impressive to employers. At the same time, you are collecting valuable information to help you in the career decision-making process.

3. **Take Action.** Evaluate all of the information that you have gathered—both personal and career-related. You may want to set up an appointment with a career services professional to help you. In addition, an academic advisor can review course requirements for certain majors so that you have a clear idea of the challenge before you. Throughout this process, you should take classes to explore your options. Choosing a major and career path (or reinforcing your choice) can bring a lot of relief. Moreover, feeling confident about your major and career can help you stay motivated and focused throughout your college career. Once you've made your decision, it is important to stay active by doing the following:

   - Seek out practical experience through volunteer experiences and internships.

   - With each new experience, update your résumé.

   - Maintain a list of contacts of professionals in the field with whom you have interacted.

   - Create a portfolio that contains descriptions of your experiences and examples of your work.

Taking these steps may require some investment of time and energy, but a well-chosen career will reap rewards for years to come.

 RESOURCES

- First and foremost, make sure you visit your campus career services office and website. Most colleges offer services and resources unique to their students—so make sure you take advantage of everything you can, while you can!

- Visit **www.mycoolcareer.com** for a comprehensive resource—you can complete self-assessments, explore careers, and get other valuable information, such as tips on volunteering and current trends in the job market.

- Want information on a certain job? Check out the U.S. Department of Labor's Occupational Outlook Handbook at **www.bls.gov/oco/**. You will find earnings, job responsibilities, the job market in each state, working conditions, and much more.

What Do You Do Now?

Exploring Careers Scenario

Zach is a Pharmacy major who always assumed that he would join his uncle's pharmacy. Recently, though, he began to have second thoughts about his decision. He is struggling with the math and science requirements and is unsure if he will be content working behind a pharmacy counter. He is in his sophomore year and has taken classes that count toward his major, and he is worried about disappointing his family if he changes his major.

1. What steps can Zach take to help him decide if he should become a pharmacist or choose a different career?

   1. _____

   2. _____

   3. _____

   4. _____

   5. _____

Now think about your own major, if you have one.

2. List all of the steps you have taken to ensure that your major matches your abilities, interests, preferences, and priorities. If you haven't declared a major, list all of the steps you have taken to search for a major.

   1. _____

   2. _____

   3. _____

   4. _____

   5. _____

3. Now list all of the steps you have taken to discover all you can about your career choice (job responsibilities, prospects, opportunity for advancement, salary, and so on).

   1. _____

   2. _____

   3. _____

   4. _____

   5. _____

4. Review all of the steps that you have taken in your career decision-making process. Do you notice any gaps? List any additional steps you should take to give you a complete picture.

   1. _____

   2. _____

   3. _____

   4. _____

   5. _____

5. Describe the career you have chosen. What is the market like right now? What is the projected market like?

_____

_____

_____

_____

_____

_____

_____

_____

_____

_____

6. Why do you want to pursue that career choice?

_____

_____

_____

_____

_____

_____

_____

_____

_____

_____

_____

_____

_____

Preparing for Exams

CHAPTER 8

In this chapter you will learn more about:

- How to set up a Five-Day Study Plan
- Active preparation strategies
- Active review strategies
- How to create study sheets
- How to study for essay exams

College Exams Are Different

As you probably have discovered, college exams are different from high school tests; they cover more material and are given less frequently. These differences require you to prepare differently, too. Many college students are shocked by their first exam grades. They aren't the easy As that they expected to receive. Even though they studied the same way they did in high school, many of them found that they didn't know the answers to the exam questions. Do you just read over the material a few times when you prepare for exams? To earn good grades on college exams, you need to do more—you need to get actively involved in the material. You need to spend more time, use more effective strategies, and monitor your learning. This chapter includes strategies for planning and organizing your study time as well as active strategies for learning course material.

Set Up a Five-Day Study Plan

Learn about the exam. The more you know about the exam, the more effectively you can prepare. You need to know what material will be on the exam—which chapters, which lectures, in addition to any videos, handouts, or labs. You also need to know what types of questions will be on the exam. Will it be all multiple choice or will there be a section of completion, short answer, or even an essay? Knowing how many questions you'll have to answer can also give you a better idea of what to expect. About a week before the exam, make a list of all of the chapters and concepts you need to review. Then review the material to see if there are any specific concepts that you really don't understand. Meet with your instructor or teaching assistant and ask for clarification. Some instructors run help sessions before the exam. These are great opportunities to review the material and to ask questions. Even if you don't have any specific questions, just listening to the questions other students ask and to the instructor's answers will help you better understand some of the more difficult material.

Increase your study time. Even though you may have spent only one to three hours preparing for high school exams, you'll need to put in more time on college exams because they cover so much material and tend to occur less frequently throughout the semester. In Chapter 4, you learned how quickly we forget. If your exam occurs after four weeks, seven weeks, or at the end of the term, you won't remember much of the material. How long did you study for your last exam? To be well prepared for a college exam, you need to study for eight to ten hours. Some students may be able to spend less time preparing (if they make word cards and/or write questions in the margin of their text and notes as they cover each chapter) and some may need more time to prepare if the subject material is very difficult or they have little prior knowledge about the topics covered.

Space your study. You also need to space out your study over a period of days to prepare well for any exam. If you study for 2 hours each day over a five-day period, you'll learn more than if you cram (study for 8 to 10 hours the day or night before the exam). Count back five days from your exam day to begin to study. The overview of the Five-Day Study Plan in Figure 8.1 shows a framework for how to set up your study plan. As you can see, you're spacing out your study of the exam material over five days and you're spacing out your study of each chapter, too. Research studies have shown that you can learn more effectively when you space your study.

By studying over a period of days, you can break down the material and work on it in smaller units, helping you focus on a few topics at a time. You'll also have time for lots of repetition of the material. Look again at the overview of the Five-Day Study Plan in Figure 8.1. You can see here that you prepare and then review the material multiple times before taking the exam. So instead of working on the material in Chapter 1 only once, you actually are spacing out your study of that material over all five days. Another great advantage of spaced learning is that you can prepare for more than one exam at the same time. Have you ever sacrificed your score on one exam to cram for another given on the same day? With the Five-Day Study Plan you'll be able to prepare for several exams at the same time. This is especially helpful when your exams seem to cluster around midterm and finals. Refer back to the calendars that you created to better manage your time (or see Chapter 2 for tips on time management) and schedule your study time.

Figure 8.1 ● Five-Day
Study Plan Overview

Tuesday			
	Prepare	CH 1	2 hrs
Wednesday			
	Prepare	CH 2	2 hrs
	Review	CH 1	30 min
Thursday			
	Prepare	CH 3	1–1/2 hrs
	Review	CH 2	30 min
	Review	CH 1	15 min
Friday			
	Prepare	CH 4	1 hr
	Review	CH 3	30 min
	Review	CH 2	15 min
	Review	CH 1	10 min
Sunday			
	Review	CH 4	30 min
	Review	CH 3	20 min
	Review	CH 2	10 min
	Review	CH 1	10 min
	Self-test		1 hr

Divide the material into chunks. The next step is to divide the material you have to study. Make a list of all of the chapters, lecture notes, handouts, and other materials you'll have to study. Then group or chunk them so that you study the lectures and text material covering the same topic at the same time. When you prepare Chapter 1 for your exam, you'll be studying the text chapter and all lectures that covered that material as well as any labs, films, or handouts. For a typical four-chapter exam, you'll prepare one chapter per day for the first four days of the study plan and review and self-test on the last day. If you have three chapters on the exam, you could use a four-day plan or you could still use a five-day plan and divide the earliest or most difficult chapter in half. If you only have two chapters on the exam, you should divide each of them in half, preparing the first half of Chapter 1 (the earliest chapter) on Day 1 and the second half of Chapter 1 on Day 2 and so on.

The Five-Day Study Plan is flexible, so you could do a four-day plan (for three chapters of material) or a six-day plan (for five chapters). However, if you have an exam on only two chapters, you should still prepare for five days. Generally, professors only test after two chapters if there is a great deal of information to learn. If you only did a three-day plan, you wouldn't have enough opportunities to practice the material. Look again at the overview in Figure 8.1. Here, the student omitted studying on Saturday. If you work on Thursday nights or have a night class, you could omit one day from your plan; however, never skip the day right before your exam.

Studying the information as a chunk helps you learn it better. You may find that information in the text helps you better understand material in your lecture notes or vice versa. Learning the information in a connected way better prepares you to answer all types of test questions. You'll also find that when you divide the material into chunks, you can focus on one section of the material at a time. That helps you stay motivated. You don't have to try to learn everything at once, so preparing for your exam doesn't seem overwhelming.

Select active study tasks. It's important to select active study tasks for your study plan. Although spacing your study and dividing the material are important components of this plan, using active strategies is the key to learning the information. Some students study for exams by reading over the material a few times or even many times. Do you? Unfortunately, just reading over the material or even copying it over and over again doesn't help you learn the material well. You may be able to answer questions that involve recognition-level learning (being able to pick out the answer when it is phrased exactly as it was in your text or notes). However, you won't be able to answer higher-level questions such as short-answer, essay, or even multiple-choice questions in which the questions or answers have been rephrased. Instead, you need to use active study strategies that involve writing (in your own words) and reciting the material. Figure 8.2 contains an example of the active study tasks that you might choose to use for two of the days in your Five-Day Study Plan. Take a look at it now. You'll learn about many other active study tasks in the next two sections of this chapter.

Use a variety of strategies. You can't learn all of the information that you need to know by studying one way. If you just focus on learning the definitions for the technical terminology for your exam, you won't be able to answer questions about the way the information is related. If you just focus on learning specific answers to

Figure 8.2 ● Actual Tasks for Five-Day Study Plan

Wednesday		
	Prepare CH 2	1. Remark highlighting
		2. Make study sheets
		3. Make word cards
		4. Make question cards
	Review CH 1	1. Recite rehighlighted material *unknowns (recite main points)
		2. Mark and recite study sheets
		3. Recite word cards
		4. Recite question cards
Thursday		
	Prepare CH 3	1. Remark highlighting
		2. Make study sheets
		3. Make word cards
		4. Make question cards
	Review CH 2	1. Recite rehighlighted material *unknowns (recite main points)
		2. Mark and recite study sheets
		3. Recite word cards
		4. Recite question cards
	Review CH 1	1. Make a list of information still not known from text or study sheets—recite
		2. Recite cards still not known
		3. Make self-test questions

specific questions from your lecture notes, you won't be able to answer a short-answer question about how the material in your notes is related to a similar topic covered in the text. To be well prepared for an exam, you need to use a variety of strategies. Some of those strategies should focus on learning information in an isolated way—learning specific definitions for specific terms or specific answers to specific questions. You also need to focus on learning some of the information in an integrated or connected way—learning all about a particular topic or about how two similar topics are different. As you write your study plan, choose at least three active preparation strategies and three active review strategies. You'll learn more about how to choose active study strategies for your study plan later in this chapter.

There are many ways to study and learn information, but some are much more effective than others. You learned in Chapter 4 about low-level rehearsal strategies (reading, saying, or copying the information over and over) and high-level rehearsal strategies (taking notes, explaining information in your own words, quizzing yourself, and creating study sheets). In this chapter, you'll learn more about using active study strategies that help you learn the material. Each day you need to get actively involved in studying the material.

Self-test. Monitoring your learning is critical to your success on exams. Have you ever walked into an exam thinking you were well prepared only to find out later that you didn't know as much of the material as you thought you did? The best way to prepare for an exam is to take the exam *before* you take the exam—to test yourself. You've already learned how to write questions in the margin of your text and in the margin of your lecture notes. Quizzing yourself by reciting or writing the answers to those questions will let you know what you do know and what you still need to practice again.

One of the greatest advantages of the Five-Day Study Plan is that it provides many opportunities to monitor your learning. As you use the review strategies each day (you'll learn more about how to do that later in the chapter), you can monitor your learning. You can monitor the outcomes of your study—ask yourself whether you know the information that you studied the previous day. You can also monitor your strategies. If you find that you don't remember much of the material you studied the day before or even two days earlier, the strategies you chose may not be working. You can then change your strategies and work on the material again. Quizzing yourself by answering your questions or reciting the definitions for the technical terms are just two ways to self-test. You'll learn more strategies later in the chapter. The important point is that you have to check your learning on a daily basis to see whether you have put the information into long-term memory and whether you can get it back out. Of course, when you self-test and know that you know the information for your exam, you'll have less test anxiety.

Active Preparation Strategies

What are they? There are many active preparation strategies that you can use. You need to decide which strategies will best prepare you for the type of exam you're going to have. For example, many students make word (definition and identification) cards to prepare for exams. Some students like writing questions in their notes while others like to write questions on index cards. It's really up to you. You could also take notes on the text material to further condense and organize it, or you could create study sheets (which will be discussed in the next section of the chapter). For an essay exam, you could predict your own essay questions, plan the answers, and practice them. For a math exam, you could make a set of formula cards or make out a set of problem cards (problem on the front and solution on the back). Look at the menu of active study tasks in Figure 8.3 for more active preparation strategies that you can use.

What's the role of preparation strategies? Preparation strategies help you identify, condense, organize, and write the information you need to learn. You can use the acronym ICOW to remember the role of active preparation strategies. Use preparation strategies the first time you work on a chapter, during the prepare stage. These strategies make you dig through the information in both the text and in your lecture notes and identify what you already know, what you don't know, and what you still need to learn for the exam. Preparation strategies are primarily writing strategies, so they work well for both visual and kinesthetic learners. Of course, auditory learners can recite the information (or mumble it) as they prepare the materials.

Figure 8.3 ● Menu of Active Study Tasks

PREPARATION STRATEGIES	REVIEW STRATEGIES
develop study sheets	recite study sheets
develop concept maps	replicate concept maps
make word cards	recite word cards
make question cards	recite question cards
make formula cards	practice writing formulas
make problem cards	work problems
make self-tests	take self-tests
do study guides	practice study guide info out loud
remark text material	take notes on remarked text
do problems	do "missed" problems
outline	recite main points from outline
take notes	recite notes from recall cues
summarize	recite out loud
chart related material	recreate chart from memory
list steps in the process	recite steps from memory
predict essay questions	answer essay questions
plan essay answers	practice reciting main points
write essay answers	write essay answers from memory
answer questions at end of chapter	recite answers
prepare material for study group	explain material to group members

Why do they work? Active preparation strategies get you actively involved with the material—they get you to work on the material. If you think back to Chapter 4, you learned that you can remember information better when you rehearse it, organize it, elaborate on it, and monitor your learning. Preparation strategies help you rehearse information, often at a higher level because when you take notes, make study sheets, write questions and answers, and even write out definitions or identifications for names, places, events, and dates, you are putting the information in your own words. You're making the information more meaningful. Preparation strategies also work because they force you to condense and organize the information that you need to learn into a more manageable format. As you know, it's easier to learn information when it is more compact and when it's well organized.

Why do you need to use a variety of strategies? As was mentioned earlier in the chapter, you do need to use a variety of strategies because you need to learn different material in different ways. You can't learn all of the information the same way. You'll also develop more cues to aid memory when you work on the material in different ways. Finally, using a variety of strategies helps you use a variety of learning styles as you prepare for your exam, ensuring that you are using the best strategy for you, for the material, and for the exam.

Active Review Strategies

What are they? There are many active review strategies that you can use. You need to decide which strategies will best prepare you for the type of exam you're going to have. The review strategies naturally must match the preparation strategies that you select. If you decide to make word cards to prepare for your exam, then you would recite them (using a flash card method) to review them. If you write questions in the margin, cover the material and recite the answers without looking. If you make study sheets, you can recite the details using the headings as cues or take out a blank sheet of paper and replicate them. If your text has a website, take any of the online tests, or take the end-of-chapter tests if your text includes them. Of course, you should also write your own test questions (planning the incorrect responses for a multiple-choice test helps you know the wrong answers, too). Look again at the menu of active study tasks in Figure 8.3 for more active review strategies that you can use. If you're working with a study group, you can discuss the material, quiz each other using the materials you each prepared, or even exchange self-test materials for more practice. If each member of your study group prepared twenty-five word and twenty-five question cards on the same chapter, they wouldn't all be the same. Each student looks at the material in a different way and will generate different questions on the material or phrase identifications or definitions in slightly different ways. By using another student's materials for self-testing, you may form different cues to aid your memory of the material and have an opportunity to monitor your own learning on each topic in a new way.

What's the role of review strategies? Review strategies help you <u>r</u>ehearse, <u>e</u>xtend, <u>u</u>nderstand, <u>s</u>elf-test, and <u>e</u>valuate your learning. You can use the acronym RE-USE to remember the role of active review strategies. Each time you practice the material that you have prepared, you're using review strategies. These strategies help you move the information into long-term memory, make the material more meaningful, add cues to help you retrieve the information during the exam, and monitor your learning. When you review the material, you get lots of repetition of it. Review strategies are primarily reciting strategies. You can write the information as you review it, but reciting is much faster and works well for auditory learners. Of course, visual and kinesthetic learners are still checking answers on paper and manipulating materials when reviewing.

Why do they work? Active review strategies provide you with many opportunities to review the material, giving you more repetition of it. They also provide you with an opportunity to monitor your learning each day. As you recite or write the information from memory, you are self-testing. You're actually practicing retrieval—going into long-term memory and pulling out the answers to questions that may appear on your exam. The daily reviews allow you to monitor the effectiveness of your strategies and also to keep the information fresh in your memory.

Why do you need to use a variety of strategies? You need a variety of active review strategies because you need to match the review strategies to each of the preparation strategies that you use. In addition, practicing the material in different ways helps you form more cues with the material and practice self-testing with a variety of cues.

Create Study Sheets

What are study sheets? A study sheet is a one-page compilation (one side of one 8.5″ × 11″ sheet of paper) of all the information you need to learn about one particular topic. Unlike long lists of isolated details that some students call study sheets, each study sheet centers around one aspect of the topic presented. By limiting yourself to one page per topic, you are more likely to both select specific topics for study and to condense the material more. For example, you could write a study sheet about the Five-Day Study Plan, another one on active preparation and active review strategies, and even one on study sheets. Generally, you would create a study sheet for each major topic covered in your text and/or lecture, so you'll have three to seven per chapter. Since a study sheet contains all of the important information on one topic, you must condense the material, organize it, and integrate the information from your text and your lecture notes.

How do you make them? Start with your textbook or your notes (whichever your instructor tends to test from the most) and jot down the major topics that were covered. Then take out one sheet of paper for each topic, or do each as a separate page in a document on the computer. At the top center of the page, write the topic. Then use either a modified-block or outline format to list headings, subheadings (if appropriate), and details in meaningful phrases. You could also use map or chart formats to create your study sheets, if you find those formats easier to learn from and remember. When you make a study sheet, include the information that you know about the topic as well as the information that you still need to learn. The previously learned information can help you learn the new information and can serve as an additional cue to help you recall the other details during the exam. Figure 8.4 contains a sample of a study sheet on Mesopotamia. As you can see, it includes a specific topic, a series of headings, and specific details. You can also add questions

Figure 8.4 ● Sample Study Sheet

Mesopotamia

I. Sumer (3500—2350 BC)
       agricultural settlements T & E valley formed towns
       first system of writing
          (signs on clay tablets – cuneiform)
       led to trade → cities
       center of life – temple
          religion – seasons – fertility Great Mother
          ex. Lady of Warka
       govern – priests

Epic of Gilgamesh (most famous ruler) fiction
       pessimistic (life struggle against disaster –
          no afterlife)
     1. quest — human is a questioner (ultimacy)
     2. death — pos & neg moments
     3. story — human is a mythmaker

II. Akkad
       Semitic King Sargon ruled (2350 to 2150)
          art – bronze head of Nineveh
           Stele of Naram – Sim
       buildings – ziggurats

in the margin of your study sheets or even write definitions for key terms used in your study sheets (see Figure 8.5). You've already learned that by adding questions in the margin, you can quiz yourself on the specific details you need to learn. By adding definitions in the margin, you can also practice them within the context of the topic to which they refer. You'll have an opportunity to practice developing study sheets with questions in the margin in Workshop 8-2.

Why do they work? Study sheets work partly because they are a type of active preparation strategy. To create a study sheet, you have to identify the important information, condense it, organize it, and write it. They are also effective because they break the course material down into individual units for study. If you've already discovered that working on one chapter at a time when you study helps you focus your learning, you'll find that breaking each chapter into its main topics will help you even more. You'll be able to concentrate on gathering and learning all of the material about each specific topic by combining the information together from your text and lecture notes. When you create study sheets you have the advantage of putting the information into your own words and organizing it in a way that makes sense to you. As you learned in Chapter 4, both of these processes help you learn and remember the material more easily. Study sheets also prepare you to answer any kind of question. Because you are learning all of the information about one topic, you can answer true/false, multiple-choice, matching, short-answer, or

Figure 8.5 ● Example of a Study Sheet with Definitions in the Margin

	Animals
Multicellular organisms that capture and consume molecules of other organisms	
	General Information
	over 1.3 million species
	greatest diversity
	include more than 30 phyla
	breathe in oxygen + exhale carbon dioxide
organisms without backbones	Invertebrates
	coral and sponges
	can be broken into separate minute
	organisms that function independently
	worms, mollusks, + microscopic organisms
invertebrates with a hard exoskeleton, specialized segments, and jointed appendages	Arthropods
	most successful phylum
crabs, shrimp, lobsters	spiders, insects, crustacea
	segmented bodies + jointed limbs
	70% of all animals
hard external covering used to support and protect	have an exoskeleton for support
	shed exoskeletons when growing
central segment with legs	body—head, thorax, and heart
have spinal cord encased in a backbone	Vertebrates
	rabbits, frogs, fish, birds
	bony fish
	skeletons made from bones
	gills supply oxygen in stagnant water
vertebrates with a body plan and reproductive mode between fishes and reptiles	Amphibians
	life cycle on land and in water
	tadpoles evolve into frogs
	3 chambered heart + circulatory system

even essay questions. Study sheets also provide you with a framework for learning the information (with loads of connections and associations) and give you layers of cues (the topic, headings, subheadings, and related details) to help you recall the specific points you need to answer exam questions. When you're ready to study for a comprehensive final exam, you'll have a set of study sheets for every chapter you've covered in the course.

How do you use them? Creating a set of study sheets is just the first step, though. You still need to learn the information on them. On each of the following days in your study plan, recite the information on the study sheets using the topic and the headings as cues. You can also use a blank sheet of paper to replicate any study sheets you anticipate will be covered heavily on the exam. By working on the material as a whole, you can practice the material in a connected or integrated way—learning all of the material related to one specific topic. If you add questions or definitions in the margin, quiz yourself using them as you did with the recall columns in your text or lecture notes. In this way you can learn the material in an isolated way—learning specific definitions for specific terms or specific answers to specific questions.

Strategies for Essay Exams

Predict questions. One of the most effective ways to prepare for an essay exam is to predict possible essay questions and then plan out the answers and learn them. You should predict broad, challenging questions that cover one or more major topics. Essay questions often ask you to describe, explain, compare, contrast, or even justify. Predict four to five times the number of questions that you'll have to answer on the exam. If you have an exam that will have two questions, predict eight to ten. That way you are increasing your odds that one of your predicted questions will be on the exam. How often are the questions that you write in the margin of your notes or text on an objective exam? You may have already discovered that the more questions you write, the more likely you'll be able to answer the exam questions. Some instructors only have students answer one essay question on an exam. If you only have one essay question on the exam, predict three to four questions from each chapter. The key is to cover all of the important topics that were covered.

Plan the answers. Many students think that writing out the answer to a possible essay question and then memorizing it is the way to prepare for an essay exam. Instead, it's actually better to create an outline of the answer. Predicting essay questions and planning the answers is a preparation strategy. As you'll see, this strategy helps you identify the information that you'll need to answer the essay questions, condense it, organize it, and write it. To plan your answer, follow these steps.

1. **Gather information.** Write the question across the top of a piece of paper and then dig through the text material and your lecture notes to find all of the information that you could use to answer that question. Then jot down all of the points using a two-column format below the question (see Figure 8.6). You want to write the information in meaningful phrases to condense it.

2. **Organize your points.** Next, look through the gathered information, decide which point you would discuss first in your answer, and label it 1. Then find any information that supports that point and label each one 1A, 1B, 1C, and so on. Continue to identify each of the main points and their related supporting details. You may find that you have a lot of support for some points but very little for others. Go back to your text and notes and look for additional points to add to your essay plan.

3. **Outline your answer.** Once you've identified all of the information you need for your answer, copy each of the meaningful phrases into an outline for your answer. By rearranging the points you've gathered, you're restructuring the information so it will be easier to learn and remember. You can also create mnemonics to cue your recall of the main points or the details you planned.

Figure 8.6 ● Sample Essay Plan

Explain the view Thomas Hobbes took on the problem of order and the social contract.

1 social order is political natural law	3 equality among people
2 state of nature	4 people form a social contract
2A people are selfish and violent	4A agreement b/w societies
2C people become power hungry	4B people give up natural liberty
2B central concept is power	4C laws tell us how to act
3A state of nature is condition of war	5 if break laws we are denied freedom
3B common fear of power	6 power of state is order

TS Thomas Hobbes viewed order in society as a hunger for power among people.

1. Social order is political <u>natural</u> law

2. <u>State</u> of nature
   A. people are selfish & violent
   B. central concept is power
   C. people become power hungry

3. <u>Equality</u> among people
   A. state of nature is condition of war
   B. common fear of power

4. People form a social <u>contract</u>
   A. agreement b/w societies
   B. people give up natural liberty
   C. laws tell us how to act

5. If we break laws, we are deprived of <u>freedom</u>

6. <u>Power</u> of state is order

1. <u>N</u>atural
2. <u>S</u>tate
3. <u>E</u>quality
4. <u>C</u>ontract
5. <u>F</u>reedom
6. <u>P</u>ower

(<u>N</u>ancy <u>s</u>ells <u>e</u>very <u>c</u>ar <u>f</u>or <u>p</u>arts.)

Practice the answers. After you develop an outline for each of your answers, you need to learn the information. You can practice your essay answers during the review stages of the Five-Day Study Plan. Each day, take a few minutes and practice reciting your outlines. Use the question as a cue and try to recall the main points in the outline first. Once you know each main point that you want to make, use the main points (headings in your outline) as cues to help you learn and recall the supporting details. If you created an acronym or acrostic to help you remember the information, practice reciting your outline using your mnemonics as cues. You can also take a blank sheet of paper and replicate your outline from memory.

Write the answers. You may want to write out some of the answers in paragraph form. It's really not necessary to do this step because if you know the outline, you'll be able to write the essay during the exam. However, some students do have a little trouble figuring out how to start the essay and string their ideas together. If you'd like a little practice, write out the answers to the most difficult questions and then ask your professor, tutor, or someone in your college learning center to look at them and give you some feedback.

WORKSHOP 8-1 Write and Critique Study Plans

In this workshop, you'll have an opportunity to critique study plans and then write your own for an upcoming exam. Review each of the study plans in Figures 8.7, 8.8, and 8.9. Then list their strengths and weaknesses in the space below. Compare your responses to those of the other members of your group. Use your own paper to write your own study plan. Consider the mistakes these students made as you write your own plan. Then critique your study plan.

SUE'S PLAN

Strengths   Weaknesses

JOE'S PLAN

Strengths   Weaknesses

MARY'S PLAN

Strengths   Weaknesses

Figure 8.7 ● Sue's Plan

Five-Day Study Plan Computer Literacy Chapters 9 and 10 Monday, February 18

Wednesday
Prepare Ch. 9

1. Remark highlighting
2. Make study sheets
3. Make question and word cards

Thursday
Prepare Ch. 10

1. Remark text
2. Make question and word cards
3. Recite lecture notes
4. Make study sheets

Friday
Review Ch. 9

1. Recite cards
2. Do test at end of Chapter 9
3. Reread marked text

Saturday
Review Ch. 10

1. Recite cards
2. Do test at end of Chapter 10
3. Recite missed test questions

Sunday
Review Ch. 9 & 10

1. Recite missed cards
2. Redo tests
3. Recite study sheets

Figure 8.8 ● Joe's Plan

Life Science – test date – March 6
The exam consists of 25 true and false and 45 multiple choice
Chapter 8 = Cellular Basis of Reproduction and Inheritance
Chapter 9 = Patterns of Inheritance
Chapter 14 = How Populations Evolve

Sunday	Read ten pages of Chapter 8 and highlight Read ten more pages of Chapter 8 and highlight later that day
Monday	Finish reading Chapter 8 and highlight Take notes on all of Chapter 8, write and recite notes, make note cards
Tuesday	Read and highlight Chapter 9, take breaks in reading Later take notes on Chapter 9, make note cards
Wednesday	Read Chapter 14 and highlight, take breaks in reading Take notes on Chapter 14 and make note cards
Thursday	Practice writing and reciting notes for the chapter = look over note cards
Friday	Practice again writing and reciting notes for all chapters Look over highlighted material again Look over note cards
Saturday & Sunday	Do everything over that I did on Friday for both of these days

Figure 8.9 ● Mary's Plan

I have prepared a Five-Day Study Plan for my American Political Process course. The test will be based on chapters six and seven. It will consist of multiple-choice questions, fill-in-the-blank questions, and one essay question. The test will be given on Monday, April 12 at 6:00 P.M.

PREPARING FOR EXAM

Tuesday, April 6
Chapter 6

1. Remark highlighting
2. Make word cards
3. Develop a part function map
4. Make up a self-test
5. Answer questions at end of chapter
6. Outline chapter

Wednesday, April 7
Chapter 7

1. Remark highlighting
2. Take notes
3. Make question cards
4. Develop study sheets
5. Answer questions at end of chapter
6. Develop an organizational chart

REVIEWING FOR EXAM

Thursday, April 8
Chapter 6

1. Review highlighted material
2. Recite main points from outline
3. Review notes
4. Draw the part function map from memory
5. Recite word cards
6. Take notes on rehighlighted material

Saturday, April 10
Chapter 7

1. Review highlighted material
2. Recite question cards
3. Review notes
4. Explain material to roommate
5. Recopy organizational chart from memory
6. Recite notes from recall cues

Sunday, April 11
Chapter 6

1. Explain material to roommate
2. Practice reciting main points
3. Take self-tests

Chapter 7

1. Recite study sheets
2. Recite main points from outline
3. Recite answers from questions at end of chapter

WORKSHOP 8-2 Integrate Material with Study Sheets

In this workshop, you'll have a chance to practice creating study sheets using the material in Chapter 5 and your own course material.

1. Go through the material presented in Chapter 5 and make a list of the major topics you would use to create study sheets. List them below.

_____

_____

_____

_____

_____

_____

_____

2. Select one of the topics you listed above and create a study sheet on the paper provided in Figure 8.10.

3. As you can see, there is a wide margin on the page. After making up your study sheet, you can use the margin in several ways:

   • Write questions in the margin and highlight the answers in the study sheet. Be sure to write the questions directly across from the answers.

   • Write definitions for the key terms you included in your study sheet and highlight the terms. Be sure to write the definition directly across from each term.

4. Compare your study sheet to that of another student who used the same topic.

   Did you use the same headings in your study sheet? _____

   Did you include the same details? _____

5. What changes would you make the next time you make a study sheet?

_____

_____

_____

_____

_____

_____

_____

_____

_____

_____

Figure 8.10 ● Study Sheet Page

WORKSHOP 8-3 Predict Essay Questions and Plan Answers

In this workshop, you'll have an opportunity to practice predicting essay questions and planning out the answers. Use the question, "Why is the Five-Day Study Plan effective in helping students prepare for exams?" Then answer each of the questions below.

1. Go through the material in this chapter and make a list of the information that you could use to answer the question. List the points in a two-column format using meaningful phrases.

   _____   _____
   _____   _____
   _____   _____
   _____   _____
   _____   _____
   _____   _____
   _____   _____
   _____   _____
   _____   _____
   _____   _____
   _____   _____
   _____   _____
   _____   _____
   _____   _____
   _____   _____
   _____   _____

2. Compare your gathered information to that of your course instructor. Did you include most of the same points? _____ Add any points that you missed to your list.

3. Go back to your list of gathered information. Label each of the main points that you would use to answer the question.

4. Compare your main points to those of your course instructor. Did you identify the same main points for your answer? _____ Did you use the same organizational structure?

5. Copy your gathered information onto the Essay Plan Sheet in Figure 8.11. Then outline your answer in the space provided.

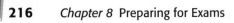

Figure 8.11 ● Essay Plan Sheet

Question: _____

_____

Gathered Information:

_____   _____
_____   _____
_____   _____
_____   _____
_____   _____
_____   _____

Outline:

WORKSHOP 8-4   What Would You Do?

In this workshop, you'll have a chance to consider a case study and make suggestions that Kimi could use to better prepare for her exams.

Kimi is a pre-med major. She hopes someday to become a pediatrician and has worked hard all through school to earn top grades. Kimi is taking Biology this term and plans to make flash cards to learn the technical terminology for her exam. She looked through the material and estimated that she would need to create about 200 flash cards for the five chapters on her exam. Two days before the exam, Kimi began to write out her flash cards. She started working on them after dinner on Wednesday and didn't finish until midnight. On Thursday, Kimi decided to make up questions about the material in her notes and text. She worked on her question cards all day Thursday when she didn't have classes. She made up about forty questions for each chapter. After dinner on Thursday, she began to review her flash cards, working on the definitions first and then on the questions. She practiced reciting them after dinner and worked until she couldn't keep her eyes open any more. She finally got to sleep about 2:30 A.M. and got up when her alarm chirped at 7:00 A.M. After she got ready for class, she did a quick review of the cards she still was having trouble remembering. She walked into her 9:00 A.M. exam feeling well prepared, though a little tired. A week later, Kimi got her exam back and was very disappointed that she had earned a low C. She knew she had to get better grades than that to get into medical school.

1. What mistakes did Kimi make in her exam preparation strategies?

_____

_____

_____

_____

_____

_____

_____

_____

2. What changes should Kimi make in the way she uses her time to prepare for her exam?

_____

_____

_____

_____

_____

_____

_____

_____

3. What changes should Kimi make in the strategies she chooses for her exam preparation?

_____

_____

_____

_____

_____

_____

_____

_____

_____

_____

_____

_____

_____

_____

_____

_____

Now think back to the last couple of exams you prepared for. What did you do? Were you satisfied with the grades you earned? What mistakes did you make in your preparation?

4. Did you make any of the same mistakes that Kimi made in preparing for her exams? What changes do you plan to make when you prepare for your next exam?

_____

_____

_____

_____

_____

_____

_____

_____

_____

_____

_____

_____

_____

_____

Taking Charge of Your Life Workshop

Managing Stress

As a college student, you are required to balance a multitude of demands while performing to a high academic standard. It is not surprising, then, that almost 30 percent of college students report that stress negatively affected their academic performance within the past year.[1] Are you experiencing the backlash of stress? Take the following assessment to check your own stress level and your ability to manage the various demands of your own life.

? Where Are You Now?

Take a few minutes to answer *yes* or *no* to the following questions.

	YES	NO
1. Do you understand the role that stress plays in your life?	_____	_____
2. Do you ignore the signals your body sends you when you are stressed?	_____	_____
3. Does stress always serve a negative function in your life?	_____	_____
4. Do you avoid addressing the stressors in your life?	_____	_____
5. Do you know how to reduce your stress level?	_____	_____
6. Do you consistently use a positive stress management technique?	_____	_____
7. Do you have trouble managing your time?	_____	_____
8. Do you consistently exercise and make healthy food choices?	_____	_____
9. Do your relationships stress you out?	_____	_____
10. Are you reluctant to ask for help when you need it?	_____	_____
Total Points		_____

Give yourself one point for each *yes* answer you gave to questions 1, 5, 6, 8, and 10 and one point for each *no* answer you gave to questions 2, 3, 4, 7, and 9. Now total your points. A low score indicates that you could benefit from learning more about the role stress plays in your life and how to better manage stress. A high score indicates that you are aware of the effects of stress and you usually manage the stress in your life in a positive way.

---

[1] American College Health Association. American College Health Association-National College Health Assessment (ACHA-NCHA) Web Summary. Updated September 2005. Available at www.acha.org/ projects_programs/ncha_sampledata.cfm.2005.

No college student is immune from feeling the effects of stress from time to time. A wide range of academic and personal stressors permeate college life, and students manage those demands with varying degrees of success. While each of you has your own unique set of challenges and varying abilities to manage stress, the following information and skills can be useful to everybody and can be adapted to fit your own set of circumstances.

Is Stress Always Bad?

Contrary to what you might think, stress can serve a positive function in your life. It can help push you to meet deadlines and perform at an optimal level. For example, when athletes feel "pumped up" for a big game, they are actually channeling the adrenaline in a positive manner. In many situations, your perception can be the deciding factor in whether you react negatively (overwhelmed, paralyzed) or positively (challenged, energized). In other words, one student might view an upcoming project worth half the class grade as terrible drudgery while another might view it as a challenge and feel excited about getting started.

The Dark Side of Stress

Unfortunately, stress more often has a detrimental impact on our lives. It is important to note that sometimes even someone with the best attitude can fall prey to stress. That's because we are all human, and life has a way of not always going as smoothly as we hope it will. Whether you experience a break-up or feel overwhelmed by three exams on the same day, stress affects us all. What are your own sources of stress?

Personal Stressors

Some of you are living with people you have known for a relatively short period of time. Others of you are living at home, perhaps under the same set of rules (and curfew!) you had when you were in high school. Some of you are trying to make long-distance relationships work, while others are navigating the always tricky waters of getting to know new people. You get the idea. Because of the nature of college, you are forced to make a variety of difficult choices on a daily basis (choices of whom to hang out with, whether to drink alcohol or not, and so on). And again, because we are human, we don't always make the best decisions— which can lead to quite a bit of stress.

Academic Stressors

Many students simply do not anticipate the amount of work necessary to perform successfully at college. And for some of you, the learning curve involves obtaining a GPA much lower than you anticipated, which means working extra hard to dig yourself out of a hole. Or you may have extremely high expectations of yourself— that only the best is acceptable. Some of you must balance demanding personal lives along with carrying your academic load. And we haven't even mentioned the stress of determining a major *and* a career path. All of this can add up to some serious stress.

Stress: Is It All in Your Head?

Stress is a normal physiological response to a perceived demand or threat—the "fight or flight" phenomenon. Think of a caveman being pursued by a saber-toothed tiger and you have a pretty good idea of what goes on in your body. While your stressors can take many forms (though probably not that of a large, threatening animal), the response of your body is the same in terms of the rush of adrenaline and the resulting experience. You also experience a psychological response to stressful situations, which could include impaired thinking and concentration as well as feeling emotions such as fear, anger, or frustration.

Other than the true crises that occur in life, there are few events that are truly stressful. We have emphasized that it is your perception that influences whether or not a situation is difficult to handle. In addition, there are some personal characteristics you may possess that trigger a negative stress response. Do you have unrealistic expectations or a negative attitude? Do you behave irresponsibly despite experiencing consequences? Your overall approach to life impacts your ability to manage stress positively.

If your stress response is triggered repeatedly and you do not employ effective stress management methods, you will experience the negative effects of stress—perhaps you already have. Stress can have both immediate and long-lasting effects on your health and well-being. Remember that we said that your body responds to stress both physically and psychologically. If your body sends you one of the following stress-induced signals, you should take action and make some changes.

Keep in mind that the following list does not represent all possible stress-related symptoms. It is also possible that your symptoms are caused by an illness. Get checked out by a health care provider to be sure. When feeling stressed do you experience any of the following physiological symptoms?

- Increased heart rate
- Tension headaches or migraines
- Upset stomach
- Weight changes
- Sleep disturbances
- Immune system suppression
- Muscle tension and back/shoulder/neck pain

How about any of these psychological symptoms?

- Confusion
- Memory problems
- Impaired problem-solving
- Anxiety
- Moodiness, depression
- Irritability
- Anger
- Sadness

These symptoms could represent a condition other than stress, so it is best to get checked out so that you get a clear idea of the source of your symptoms—and to be treated appropriately. When you experience any of the mentioned stress-related symptoms, it is likely that your relationships will suffer. An increase in conflicts and arguments with people in your life can also be cues that you are suffering from the negative effects of stress.

Strategies for Managing Stress

So how can you ensure that stress doesn't get the better of you? Asking yourself the following questions can help you manage the stress in your life:

1. **Am I feeling stressed?** As simple as this question may seem, too many people speed through life, ignoring the signals of stress. Be aware of the messages your body and mind send you. Recognize your unique physical and emotional reactions to stress. Realizing that you are feeling stressed can help you get a grip on the situation before it worsens.

2. **What is causing the stress?** While we sometimes ignore the stress signals, we also may not slow down long enough to consider what exactly is producing our stress response. Pinpointing the source of your stress helps you avoid feeling overwhelmed and enables you to take appropriate action.

3. **Why am I reacting to the stressor?** A better question might be: Am I *overreacting* to the stressor? Do some introspection to figure out what you find demanding or threatening about the situation. Why are you feeling this way? Can you shift your perception? This process will require you to be honest with yourself and to face reality. For example, it takes courage to realize that a relationship is causing you more stress than joy, or that you won't be able to proceed in a certain major. After you make such realizations, you then need to figure out what you can do about it by asking yourself the next question.

4. **How can I manage the stress?** Don't wallow in your misery. Taking some kind of action helps you feel more in control of the situation. Perhaps you need to manage your time better to avoid feeling overwhelmed by the demands of your coursework. Maybe you need to have an honest discussion with your roommate. Whatever the circumstance, taking action means that you are doing something to change your situation and can go a long way in relieving stress. You also have the choice of reducing your exposure to the stressor or eliminating it altogether. In the case of a toxic relationship, this might mean ending it. In the case of realizing that your major is too tough for you, it may mean finding a career that is related to what you originally wanted to pursue. The point is that you need to be active instead of feeling victimized by stress, which can be accomplished by focusing on the things that you can change and not on what you cannot.

Many resources on managing stress are available. The key is to find something that works for you. One size definitely does not fit all when it comes to stress management. For example, your friend may find it very relaxing to take a yoga class, while you may benefit more from an intense kickboxing session. The following tips are some general guidelines that can be adapted to fit your needs.

Manage Your Time

Often, students feel overwhelmed and stressed out about the sheer number of demands in their lives. Getting organized and utilizing some time management strategies can help you stay on task (see Chapter 2). Stress is reduced because you feel more aware and in control of the tasks that you need to complete. Using a planner, making weekly and daily To-Do lists, and setting study goals are all techniques that can help you stay focused.

Take Care of Yourself—Body and Mind

Your mind and body are intricately related when it comes to your response to stress. Taking care of your physical well-being strengthens emotional well-being. The old adage, "You are what you eat," is particularly true when it comes to stress. A steady diet of high-fat, high-sugar, and/or high-calorie foods makes you feel sluggish, both mentally and physically. Doing your best to maintain a healthy balance of all food groups can help you be at your best. Likewise, trying to get in regular exercise helps your cause. A Harvard report states that you can ". . . use exercise to stifle the build-up of stress in several ways. Just about any form of motion helps relieve pent-up muscle tension. And certain activities, such as yoga and tai chi, and repetitive exercise, such as running or rowing, elicit the relaxation response."[2]

Take a Time Out

Even the busiest college student can, and should, schedule some down time daily. You can benefit tremendously from getting away from the source of your stress and doing something that you love and that makes you feel calm. Take a quick walk, join a friend for a cup of tea, chat online for a while—you know what works best for you. Whatever you choose, make sure that it is a positive way of dealing with stress. Too often, college students turn to methods of reducing stress that serve to bring them down further. Turning to alcohol and drugs provides a brief escape from the daily stress of life, but it is only temporary. Then, throw in a hangover and some of the other consequences of substance abuse, and you end up feeling more stressed out. If you tend to use alcohol or another drug to "blow off steam" or to escape from life's pressures, you may benefit from seeking out a counselor to help you deal more positively with stress.

Pledge for Positive Relationships

Every once in a while, it is beneficial to do an inventory of your current relationships. What role do your relationships play in your life? If you are in a relationship filled with arguments and conflict, what can you do to change the situation? The point is this: Relationships should serve to support you and bring you happiness. When you are feeling the effects of stress, you should be able to count on your relationships (with friends, family, or your significant other) to boost and help you get through the difficult time. Instead, too many students are involved in relationships that actually add to the stress in their lives. Resolving to end an unhealthy relationship can dramatically reduce the stress in your life.

It is normal to feel "stressed out" every once in a while. If you find that you are consistently feeling overwhelmed and burdened by the stress in your life, seek out a support person to help you. Talking about your stressors with someone who is unbiased and uninvolved in your life can provide you with much-needed perspective.

[2] Coltrera, Francesca. *Stress Control: Techniques for Preventing and Easing Stress.* Ed. Ann Marie Dadoly. Boston: Harvard Health Publications, 2002.

RESOURCES

- Visit **www.campusblues.com**, a website designed specifically for college students to help address the issues that you face.

- Check out **wellness.uwsp.edu/Other/stress**, a stress self-assessment from the University Health Services at the University of Wisconsin-Stevens Point. The assessment will help you to evaluate the sources of stress in your life.

What Do You Do Now?

Managing Stress Scenario

Jon is a Political Science major and is in his junior year. He has been working hard this semester because he is on academic probation and must bring up his GPA or face dismissal from the university. He has borderline grades in a number of his classes as he approaches the last few weeks of the semester.

1. Describe a possible negative response to this stressor.

_____

_____

_____

_____

_____

2. How will this response serve him in meeting his goals?

_____

_____

_____

_____

_____

3. How could Jon react more positively to the situation?

_____

_____

_____

_____

_____

4. How would this response better serve him in meeting his goals?

_____

_____

_____

_____

Now think about your own life.

5. List three stressful situations that you are currently dealing with or have had to deal with during the past three months. Briefly describe each of the three situations. Be sure to include at least one academic stressor.

Stressful Situation A:

_____

_____

_____

_____

Stressful Situation B:

_____

_____

_____

_____

Stressful Situation C:

_____

_____

_____

_____

6. Select one of the three situations you described and respond to the questions included in the stress-management process.

a. Was I feeling stressed out? (List any physical or emotional stress-related signs that you experienced.)

_____

_____

_____

_____

_____

b. What was causing the stress? Was it academic, personal, or career related? Describe the cause of the stress.

_____

_____

_____

_____

_____

c. Why was I reacting to the stress?

_____

_____

_____

_____

d. How did I manage the stress? (Were you able to change the way you were thinking about or responding to the situation? What stress management techniques did you use?)

_____

_____

_____

_____

10. Describe a current stressor that you are experiencing.

a. Am I feeling stressed out? (List any physical or emotional stress-related signs that you experienced.)

_____

_____

_____

_____

b. What is causing the stress? Is it academic, personal, or career related? Describe the cause of the stress.

_____

_____

_____

_____

c. Why am I reacting to the stress?

_____

_____

_____

_____

d. How can I manage the stress? (Can you change the way you are thinking about or responding to the situation? What stress management techniques do you think will benefit you?)

_____

_____

_____

_____

_____

Taking Tests

CHAPTER **9**

In this chapter you will learn more about:

- General test-taking strategies

- Strategies for true/false tests

- Strategies for multiple-choice tests

- Strategies for matching tests

- Strategies for essay tests

- Strategies for problem-based tests

? Where Are You Now?

Take a few minutes to answer *yes* or *no* to the following questions.

	YES	NO
1. Do you always read the directions before you begin to answer the questions on an exam?	_____	_____
2. Do you eliminate wrong answers on multiple-choice exams?	_____	_____
3. Does test anxiety interfere with your performance on exams?	_____	_____
4. Do you ever leave blanks on exams?	_____	_____
5. Do you use strategies to help you figure out the correct answer when you are unsure of it?	_____	_____
6. Do you ever find that you're unable to finish an exam before time runs out?	_____	_____
7 Do you go back over the entire exam before you turn it in?	_____	_____
8. After your exam is returned, do you go over it to evaluate your preparation and clarify your errors?	_____	_____
9. When you get your exam back, are you often surprised by the grade that you received?	_____	_____
10. Do you usually score lower an essay exams than objective tests?	_____	_____
Total Points	_____	

Give yourself 1 point for each *yes* answer to questions 1, 2, 5, 7, and 8, and 1 point for each *no* answer to questions 3, 4, 6, 9, and 10. Now total up your points. A low score indicates that you need to develop some new skills for taking tests. A high score indicates that you are already using many good test-taking strategies.

General Test-Taking Strategies

Preview the exam. As soon as you get your exam, take a look through it. Check to see how many questions you have to answer, what types of questions are included, and whether some sections are worth more than others. If your instructor gave you a description of the exam prior to it, look to see if the exam matches what you expected.

Follow directions. Reading and following directions is critical on any exam. Some students are so nervous at the beginning of an exam that they forget to read the directions carefully. Others plunge into the exam as soon as they get it and don't listen as the instructor gives oral directions related to the exam. The directions provide you with information on how many questions to answer on an essay test, what form answers must take, point values for different questions, and other special directions. Most students expect all exam directions to be the same, but they aren't.

Some instructors ask you to find the best answer on a multiple-choice test and others ask for all correct answers. If there are three correct answers for some of the questions and you only mark one correct, you'd lose a lot of points on the exam. As you read the directions, you should underline key words that tell you what you're expected to do. You may also find it helpful to use a monitoring device; put a check-mark in the margin after reading the directions so that you can look back later to see if it is there.

Budget your time. Some students fail exams because they aren't able to complete all of the questions in the time provided. If you leave five questions blank (out of fifty) and each is worth two points, you would lose a whole letter grade on the exam. To finish the test, you need to pace yourself as you take the exam. To maximize your score, you also need to put the correct amount of time into each question on the test.

● *Consider the point values.* Count the total number of questions that you have to answer. Then look at each section of the exam and check the point value for each question. If you had to answer four short-answer questions (each worth five points) and forty multiple-choice questions (each worth two points), how much time would you need to spend on the short-answer questions if you had 50 minutes to complete the exam? If you said about 10 minutes, you were correct. Because the four short answer questions total twenty points of 100 points, they are worth 20 percent of the points. You should spend 20 percent of the time, or 10 minutes, on that section. That would leave you with 40 minutes to spend on the multiple-choice section (80% of the points = 80% of the time). If you have to answer ten (five-point) identification questions and one fifty-point essay, how much time would you spend on each section of the test? Consider the formula below.

> Percentage of total points = Percentage of total time

● *Pace yourself.* Let's say you had 60 minutes for the exam described previously. You would need to spend half of your time on the identification questions and the other half on the essay question. Since each section of the exam is worth fifty points, you would need to divide your time in half, spending 30 minutes on each section of the exam. To be sure that you stay on track, jot down the amount of time you want to spend on each section on the exam and keep track of the time as you move through the test. If you had forty multiple-choice questions with only 50 minutes to complete the exam, you would need to spend about 1 minute on each question and 10 minutes to review the exam. That sounds easy enough; however, it's also easy to get behind early in the exam. Instead divide the number of pages on the exam (let's say there are five) into the total time. You would need to spend about 8 minutes per page. If you wrote the time at the bottom of each page (2:08, 2:16, and so on), the written time would serve as a cue to check your watch and either slow down or speed up as you moved through the test.

Reduce test anxiety. Many students experience some test anxiety before and during exams. A low level of test anxiety, called *facilitating test anxiety*, is actually motivating and helps you prepare well for the exam and work hard when taking it. A high level of test anxiety, called *debilitating test anxiety*, can interfere with a student's ability to prepare for and take exams. When students are very nervous about exams, they typically experience mental and physical symptoms. Some of the more

Figure 9.1 ● Test-Anxiety Cycle

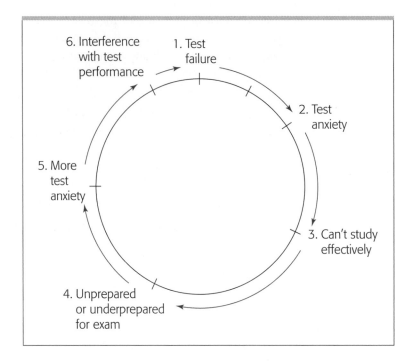

common symptoms associated with test anxiety are negative thoughts, worry, headaches, nausea, sweaty palms, rapid heartbeat, and difficulty breathing, just to name a few. These symptoms often occur when students think about the exam, and they can interfere with test preparation. When you can't stop thinking about failing the exam or worrying about whether you will be permitted to return to school next term, it's difficult to concentrate on the material you are trying to learn. In the same way, when you have a headache or feel sick to your stomach, that also interferes with your ability to study effectively.

Typically students with high levels of test anxiety come to the exam either unprepared or underprepared. Knowing they are not adequately prepared then leads to even more anxiety about the exam. This leads to more symptoms and subsequently more interference with test performance (see Figure 9.1). In much the same way, when you're thinking about failing the exam, you're not thinking about the questions and retrieving the answers. When you become physically ill during the exam, you may lose time trying to control your physical symptoms or by being out of the classroom throwing up.

There are a number of strategies that you can use to reduce your test anxiety. Some are listed here. You can find many others by doing a search on the Internet.

- **Prepare well.** The best way to lower your test anxiety level is to be well prepared for the exam and to know that you are well prepared. A structured study plan such as the Five-Day Study Plan can help you prepare well.

- **Monitor your learning.** If you test yourself as you study for the exam, you'll know what you do know and what you don't know. Then you can work more on the material until you do know it. Knowing you know the material will help you feel more confident and less anxious when you begin the exam.

- **Use relaxation strategies.** Use some type of deep-breathing or muscle-relaxation strategies at the beginning of the exam to calm yourself. Just taking a few deep breaths can reduce your anxiety.

- **Use positive self-talk.** If you begin to think negative thoughts during the exam, you need to push them aside by substituting positive self-talk. Practice a positive script that you can recite to focus your thinking and calm yourself.

- **Answer the easiest questions first.** If you skip the hard questions and answer the easy ones (the ones you know) first, you'll actually reduce your anxiety. You'll know after a few minutes that you do know some or even many of the answers and begin to relax. Once you've reduced your anxiety level, you'll find that you can go back to some of the harder questions and they won't seem as hard as they seemed at first.

- **Identify your triggers.** Find out what things tend to trigger your anxiety and avoid them. If you tend to get nervous when you read the first question on the exam, start with the second page or last page of the exam. If you tend to worry about the essay questions at the end of the exam while you're working on the first part of the exam, do them first instead.

Work logically through the exam. To maximize your score, you should work logically and methodically through the exam. Answer the questions that you know first (the easy ones for you), use specific test-taking strategies (presented later in the chapter) to figure out the answers to others, and then search your memory and the test to answer a few more. When you come to a difficult question, don't panic. There are difficult questions on tests. Instead, say, "Oh, that's a hard one; I'll come back to it later." In the process of completing other questions on the test, you may find that you can pick up a clue or cue to one of those harder questions.

Use strategic guessing to pick up more points. After you complete all of the questions you know, you may still have some questions you can't answer. Instead of just randomly filling in the blanks, you can pick up a few points on your exam by using some strategic guessing strategies. In Workshop 9-1, you'll have a chance to try out some of them. One of the most important things you need to remember is that you need to be well prepared for the exam to benefit from strategic guessing. It only works when you are well prepared—when you only have a small number of questions that you can't answer correctly. You also need to remember that you should only use these strategies when none of your test-taking strategies work.

● *Look for patterns.* One of the most commonly used strategic guessing strategies is to look for patterns in the answers. Many professors are careful about how they structure the exam. They like to mix up the letters for the correct answers on multiple-choice and true/false exams. Have you ever answered two multiple choice questions you were sure of with the same letter (B for example) and then switched to a different letter when you weren't sure of the correct answer for the next question? This strategy only works, though, if you are well prepared for the exam, because you need to get most of the questions correct for the patterns to emerge.

● *Check for balanced answer keys.* Many instructors balance their answer keys— they include exactly the same number of A, B, C, and D answers on the exam. If you know that your professor balances his or her answer keys, count the number of each answer you've already used on the exam and then guess strategically. For example, if you have six questions that you can't answer on your exam and you've already used six As, eight Bs, ten Cs, and ten Ds, how would you answer the remaining questions? When I use this example in class, most students choose four As and two Bs to complete the answer key. Unless you are extremely lucky, that's not the best strategy to use. Two of the As could be Bs and the two Bs could be As. If that were the case, you would get only two questions right. A better choice would be to put all As for the six answers resulting in four correct answers. The first rule of strategic guessing is don't be greedy. Instead of trying to get them all right (which probably won't happen) try to get some right—try to pick up just a few more points. Again, the more questions that you can answer correctly, the better your odds of guessing strategically.

Review the exam before turning it in. Before turning in your exam, you need to take a few minutes and review the exam. First, check to make sure that you answered all of the questions. Leaving blanks costs you points. Next, go back over your responses to each question. Check to be sure that you didn't misread any of the questions or answers. How many times have you gone over an exam in class and realized that you lost points due to careless mistakes? Finally, check the answers that you marked on the exam (circle the correct answer if you're allowed to write on the test) against your answer key. Be sure that the answer to each question that you marked on the exam matches the answer you coded in on the answer sheet.

Learn from your mistakes. When you get your exam back, take a good look at the mistakes you made. Take some time to figure out why you got each question wrong. Consider the following questions as you review your exam:

- Did you make careless errors because you spent too little time on each of the questions?
- Did you run out of time and have to just mark down any answer at the end of the exam?
- Were there specific sections of the exam that caused you problems?
- Did you spend too much time on questions you really couldn't answer anyway?
- Did you miss questions that were taken from the text? Lecture? Other materials?
- Did you earn a low score on one, or all, of the essays?

If you earned a low score on all of the essay questions, you may not know how to write a good essay answer—you may not know what your professor expects. You could ask a classmate who earned an A on the exam to allow you to read his or her answers so that you have a better idea of what your professor expects. You could also meet with your professor during office hours to get more feedback on what you need to do differently. To be sure that you will do better the next time, rewrite one or two of the answers (using your text and lecture notes) and ask your professor to review the answers with you.

Strategies for True/False Tests

True/false tests are often the easiest type of test because there are only two options—it's either true or it's false. Many professors avoid using true/false items because of that. True/false items lend themselves to guessing because you have a fifty-fifty chance of being correct. But some true/false items can be challenging. There are a number of strategies you can use to arrive at the correct answer.

Identify key words. Many professors make a statement false by substituting one word or phrase for the correct one. When you take a true/false test, underline the word or phrase that makes it wrong. If any part of the statement is false the entire statement is false. Even if a statement is composed of two or three parts or entire sentences, if one part or even one word is incorrect, the entire statement is false. Occasionally, a statement is false by omission—a key word is left out—but most of the time the instructor simply changes a key word.

Look for absolute words. Statements that contain absolute words are usually false. *Always, never, only, all, none,* and *every* are just a few examples of absolute words. Each of these words implies that there are no exceptions. When you see an absolute word in a true/false statement, underline it. Most of the time, absolute words make a statement false. Adding absolute words is another way instructors make statements false.

Look for qualifying words. Statements that contain qualifying words are usually true. Words like *usually, often, may, can, sometimes, frequently, rarely, most, some, many, few,* and *generally* are examples of qualifying words. These words qualify or "temper" the statement to allow for exceptions and are generally associated with true statements. However, if you know that the statement is false for some other reason, mark it *false,* even though it contains a qualifying word.

Eliminate double negatives. Some professors use double negatives in true/false statements just to make them harder. Generally these statements contain the word *not* and another word that contains a negative prefix, such as *in, il, ir, un,* and so on. To better decide whether or not the statement is true, simply cross out the double negatives and reread the sentence. Look at the following example: *It is not illegal to smoke in the dormitory rooms.* By eliminating the double negative, the statement reads: *It is legal to smoke in the dormitory rooms.*

Correct false statements if you have time. If you have time at the end of the exam, go back and make notes on how you would correct the false statements. When you get the exam back, you may not recall why you thought the statement was false. If your instructor marked your answer wrong, indicating that the statement was true, you could then approach him or her and explain your reason for marking it false.

Professors include more *true* items. Most professors like to use tests to reinforce the main points that were made in the course—essentially an exam is one last chance to teach. So most professors include more *true* than *false* items on tests. Look at each of your exams to see if your professor is using that strategy.

Strategies for Multiple-Choice Tests

Multiple-choice items are the most commonly used types of test questions in college. Most contain a stem, which is composed of a question or incomplete statement, and several alternatives or possible answers. Some professors use four alternatives and others use five (which, of course, is more difficult). There are a number of strategies, though, that can help you succeed on multiple-choice exams.

Problem-solving strategies. Use problem-solving strategies to figure out the correct answer when you don't know it immediately.

● *Consider all answers.* Many students lose points on multiple-choice exams because they don't consider or even read all of the answers before choosing the "correct" one. Most multiple-choice tests direct you to choose the best answer. That means that two or more answers could be correct, but one is the "best" answer.

● *Underline key words in the question.* By underlining key words in the question, you can better focus your attention on what you are being asked to do. In some ways, you are forcing yourself to slow down and look carefully at what the question is asking. This can help you avoid careless errors resulting from misreading. Moreover, if you underline the key words in the question, you're also helping to trigger cues to long-term memory.

● *Underline key words in the answers.* Underlining key words in the answers (as you did with true/false tests) helps you identify the word or phrase that makes a statement incorrect. After all, multiple-choice tests are really made up of a series of true/false items.

● *Eliminate wrong answers.* Instead of looking for the correct answer, go through each of the alternatives and work to eliminate the ones that are wrong. Once you have eliminated all of the incorrect alternatives, only one should be left. Many students can easily eliminate two of the choices and find themselves left with two that seem correct. Even doing this can help you focus more on the differences between the two.

● *Search the test for clues or cues.* You can often find the answers to difficult questions in other test questions. When you aren't sure of the correct answer, circle the number and come back to it later. Haven't you ever found the correct answer to one question in another question? Many students pick up a clue to an earlier question later in the test. You may find that the incorrect answer to question 21, for example, is the correct answer to question 3. You may also find a cue in a later question that triggers your memory and, just like that, you know the answer to one of the questions you skipped.

● *Do a memory search.* You can also search your memory for cues. Look at the question and ask yourself: Which chapter did this question come from? (You may even try thinking of the titles of each chapter or topics of each lecture.) What was the main topic? Which night did I study this? Was it on a study sheet? What was the topic? What were the headings? By asking yourself a series of questions, you can search your memory for the cues you used and now need to unlock the file in your long-term memory to find the answer.

● *Cover the alternatives to avoid confusion.* Some students allow the professor's incorrect alternatives to distract or confuse them. If you find yourself less sure of the answer after looking at the alternatives, don't look. Read the question and cover the alternatives with your hand and try to recall the answer from memory. Then go find it. Compare each alternative to the answer you know is correct.

● *Watch for* all of the above *and* none of the above *choices.* Some professors like to use *all of the above* and *none of the above* when writing their alternatives. If you can eliminate even one alternative, you can eliminate *all of the above*, too. If you know that at least one alternative is correct, you can eliminate *none of the above*.

However, if you know that two alternatives are correct but aren't sure of the third (and you can only pick one answer), *all of the above* must be correct.

Test-wise clues. Use test-wise clues to pick up a few points when you can't figure out the answer. There are a few test-wise clues that occasionally can help you pick the right answer, but most have lost their effectiveness with the use of computers. Few professors make typos, spelling errors, or even grammatical mistakes on tests now. However, there are a couple of clues that may still work. Never use them, though, when you know the correct answer.

- An answer that contains more specific, detailed information is probably correct. Vague or general alternatives are often used as distractors.
- An answer that contains the most words, especially if it also contains the most specific information, probably is correct.
- An answer that's about in the middle numerically is probably correct.
- An answer that contains an unfamiliar term probably is wrong.
- If a question contains two opposite alternatives, one of them is probably correct.

Strategies for Matching Tests

Matching tests generally focus on definitions of technical terms or identifications of key people, places, events, or dates. Matching tests only require you to recognize the correct answer from a list of given alternatives, making them a bit easier than some other types of tests. Generally, you are expected to use each alternative once, but some instructors allow for or require the repeated use of some alternatives. In either case, the strategies described here can help you earn top scores on matching tests.

Work from one side only. Matching tests generally have a list of terms or names to be described or defined on one side and the descriptions or definitions on the other side. It's a good strategy to work from the side with the most words. Then, when looking for a match, you would have to scan through a shorter list of terms each time. This saves a lot of time. In the example shown in Workshop 9-1, you would have to scan only thirteen words instead of more than eighty. Also, you want to always work from one side, so that you don't become confused about which alternatives you've already used.

Do the ones you know first. To minimize errors, it's a good strategy to match only the ones you're completely sure of first. Skip any that you aren't sure about because once you make one mistake on a matching test, you're bound to make more. Even though you may only get two or three correct the first time through, you've now eliminated several of the choices for your next pass through the list. Most instructors mix terms, people, events, and so on, so you may find that one of the words will only make sense matching one of the descriptions.

Eliminate and cross off alternatives. As you make a match, put a single diagonal line through the letter (or number) of the term you use. Keep moving through the list, eliminating more and more terms as you go. At the end of the test, you may find that you have only one word left and one description. If they don't match, you've made a mistake. Go back and check to be sure that you didn't make any errors. If necessary go through the test again. This time as you use one of the terms, put another line through the letter or number, forming an X.

Strategies for Essay Tests

Essay tests aren't as difficult as they sound. On the positive side, essay tests don't tend to be tricky. On the negative side, they require recall learning. There are no correct answers to find on the test, and they don't lend themselves to guessing. However, if you are well prepared, you can do very well on essay tests. Even if you don't know all of the information to earn a perfect score, you can earn partial credit on essays. Using some test-taking strategies can help you earn more points on essay tests.

Jot ideas in the margin. One of the best strategies for essay tests is to jot ideas in the margin before you even begin to answer the question. Write down any words, phrases, or even mnemonics that pop into your mind as you read each question. In fact, if you are permitted to choose which questions you want to answer from a list of questions, jotting ideas in the margin can actually help you decide which questions to answer.

Firm up your essay plan before writing. Once you've chosen which questions you plan to answer, look back at the question and add any additional ideas to your notes in the margin. Use the ideas you already jotted down as cues to search your long-term memory for more main points or supporting details. Also, pay careful attention to multi-part essay questions. Go back and reread the questions and be sure that your notes in the margin reflect your answer to all parts of the question.

Organize your ideas. If you have limited time to write your essay answers, you can quickly organize your points by labeling each of the notes you've written in the margin. Look for the first point that you want to make and mark it 1. Find any related details for that point and mark them 1A, 1B, 1C, and so on. Continue marking each of your main points and supporting points. If you have sufficient time, you can rewrite your notes into an outline, but you'll find that a quick organization as described here will guide you through writing your essay just as well. Checking off or crossing off each idea as you use it in your answer will keep you from leaving anything out.

Use a basic essay design. Many essay questions can be answered within one paragraph; others may take two, three, or more paragraphs or several pages. How much you write is dependent on how much space the professor provides, space limitations listed in the directions, or even the point value of the question. For a one-paragraph essay answer, you should begin with a topic sentence that restates the question and includes the main points of your answer. Follow it with a main point sentence and then as many supporting sentences as you can write, based on the information that you have acquired. Continue listing each additional main point and related details. Finally, complete the paragraph with a concluding sentence that restates the main points you made in your essay. For a longer essay, write an introductory paragraph that includes your thesis statement and the main points for your answer. Then begin each of the body paragraphs with a topic sentence for each of the main points in your answer. Next, add details to support each of the main points. Finally, add a short concluding paragraph that restates the main points you made.

Add all relevant details. When writing your essay answer, it's important to include all of the information that you know about the topic that is relevant to the question. Include definitions of key terms; descriptions of key people, events, dates, and so on; any examples that may explain some of your points; and reasons, facts, or details about the points you are making. Some students tend to leave out information, assuming that it's rather obvious. By pretending you're writing your answer for someone who doesn't know the answer, you may find that you go into more detail. On the other hand, do not include information about the topic (even though you spent a lot of time learning it) that is not related to the question. Some professors will simply ignore those points, but other professors may think that you don't know the answer as well as he or she thought you did.

Include transitional words. To help your instructor clearly note the points you've made, you should begin each main point of your answer with a transition word. The easiest system to use is to write words such as *first, second, third, next,* and *finally* at the beginning of each main point sentence. You can also use transitions such as *moreover, in addition, additionally,* and *furthermore* to indicate that you are adding more points to the previously stated point. Words like *consequently, therefore,* and *thus* indicate that you've reached a conclusion based on previous information.

Consider the factors that influence your grade. Most students would agree that the best essay answer is the one that best answers the question. However, there are a number of factors that contribute to making an essay answer the best answer.

● *Content.* The best answer should be one that answers the question and includes all of the information presented in the course material. Most professors look first at the content of the answer when determining the grade.

● *Organization.* The organization of your answer is also an important factor in determining your grade. A well-organized answer helps your instructor find the information that you wrote. Poorly organized answers are harder to follow, and most instructors will not go back and read your answer three or four times, checking to see if you did include the relevant points.

● *Format.* Some professors are very particular about how they want the essay to be written. If you're told to use paragraph form but you list the points in your answer instead, you may receive a failing grade. If you're told in the directions to use ink, write every other line, or limit your answer to one side of the page, but you don't, you could lose points on your answer.

● *Mechanics.* Mechanics—sentence structure, grammar, spelling, and punctuation—all contribute to or detract from your answer. If your instructor can't understand what you're saying in your essay, he or she can't award you points for the information you wrote. Poor mechanics also sends a message about you as a student—that you're not very well-educated. Unfortunately, that impression of you can "spill over" to the evaluation of the content of your answer. Some professors may find themselves thinking, "If he can't even write a complete sentence, how can he possibly understand this material?"

● *Neatness.* Most professors expect you to write clearly and neatly, observe margins, and present the material in a "professional" manner. Very few are willing to spend hours trying to decipher unreadable handwriting. If your professor can't read your essay, you'll lose points. You can also lose points just because you make a "bad impression" by writing in an awkward and messy manner. Nicely written papers have been getting better grades for years. Teachers seem to believe that good students care about what they are writing and make the effort to present their answers in a careful and skillful manner.

What if you run out of time? Most professors expect you to complete the exam within the designated time frame. When the professor announces that you only have 5 minutes left, you need to quickly list or outline the other points that you wanted to make instead of just trying to write a few more sentences. This is a better strategy than answering only half of the question.

Strategies for Problem-Based Tests

Problem-based exams such as those given in math, science, and business courses are a lot like essay exams. You won't recognize the correct answer on the test because it isn't there and you can't just guess; you have to know the answer or how to figure it out instead. There are number of strategies that can help you earn a high grade on problem-based exams.

Preview the exam. When you first get the exam, read the directions and then look through the test. Check to see how many problems you will have to solve and look at the point values to see if some have higher point values than others.

Do the easy ones first. Look at the first problem on the test. If you know how to do it, go ahead and solve the problem. If you don't, skip it and move on. Trying to solve a problem when you don't even know where to begin will frustrate you and waste valuable time. By completing all of the problems that you know how to do immediately, you'll maximize your score. If you run out of time (which often happens on problem-based exams), you may never even get to some of the problems that you could have solved.

Identify the type of problem. When you first look at the problem, try to determine what type of problem it is. Then think about the problems you practiced and consider the examples of the same type of problem. Picture the problems you have already solved as you solve the new one.

Jot down notes or draw diagrams. Drawing a diagram can help you solve some types of problems. Write down what you are given and what you need to find. You could also jot down a sample problem that you practiced and then follow the same steps as you solve the new problem.

Show all of your work. When taking a problem-based test, your grade depends more on how you solve the problem than the exact answer you get. Show all of the steps as you complete the problem. If you make a careless mathematical error, you may still get credit for knowing how to solve the problem.

Check your work. If you have time, go back and check your work. Don't just look at the problems, though; you won't catch many mistakes that way. Instead, cover the solution with your hand and rework the problem in the margin or on scrap paper. If you get a different answer, check each line until you find your error.

WORKSHOP 9-1   Practice Test-Taking Strategies

In this workshop, you'll have an opportunity to practice using some of the test-taking strategies that you learned in this chapter. True/false, multiple-choice, and matching tests are provided for practice. First, consider the strategies you use now. After taking each of the tests, list the strategies you used in the space below the test. Your instructor will provide you with the correct answers. Then try two tests to practice strategic guessing.

1. What strategies did you use when you took your last true/false test?

_____

_____

_____

_____

_____

_____

_____

_____

_____

2. What strategies did you use when you took your last multiple-choice test?

_____

_____

_____

_____

_____

_____

_____

_____

3. What strategies did you use when you took your last matching test?

_____

_____

_____

_____

_____

_____

_____

_____

True/False Test

Work with a partner to indicate whether each item in the following section is true or false. If it is false, underline the word or words that make it false and then correct the statement. Circle any absolute words. Compare your responses to those of the students in another group.

———— **1.** Reading and active reading involve exactly the same processes.

———— **2.** You should always make maps when studying for exams.

———— **3.** You may find it helpful to read the summary before reading the chapter.

———— **4.** Sitting in the front of the room will ensure that you get a good grade.

———— **5.** When skimming a chapter, you should have complete comprehension.

———— **6.** Once you learn something, you never have to review it again.

———— **7.** Some students use recall columns when they take lecture notes.

———— **8.** Recopying notes verbatim is an active study strategy.

———— **9.** All students should take self-tests to reduce test anxiety.

———— **10.** All students who fail exams have high levels of test anxiety.

What strategies did you use to figure out the correct answers?

_____
_____
_____
_____
_____
_____
_____
_____
_____
_____

Which of your strategies was the most successful in helping you score more points?

_____
_____
_____
_____
_____
_____
_____
_____
_____
_____
_____

Multiple-Choice Test

Circle the letter of the best answer for each question.

1. Underlining key words and eliminating wrong answers are examples of
   a. test-wise strategies.
   b. absolute strategies.
   c. guessing strategies.
   d. problem-solving strategies.

2. Choosing an answer that's in the middle and has the most specific information is an example of
   a. a test-wise strategy.
   b. an absolute strategy.
   c. a guessing strategy.
   d. a problem-solving strategy.

3. Which of the following is a good strategy for a true/false test?
   a. Statements with absolute words are always correct.
   b. Statements with qualifying words are usually correct.
   c. Statements with negative words are always incorrect.
   d. Statements that seem very simple are generally tricky and incorrect.

4. When taking a matching test, you should
   a. eliminate wrong answers.
   b. work straight down the left column.
   c. match the definitions to the words.
   d. eliminate the answers only when you're absolutely sure of them.

5. If you had 60 minutes to take an exam and Part I contains twenty multiple-choice questions and Part II contains two essay questions, how would you decide how much time to spend on each multiple-choice question?
   a. You would divide up the test time and spend half on the multiple-choice and half on the essays.
   b. You would spend 20 minutes on multiple-choice and 40 on the essays.
   c. You couldn't decide on the time to spend because you don't know how much the multiple-choice and essay questions are worth.
   d. You wouldn't decide ahead of time anyway. You would do the multiple-choice questions first and just use the remainder of the time on the essays.

6. Before you begin to write your essay answer, take a minute to number each point that you jotted down in the margin so that your answer is more
   a. clear.
   b. complete.
   c. detailed.
   d. organized.

7. The first main point in a one-paragraph essay would be the _____ in a multi-paragraphed essay.

   a. first paragraph

   b. topic sentence of the first paragraph

   c. thesis statement of the essay

   d. conclusion of the introductory paragraph

8. One mistake that students make when answering essay questions is

   a. spending more time on the questions that are worth the most.

   b. spending too little time on the questions that are worth the least.

   c. including all of the relevant information in their answer.

   d. including irrelevant information in their answer.

What strategies did you use to figure out the correct answers?

_____

_____

_____

_____

_____

_____

_____

_____

_____

_____

_____

_____

Which of your strategies was the most successful in helping you score more points? Why?

_____

_____

_____

_____

_____

_____

_____

_____

_____

_____

Matching Test

Work as a group to take a matching test. Write the letter of the correct grammatical term on the line next to each definition. Each letter is used only once.[1]

Definitions

———— **1.** A class of words that relate a noun (or equivalent) to the rest of the sentence

———— **2.** Words that connect two or more sentence elements

———— **3.** A class of words that can take the place of nouns

———— **4.** A class of words that can point out a quality of a noun (or noun equivalent)

———— **5.** A grammatically independent element used to express attitudes or emotion

———— **6.** A class of words that name or classify people, animals, things, and ideas

———— **7.** A class of words that answer questions like *how, when,* and *where*

———— **8.** A class of words that signal the performance of an action, the occurrence of an event, or the presence of a condition

Parts of speech

A. noun

B. pronoun

C. verb

D. adjective

E. adverb

F. preposition

G. conjunction

H. interjection

What strategies did you use to figure out the correct answers?

_____

_____

_____

_____

_____

_____

_____

_____

Which of your strategies was the most successful in helping you score more points?

_____

_____

_____

_____

_____

_____

_____

[1] From *New English Handbook*, 2nd edition by GUTH. 1985. Reprinted with permission of Wadsworth, a division of Thomson Learning: www.thomsonrights.com Fax 800-730-2215.

Practice Strategic Guessing

Look at each of the answer keys below. In each case, the student completed all of the questions he or she knew and then guessed on the others. The guesses have been removed so that you can practice some of the strategic-guessing strategies that you learned about earlier in the chapter. See how much you can improve the score on these exams by guessing. Your instructor has the actual answers for each of the exams.

Guess on a true/false test:

1. T	6. F	11. T	16. ___	21. F
2. ___	7. F	12. T	17. F	22. F
3. F	8. ___	13. F	18. F	23. T
4. F	9. T	14. ___	19. F	24. ___
5. ___	10. F	15. T	20. ___	25. T

What strategies did you use? _____

_____

_____

_____

_____

Guess on a multiple-choice test:

1. A	11. B	21. D	31. ___	41. ___
2. ___	12. A	22. D	32. B	42. C
3. C	13. C	23. A	33. ___	43. ___
4. C	14. ___	24. ___	34. B	44. D
5. B	15. B	25. A	35. D	45. A
6. D	16. ___	26. C	36. ___	46. B
7. C	17. C	27. A	37. ___	47. A
8. ___	18. C	28. B	38. D	48. ___
9. B	19. D	29. D	39. A	49. D
10. D	20. A	30. ___	40. ___	50. C

What strategies did you use? _____

_____

_____

_____

_____

WORKSHOP 9-2   Practice Writing Essay Answers

In this workshop, you'll have a chance to practice writing out essay answers. You'll have an opportunity to practice writing main points and supporting points for an essay answer.

1. Label each point to organize the information and then write main point sentences for each idea jotted in the margin for the question:

   Why is the Five-Day Study Plan so effective in helping students prepare for exams?

2. Plan in the margin:

   Spaced study   Built-in repetition   Active preparation strategies

   Divided material   Self-testing   Active review strategies

3. *Main point 1:* _____

   _____

   _____

   Main point 2: _____

   _____

   _____

   Main point 3: _____

   _____

   _____

   Main point 4: _____

   _____

   _____

   _____

   Main point 5: _____

   _____

   _____

   _____

   Main point 6: _____

   _____

   _____

   _____

4. Write supporting sentences for each of the main point sentences for the question:

Why do some students have difficulty during their first semester in college?

Main point 1: First, many students don't make academics their first priority.

Supporting point 1: _____

_____

_____

Main point 2: Second, some students don't put enough time into their work.

Supporting point 2: _____

_____

_____

_____

Main point 3: Third, some students don't attend classes on a regular basis.

Supporting point 3: _____

_____

_____

_____

Main point 4: Next, some students have difficulty because they don't know how to take lecture notes.

Supporting point 4: _____

_____

_____

_____

Main point 5: Another reason that students have difficulty during their first semester in college is because they have trouble reading their textbooks.

Supporting point 5: _____

_____

_____

_____

Main point 6: Finally, students have difficulty during their first semester because they don't know how to study for exams.

Supporting point 6: _____

_____

_____

_____

WORKSHOP 9-3 Critique Essay Answers

In this workshop, you'll have an opportunity to critique some essay answers written by other students. This activity should help you become more aware of the factors that contribute to your grades on essay tests.

Part 1: Writing Essay Answers

Answer the following essay question before you continue with the workshop.

What strategies should students use when taking an objective test?

_____

_____

_____

_____

_____

_____

_____

_____

_____

_____

_____

_____

_____

_____

_____

_____

_____

_____

_____

_____

_____

_____

_____

_____

Part 2: Evaluating Essay Answers

Below is a series of essay answers for you to evaluate. There are only five answers, which were assigned the following grades: 1, 3, 5, 7, and 9 points. Write a sentence or two explaining the strengths and/or weaknesses of each answer. Then assign one of the grades to each of the five sample answers. Each grade can be assigned to only one of the answers. Assign a grade to your own answer as well.

1. Strategies that students should use when taking objective test include looking for key terms and their definitions, major lists of items, points emphasized in class or in the text, specific examples given in class, and important people and dates.

   By using these strategies a student should do very well on an objective test and be able to answer the questions very reasonably.

   Evaluation: Grade _____

   _____

   _____

   _____

   _____

   _____

2. When taking an objective test there are certain strategies that a student should take advantage of. First, basic rules should be recognized. A student must read all the directions and look over the test. This will assure a complete understanding of what is expected. Strategies on answering questions vary from matching, multipul choice and true/false. There are however certain items which are the same. First read and reread the question so that it is completely understood. Second think of a possible answer. Look on the list to see if it is there. If it is not see if there is one which has the same meaning. If you do not know the exact answer, look and see if you can at least eliminate one or two as being definitely wrong. Look to see if you can choose one of the remaining answers to be correct. If there is no penalty for wrong answers and you have eleminated all but two answers guess. Another strategy is that the correct answer is usually in the middle of the possible answers. For example, if you are taking a multipul choice test and there are four possible answers, the one's to be most likely correct are B or C, because they are in the middle. Another strategy is if there are two answrs that are totally opposite, one them are right. Finally, if there are answers with more than one word, the longest is usually right. There are many strategies a student can learn to take an objective test. The one's listed are just a few.

   Evaluation: Grade _____

   _____

   _____

   _____

   _____

   _____

3. We learned many different strategies that a student can use when taking an objective test. While the student is studying for the test, she can do somethings that can make the test much easier. Predicting questions, quizzing yourself, making flash cards, and making study guides (with notes from the text and the lecture).

There are many strategies to use when actually doing the test too. A student should always preview the test before hand so she can pace herself. It does come in handy to know the material too. When taking an objective test, you should always do the ones you know first, then go back and do the more difficult ones. You may find a clue later in the test, that will help you answer another question.

Evaluation: Grade _____

_____

_____

_____

_____

_____

_____

_____

_____

_____

_____

4. First, you should read the statements carefully. In order to be false the statement must be totally false. When you encounter a false statement you should be able to circle a word or words that make it false, however, there are some exceptions. Students should also look for absolute or 100% words such as all, every, and none. Statements with these words in it usually are false, because if you can think of one exception then it is definatly false. Statements using qualifier words such as most, some and usually are often true. Last a student should remember that teachers want to put correct statements in a students mind so most of the statements are usually true.

Evaluation: Grade _____

_____

_____

_____

_____

_____

_____

_____

_____

_____

5. When taking an objective test it is important to remember that there may not be a perfect answer so look for the best one. Never choose an answer before you read all the possible choices. You may think that you found the right one but there might be a better one. Do all the questions you are sure of first then go back. This saves time that would otherwise be used to stare blankly at the paper. Also it may help in another way. If you read a question and you just cant figure it out you might find a clue later in the test. If this fails, try to eliminate the answers you know are wrong. For example you have the question: which animal has 4 legs, fur, and purrs. A.) snake B.) cat C.) dog D.) bird. You could eliminate snake and the bird right off. That will make your decision easier and then your chances of getting it right went from 1/4 to 1/2 or 50 - 50. If you cant eliminate this way try to change the multiple choice into true-false, ex. a snake has 4 legs, fur, & purrs. That would be false. Do that with all 4 choices—if this fails there are other ways. Longer, detailed answers are often right. If every answer list doesn't contain it "all of the above" or "none of the above" are usually right. Look for answers containing—generally, often, some, sometimes, usually. Avoid answers with always, never, all none. In answers that are opposite each other one is usually correct ex. answers A.) he was on both sides B.) he wasnt on either side. Answers in the middle (B & C) are sometimes correct when nothing else is present. Also when taking these tests cover up the answers and think of your own answer then uncover them and see if yours is there. And when all else fails pick one. You have a better chance of getting it right than if you didnt put anything at all. One more clue. Dont change your answer unless you misread the question.

Evaluation: Grade _____

_____

_____

_____

_____

_____

_____

_____

_____

6. Your answer:

Evaluation: Grade _____

_____

_____

_____

_____

_____

_____

_____

_____

WORKSHOP 9-4   **What Would You Do?**

In this workshop, you'll have a chance to consider a case study and make suggestions that Jessica could use when taking exams.

Jessica is majoring in Journalism and hopes to write for a newspaper or magazine after graduation. She is a skilled writer and generally does quite well on essay exams. However, she has had some difficulty taking multiple-choice exams this term. As soon as the professor announces the exam, she starts to panic. No matter what she does, she just can't seem to pick the right answer. As soon as she touches the exam, she gets nervous and then it's all downhill from there. When Jessica took her last Sociology exam, she worked carefully through the test, reading each of the questions, looking at all four of the possible answers, and then deciding on the one she thought was correct. She thought she was moving through the exam at a good pace until she noticed other students turning in their tests. She decided that she had better work faster when she saw her three friends leave the classroom. Jessica knew they were waiting for her in the hall and that made her feel even more uncomfortable. On the last four questions, Jessica simply wrote down A, B, C, and D. She wanted to get to lunch just as much as her friends and thought that guessing might get her a few more points. This test was much harder than she expected it to be. When her friends were discussing the test questions at lunch, Jessica knew she was right. She got a lot of them wrong. Multiple-choice tests were just too tricky—that was the problem.

1. What was really Jessica's problem?

_____

_____

_____

_____

_____

_____

_____

2. What mistakes did Jessica make when taking her Sociology exam?

_____

_____

_____

_____

_____

_____

_____

3. What changes should Jessica make when taking multiple-choice exams?

_____

_____

_____

_____

_____

_____

_____

_____

_____

_____

_____

_____

_____

_____

_____

_____

Now think back to the last couple of exams you took. What did you do? Did your grade accurately reflect your knowledge of the material?

4. What types of errors did you make when taking your last exam? What new strategies would you use now to maximize your score?

_____

_____

_____

_____

_____

_____

_____

_____

_____

_____

_____

_____

_____

Taking Charge of Your Life Workshop

Staying Healthy

Sleep, nutrition, exercise . . . perhaps these areas are not top priorities in your life right now. Staying healthy, however, is critical to being your best both in and out of the classroom. Becoming aware of your sleeping, eating, and exercise habits and making small changes in your lifestyle can help you experience a higher level of health and well-being—and a more enjoyable life. The goals of this workshop are to help you assess current habits, learn basic tips, and explore ways to improve upon your own health habits.

? Where Are You Now?

Take a few minutes to answer *yes* or *no* to the following questions.

	YES	NO
1. Do you get at least 8 hours of sleep each night?	_____	_____
2. Do you go to bed and wake up at about the same times most days of the week?	_____	_____
3. Do you feel well-rested throughout the day?	_____	_____
4. If you take naps, do you limit the duration of your naps to no more than 30 minutes?	_____	_____
5. Do you know how to improve your sleep pattern?	_____	_____
6. Do you know what constitutes a serving size of food?	_____	_____
7. Do you limit your consumption of junk foods (foods high in fat and/or calories)?	_____	_____
8. Are you aware of the opportunities your campus offers for physical activity?	_____	_____
9. Do you exercise for at least 30 minutes three times a week?	_____	_____
10. Do you recognize the benefits of establishing healthy sleep, eating, and exercise patterns?	_____	_____
Total Points	_____	

Give yourself one point for each *yes* answer and zero points for each *no* answer. Now total your points. A low score indicates that you need to improve upon these health habits. A high score indicates that you are doing well.

Consider Your Sleep Patterns

Scan any college classroom and you will observe students who are suffering from the results of inadequate sleep. It's likely the instructor also is observing these sleep-deprived souls as their heads nod and eyelids droop. Perhaps you know firsthand what it is like to struggle to stay awake in class. Feeling alert and rested is essential to academic success, but some students seem to believe that a good night's sleep won't take place until after graduation. Making some simple changes to your daily routine can bring you those much needed zzzzzz's.

- **Think about your current sleep pattern.** Do you get enough sleep? Do you have difficulty falling or staying asleep? Do you feel rested when you wake up? Does your sleep pattern vary widely from day to day? Track what time you go to sleep, what time you wake up, and the total number of hours you sleep each night for a week. Also, make note of how you feel over the course of the day. Becoming aware of your personal sleep pattern will help you identify what you need to change.

- **What is your daily sleep requirement?** Most college students function optimally on 8 to 9 hours of sleep. Some people do well with less, but most of us cannot skimp on the quantity of sleep we get. Inadequate sleep results in difficulty concentrating, diminished motivation and reaction time, weakened immune system, and irritability. No college student can afford to experience any of these effects on a regular basis.

- **Don't incur a sleep debt.** If you don't get an adequate amount of sleep over the course of a few days, you begin to build a sleep debt. The best strategy to get back on track is to try to get at least 8 hours during your next night of sleep. If you do not begin to get back on track, your debt continues to accumulate and you experience the backlash.

- **Too many students fall into the *nap trap*.** The nap trap strikes students who end up taking a 2- or 3- (or more!) hour nap during the day. How many times have you heard someone say, upon exiting the classroom, that he or she is going home to take a nap? Sure, a 20- to 30-minute power nap can refresh and rejuvenate you to take on the challenges of the rest of the day. Too often, though, students slumber away the afternoon—misusing valuable study time and ruining any chances of going to bed at a reasonable time. A prolonged daytime siesta results in a disrupted and unhealthy sleep pattern.

- **What else is throwing off your sleep pattern?** Do you have varying bedtimes depending on your class schedule, social life, or other factors? The schedule of a college student can, by all means, be an unpredictable, erratic ride, but doing your best to keep a consistent sleep schedule can help reduce negative effects of sleep deprivation.

- **Are you sleeping to avoid responsibilities?** Some students actually use sleep as a way to avoid doing work. Whether sleeping for 10 or more hours at night or taking endless naps, these students end up accomplishing little else. If you find yourself sleeping an exorbitant amount, consider scheduling your sleep as you would other activities. Commit to a reasonable 8 or 9 hours—and no naps. Excessive sleep (or insomnia) could be a sign of depression. Consult a counselor or physician for help.

The quality of your sleep is also very critical to feeling well-rested. And while some students can nod off—anytime, anywhere—others have a difficult time

falling and staying asleep. Some variables may be beyond your control if you live in a residence hall, but taking charge of the following factors can help your cause.

- **Watch your alcohol consumption**. Yes, alcohol is a central nervous system depressant and can make you feel drowsy, but drinking in excess disrupts the quality of sleep you get. You can snooze for several hours and still not feel well-rested. In addition, those multiple trips to the bathroom over the course of the night interfere with a good night's sleep.

- **Reduce caffeine intake**. Many college students turn to quick caffeine fixes in the form of coffee, soda, and other drinks, or powerful caffeine pills. Think about your own consumption over the course of the day, and remember that caffeine is a powerful stimulant that speeds up your central nervous system. At a minimum, avoid caffeine at least 2 hours before you go to bed to help you fall asleep more quickly.

- **Try to resolve any lingering issues.** Having an argument or passionate debate with a loved one, roommate, or friend right before you turn in can make falling asleep seem like an impossibility. Likewise, if you have a problem that is bothering you, it may be difficult to get to sleep. Try to work through your problem with a support person or write out your feelings to try to clear your head before bed.

- **Establish a bedtime routine.** Even if you live in a residence hall room, you can still develop a way to wind down at the end of the day. Take some time to relax and enjoy some quiet time. The lives of most college students are fast-paced and inundated by almost constant stimulation via cell phone chats, instant messaging, video games, and so on. A peaceful moment before bed can help relax and prepare you for a restful snooze.

Evaluate Your Eating Habits

What you put into your body also has a direct impact on your energy level, mood, and ability to concentrate. Eating healthy can seem like a monumental challenge when faced with busy schedules, late-night pizza runs, and dining-hall dinners (instead of home-cooked meals). Whether you've gained that notorious "freshman fifteen" or feel rundown from making poor food choices, you can benefit from adopting some basic guidelines.

- **Don't "super-size" portions.** Learning appropriate serving sizes is vital to healthy eating. Many of us underestimate how much we really consume. We tend to think that whatever lands on our plate is a legitimate serving. Consider this: one serving of meat should be the size of a deck of cards (about 3–4 oz.), one serving of spaghetti is the size of a scoop of ice cream (about ½ cup) and one serving of cheese is about the size of a pair of dominoes (2 oz.). Learning accurate portion sizes and recommended food group servings per day as well as adjusting food intake will help you make great strides toward a healthier diet.

- **Balance your choices.** Too many students get stuck in some kind of nutritional rut, such as eating too many fried foods and too little fruits and veggies. Your favorite fried food won't hurt every once and a while—but moderation is truly the key. Eating fried mozzarella sticks every day for lunch is just not the wisest choice. Make it a priority to eat a balance of foods each day, with emphasis on fruits and veggies.

- **Plan ahead.** Whether you commute or live on campus, make sure healthy food choices are readily available, which may mean stocking your room or packing snacks that are convenient when you are hungry. College students tend to reach for whatever is there, so that means being prepared. Likewise, before you enter the campus dining hall or you make a quick trip to your favorite fast food destination, decide to choose a healthy selection and stick to your plan!

- **Watch for snack attacks.** Yes, late-night pizza deliveries almost seem to be the standard fare of college students, but again, too much of anything can lead to problems. College students tend to gain weight as a result of poor snack choices—late at night, while studying, and so on. Balance junk foods with healthier choices that you also enjoy. Remember: If you don't really like something, you won't eat it and will end up reaching for the junk.

- **Try not to skip meals.** Students are notorious for skipping breakfast—choosing to hit the snooze button instead up waking up a bit earlier to eat something. Going several hours without food will drop your metabolism significantly, which affects your energy and concentration levels. Grabbing a piece of fruit or a granola bar on the way out the door requires no extra effort, but you will experience a much-needed boost.

- **What's your beverage of choice?** Drinks laden with calories, sugar, or other additives can make you feel sluggish and cause you to gain weight. The average soft drink has about 150 calories and 10 teaspoons of sugar. How many sodas do you drink in one day? And is the beer belly a myth? Think about the fact that 12 oz. of regular beer has about 145 calories per serving, and then think about this . . .

- **It takes about 3,500 calories to equal one pound.** Therefore, if you progressively take in more calories but don't burn them through exercise, weight gain is inevitable.

Make Exercise Part of Your Routine

We've established that the busy lives of college students can make it challenging to maintain physical well-being, and for many of you, exercising isn't a part of the weekly schedule. It may be that in high school you participated in sports, dance classes, aerobics, or some other activity, but now find that the most exercise you get is walking from class to class. Or it may be that your rather sedentary ways in high school have become more ingrained in college. Regardless of your past experience, getting active now will improve the quality of your life. Sure, there are the obvious physical benefits of exercising (burn calories, build muscle, improve heart rate, and so on), but the emotional payoff is significant as well. Becoming more active can be the perfect antidote to the hectic, stress-filled life you lead. Exercise improves mood, diminishes stress, and improves self-esteem.

- **But I don't have time!** Saying you can't fit 30 minutes of exercise into your day is a cop-out. Some of the most successful (and busy) people in our society are consistent exercisers. As you set your schedule each day, carve out time to exercise. Make sure you write it into your daily planner, and then do it!

- **Pick something you enjoy.** Studies show that the more you enjoy exercising, the more likely you are to stick with it. Check out what your campus offers. If you enjoy competition and team sports, get involved in intramurals. Do you like music and dancing? Find out what aerobics classes are offered. The point is . . . just pick something you like and get moving!

- **Find a partner.** Having the support of a friend can be a great motivator. He or she can help you on days when you don't feel like working out and he or she can expect the same from you. You can support and push one another to meet your exercise goals.

- **Make sure those goals are realistic.** Setting goals is another great way to stay motivated, as long as you have created a reasonable time frame and end result. If you've never run and you expect to finish a marathon at the end of the month, you are likely to experience a major disappointment. As you meet your goals, establish new ones to keep your motivation level high.

Some of you may be experiencing a more severe problem with sleeping, eating, or exercising than described in this workshop. Please seek help from a health care provider for advice and support for your particular issue.

 RESOURCES

Sleep

Check out the sleepiness diary, the sleep IQ test, and other resources at National Sleep Foundation's website: **www.sleepfoundation.org**

To find out just how sleepy you really are, take the Epworth Sleepiness Scale at **www.stanford.edu/~dement/epworth.html**

Nutrition

This book's author understands the lifestyle of college students and offers practical advice: *The College Student's Guide to Eating Well on Campus* by Ann Selkowitz Litt, available from Tulip Hill Press.

Go to **www.mypyramid.gov** for personalized nutrition recommendations based upon gender, age, and activity level.

Exercise

Visit the American Council on Exercise's education center for sound advice about a variety of fitness topics: **www.acefitness.org/educationcenter/**

To help jumpstart your exercise plan and find great tools like the Body Mass Index calculator, check out **www.nhlbisupport.com/bmi/**

What Do You Do Now?

Staying Healthy Scenario

Kayla is a first-year student majoring in Secondary Education. She had a good first semester but now is feeling rundown (low energy, falling asleep in class, and so on), which is taking a toll on her class work. Kayla was a soccer player in high school and is not nearly as active as she was a year ago. In addition, she eats just one meal a day, missing breakfast because she sleeps in and has to rush to class in the morning.

1. Name a strategy for each of the health areas that Kayla could implement for a much-needed energy boost.

   Sleep Strategy:

   _____

   _____

   _____

   Nutrition Strategy:

   _____

   _____

   _____

   Exercise Strategy:

   _____

   _____

   _____

2. We've covered the basics of staying healthy in terms of your sleep, nutrition, and exercise habits. What do you need to do in order to take action? Describe your biggest challenge with each of the following health behaviors, and come up with a strategy that will help you overcome the challenge.

EXAMPLE

Sleep

My Challenge: I take 2-hour naps after history class and don't feel tired later on at bedtime.

Strategy: I will set my alarm for 30 minutes when taking a nap.

Desired Result: Go to bed by 11:30 P.M. and improve overall sleep pattern.

Sleep

My Challenge: _____

Strategy: _____

Desired Result: _____

Nutrition

My Challenge: _____

Strategy: _____

Desired Result: _____

Exercise

My Challenge: _____

Strategy: _____

Desired Result: _____

Preparing for Finals

CHAPTER 10

In this chapter you will learn more about:

- How to manage your time before finals
- How to set priorities for finals
- How to set up a Final Exam Planning Calendar
- How to plan properly for comprehensive finals

Where Are You Now?

Take a few minutes to answer *yes* or *no* to the following questions.

		YES	NO
1.	Do you work ahead before finals to free up study time?	_____	_____
2.	Do you tend to give up at the end of the term and spend little or no time preparing for finals?	_____	_____
3.	Do you usually score lower on final exams than on the other exams given during the term?	_____	_____
4.	Do you set up a plan to prepare for your finals?	_____	_____
5.	Do you put most of your effort into the course in which you have the lowest grade?	_____	_____
6.	Do you generally spend a lot of time partying at the end of the term when you know you should be studying?	_____	_____
7.	Do you calculate the grade you need on your final?	_____	_____
8.	Do you use a four- or five-day study plan to prepare for each of your finals?	_____	_____
9.	Do you put so much effort into one exam that you don't have the time or energy to prepare for one or more of the others?	_____	_____
10.	Do you realistically consider your chances of success before preparing for final exams?	_____	_____
	Total Points		_____

Give yourself 1 point for each *yes* answer to questions 1, 4, 7, 8, and 10, and 1 point for each *no* answer to questions 2, 3, 5, 6, and 9. Now total up your points. A low score indicates that you need to develop some new strategies for preparing for final exams. A high score indicates that you already are using many good strategies.

What Are Final Exams?

Final exams are end-of-term tests that help professors evaluate your progress. They are used by some professors to monitor your mastery of the concepts and ideas presented in the course. Others use them to make decisions about grades, to determine whether students should move on to the next class, or even to monitor their own teaching. Although final exams may be one of the many routine exams given during the semester, they are often longer, both in number of questions and in time allotted for the test, and more difficult. Finals often carry more weight than regular exams and in many cases determine your grade in the course. Although finals are more challenging than most of the regular exams that you have during the term, you can still use many of the same strategies that you used for your other exams to prepare for them. However, because you may have four or five exams in a one-week period, you need to use some special strategies, too. In this chapter, you'll learn how to manage your time, set your priorities for study, set up a final exam study schedule, and prepare properly for comprehensive finals.

Time Management for Finals

List all outstanding assignments. The first step in preparing for finals is managing your time carefully at the end of the semester. About two weeks before your first final, make a list of all of your outstanding assignments. Make a list of each reading assignment, math assignment, quiz, paper, project, and exam that you have coming up for the remainder of the term. You can group the assignments according to the course or you can list them based on the date each is due.

Create a new Fixed Commitment Calendar. Make up a new Fixed Commitment Calendar for the last two weeks of the term. Use the blank copy in Figure 10.1 or create your own on the computer. Fill in all of your classes, any work hours, meal times, meetings, appointments, practices, and even special television shows you want to watch. Box in the remaining available study time and begin to schedule the study tasks that you still need to complete.

Work ahead to complete tasks. One of the biggest mistakes that students make before finals is deciding to rest up before finals week. Some students take so much time off that they even get behind in their work just when they need to be pushing harder to get ahead. Rather than easing off at the end of the term, you need to push hard. If you work as hard as you can for one week about two weeks before your first final, you'll be able to complete many of the assignments on your list and clear time to study for your finals. Go through your list of outstanding assignments and select any that you can complete early. Two weeks before finals tends to be a rather slow week for exams, papers, and projects; however, the last week of the semester is much more demanding. Any work that you can complete early will take some of the pressure off of you during that last week.

Set Priorities for Finals

Make academics your top priority. Many students get serious about their studies toward the end of the semester. They know that their grades are on the line and that they need to buckle down and get to work. The dorms get quiet, the library fills with students who want to do well, and the computer labs are filled with students completing papers and projects. To be successful on your finals, you need to make academics your top priority. Put away the video games, pack up your television, cut back on your social time, and reduce your work hours if possible. If you have household responsibilities, let the cleaning (laundry, shopping, ironing) go for a week or two. Once finals are over, you'll have lots of time to catch up at home, watch TV, socialize, relax, and put in extra time at work.

Set priorities for your exams. You can increase your overall GPA if you set priorities for study. Although you need to properly prepare for all of your exams, you'll probably find that you should put more time into some of your exams than others.

Figure 10.1 ● Fixed Commitment Calendar

	Monday	Tuesday	Wednesday	Thursday	Friday	Saturday	Sunday
5:00 A.M.							
6:00 A.M.							
7:00 A.M.							
8:00 A.M.							
9:00 A.M.							
10:00 A.M.							
11:00 A.M.							
12:00 P.M.							
1:00 P.M.							
2:00 P.M.							
3:00 P.M.							
4:00 P.M.							
5:00 P.M.							
6:00 P.M.							
7:00 P.M.							
8:00 P.M.							
9:00 P.M.							
10:00 P.M.							
11:00 P.M.							
12:00 A.M.							
1:00 A.M.							
2:00 A.M.							
3:00 A.M.							
4:00 A.M.							

Hours Available for Study _____   Hours Needed for Study _____

● *Calculate your current grade.* You can determine which courses to put more time into by calculating your current grade in the course and determining what you actually need on the final. If your course grade is determined by exams only, it's fairly easy to calculate your grade. If all of the exams count the same, add up the grades that you have on the first three, for example, and divide by three to get your current average. Let's say you have an 85% average and 80% is a B and 90% is an A. That's a pretty solid grade. What would you need on the final to keep your B? Add up your grades: $84 + 82 + 89 = 255$. To earn a B, you would need 320 points (80×4). Subtract your current points from the points you need $(320 - 255 = 65)$ to find the grade you would need to maintain your B.

If your grade is more complicated—many other factors such as attendance, homework, quizzes, exams, and a paper, for example, determine your grade—you will need to add up the total points you have in the course and divide that number by the total possible points you could have earned. To calculate what you need on the final, determine the total points you need to earn for the next highest grade. If you have 420 points before the final out of a possible 500 points (not counting the final yet), you would have an 84% in the course. If the final exam counts 100 points, you would need 80% of 600 (total possible points in the course) or 480 points. To calculate what you need on the final, you need to subtract the points you have prior to the final from the points you need for a B $(480 - 420 = 60)$. Would it be possible to earn an A in the course if 90% equals an A?

● *Make borderline grades your top priority.* One of the reasons that you need to calculate your current course grade is to see whether or not you have a borderline grade going into the final. The final exam will have the greatest impact on a borderline grade. Let's say you have a 92% in a course before the final and you need a 92% to get an A in the course. It's obvious that if you do well on the final, you could earn an A in the course, and that if you don't do very well you could lose your A and get a B or even a C. On the other hand, if you have a 98% in the course, you are less likely to lose your A in the course. Once you determine which courses have borderline grades, you can put more time and more effort into those finals. In the first example, you only needed a 65% to maintain your B in the course. What would you need to earn an A in that course? If an A in that course is a 90%, you would need a total of 360 points to earn an A. If you subtract your 255 current points from 360, you'll notice that you would need a 105% on the final—impossible to achieve. If your instructor doesn't use plus/minus grading, you're likely to earn a B in the course. Since you would need only a 65% on the final (having already earned an 84%, 82%, and 89%), you probably can spend a little less time and effort on that course.

Consider all of your options. It's also important to look realistically at classes in which you have low grades. Some students foolishly decide to let all of their other finals go just to bring up a low grade. Sometimes, though, even the final won't help. If you need more than a perfect grade on the final to pass the course, forget it. One student determined that getting a 95% on the final would earn him a passing grade. However, he had only had a 39%, 50%, and 56% on his previous exams. Earning a 95% on the final seems pretty unrealistic. If you can't possibly pass the class, you should withdraw from it to protect your overall GPA. If it's too late to withdraw, check with your professor to see if there is any chance that you can pass the course. Some professors take improvement into consideration or will even drop your lowest exam grade. If your professor indicates that there is no way that you can pass the course, don't even study for the final and don't take it. Put your time instead into your other courses. However, if you do plan to repeat the course, you should go to the final just to see what it's like. That information can be useful when you prepare for the final the next time you enroll.

Prioritize your study.   Once you know which courses have borderline grades, you need to set priorities for study. The classes with borderline grades should be your highest priority classes. If you have several borderline grades, you should make the courses in your major a higher priority than those that are electives. Rank each of the courses so that you know which course is number 1, 2, 3, and so on. When setting up your study plan, you need to put more time and effort into the courses that are your highest priority classes. You'll have an opportunity to practice ranking classes in Workshop 10-1.

Set Up a Final Exam Planning Calendar

Set up a Final Exam Planning Calendar.   About ten days before your first final, you should make out a Final Exam Planning Calendar (See Figure 10.2). Write in your classes and other fixed commitments, but don't put in your meal times yet. Meal times work very well as breaks between study sessions, so you may need to eat a little earlier or later to make your exam plan work. You'll have a chance to set up your own Final Exam Planning Calendar in Workshop 10-3.

Block in each exam.   The next step in making out your exam plan is to write in each of your final exams. Once you put them on your calendar, outline each exam block with a different color. Do you have more than one exam on the same day? Some students have two exams on the same day; that's okay. You can easily prepare for and take two exams on the same day. Look at Hollie's Final Exam Planning Calendar in Figure 10.3. Although she had two exams on Wednesday, she had no problem setting up her study plan. However, taking three exams on the same day is not in your best interest. Check with one of your instructors about taking your exam at a different time.

Set up Five-Day Study Plans.   Instead of trying to cram for one exam after another, you need to schedule overlapping Five-Day Study Plans for each of your exams. Plan to study for 2 hours each day for each of your exams. Most students find that scheduling a five-day plan works well, but you can set up a four-day plan for an easy exam that covers only a few chapters or a six-day plan for a more difficult exam that covers a lot of chapters. Count back from each of your exams to determine the correct day to begin your study. You'll be working on Day 1 for one exam at the same time that you're on Day 3 for another one.

Split your day to schedule your study.   One of the easiest ways to schedule each of your exams is to split your day. Study for one exam in the morning, another in the afternoon, one in the early evening, and one late at night. Of course, if you're a morning person, you may want to prepare for one exam early in the morning and another later in the morning and so on. It's a good idea to work on your hardest or highest-priority exam early in the day and leave your easier or lower-priority exams for later in the day when you're already tired. You also want to be consistent in scheduling the time blocks for each exam. One of the problems students experience during finals week is a lack of structure in their time schedules, which

Figure 10.2 ● Final Exam Planning Calendar

	⑨ Wednesday	⑩ Thursday	⑪ Friday	⑫ Saturday	⑬ Sunday	⑭ Monday	⑮ Tuesday	⑯ Wednesday	⑰ Thursday	⑱ Friday	⑲ Saturday
7:00 A.M.											
8:00 A.M.						Extra Review Algebra		Extra Review English			
9:00 A.M.	English		English		Day 5	Algebra Final		English Final	Extra Review	Extra Review	
10:00 A.M.					Algebra				Biology	Study Strategies	
11:00 A.M.	Biology		Biology							Lunch	
12:00 P.M.	Lunch	Lunch	Lunch	Lunch	Lunch	Lunch	Lunch	Lunch			
1:00 P.M.	College Algebra		College Algebra	Day 1	Day 2	Day 3	Day 4	Day 5	Biology Final	Study Strategies Final	
2:00 P.M.		Study Strategies		Biology	Biology	Biology	Biology	Biology			
3:00 P.M.				Break	Break	Break	Break	Break			
4:00 P.M.			Day 1	Day 2	Day 3	Day 4	Day 5				
5:00 P.M.			English	English	English	English	English				
6:00 P.M.	Dinner	Dinner	Dinner	Dinner	Dinner	Dinner	Dinner	Dinner	Dinner	Dinner	
7:00 P.M.	Day 1	Day 2	Day 3	Day 4	Day 1	Day 2	Day 3	Day 4	Day 5		
8:00 P.M.	Algebra	Algebra	Algebra	Algebra	Study Strategies	Study Strategies	Study Strategies	Study Strategies	Study Strategies		
9:00 P.M.			Break	Break	Break	Break	Break	Break	Break		
10:00 P.M.			Optional	Optional	Optional	Optional	Optional	Optional	Optional		
11:00 P.M.			Study Time	Study Time	Study Time	Study Time	Study Time	Study Time	Study Time		

Note: Do not use the words *Optional Study Time* on your plan. Instead, indicate how that time will be used.

Figure 10.3 ● Hollie's Final Exam Planning Calendar

	Wednesday	Thursday	Friday	Saturday	Sunday	Monday	Tuesday	Wednesday	Thursday	Friday	Saturday
7:00 A.M.											
8:00 A.M.									Extra Review SS		
9:00 A.M.	Math	Educational Psychology	Math	Day 2	Day 3	Day 4	Day 5	Extra Review	Study Strategies Final	Extra Review	
10:00 A.M.	Study Strategies		Study Strategies	Educational Psychology	Educational Psychology	Educational Psychology	Educational Psychology	Educational Psychology		Science	
11:00 A.M.	Lunch	Lunch	Lunch	Lunch	Lunch	Lunch	Lunch	Lunch	Lunch	Lunch	
12:00 P.M.				Day 1	Day 2	Day 3	Day 4	Educational Psychology Final	Day 5	Science Final	
1:00 P.M.	Comp		Comp	Science	Science	Science	Science		Science		
2:00 P.M.	Science		Science								
3:00 P.M.			Day 1	Day 2	Day 3	Day 4	Day 5	Math Final			
4:00 P.M.			Math	Math	Math	Math	Math				
5:00 P.M.	Dinner	Dinner	Dinner	Dinner	Dinner	Dinner	Dinner	Dinner	Dinner		
6:00 P.M.			Day 1	Day 1	Day 2	Day 3	Day 4	Day 5		Dinner	
7:00 P.M.			Educational Psychology	Study Strategies	Study Strategies	Study Strategies	Study Strategies	Study Strategies			
8:00 P.M.							Extra Review				
9:00 P.M.			Extra Review	Extra Review	Extra Review	Extra Review					
10:00 P.M.			Educational Psychology	Educational Psychology	Educational Psychology	Educational Psychology	Educational Psychology				
11:00 P.M.											

Note: Hollie did not have a final in English Composition.

increases their feelings of stress. By setting up consistent study blocks for each exam, you're creating a more structured study schedule. Color-code each of your Five-Day Study Plans to match the color you used for the exam. You'll be able to look at your calendar and see the sequence of study for each exam.

Plan study breaks. Taking breaks is very important during finals preparation. You need time to let the information that you studied consolidate in long-term memory and reduce interference. You also need to take time to relax a bit during the day so that you can maintain your motivation to work on one exam after another. Plan one-hour breaks between your study blocks. If you aren't working this semester, you may find that you have additional time to relax during the day. If you complete some of your regular assignments early, you won't need to study every hour of the day.

Make use of optional study time. Take another look at the sample Final Exam Planning Calendar in Figure 10.2. You'll notice that there is a block for optional study time from 10 P.M. to 12 A.M. Don't write *optional study time* on your calendar. Instead, you need to designate how you plan to use that time, as Hollie did on her calendar in Figure 10.3. You could use that time block to prepare for a fifth exam, if necessary, to meet with your study group, or for additional review for your highest-priority class or classes.

Add extra reviews the day of the final. If you have an afternoon or evening exam, it's critical that you set up an extra review the day of the final. Depending on how you set up your study plan, you may be taking your final more than 24 hours after your last review of the material. As you know, we forget rapidly. Doing an extra review of the material just before the final will help make the information more accessible during the exam and help you practice again some of the material that you're still not quite sure about. If you have a morning exam, getting up a little earlier will help you do better on the exam. Don't make the mistake, though, of waiting until the day of the exam to do your final review and self-test. Some students who used that strategy did just fine on the final, but others (who didn't quiz themselves each day) found that they didn't know as much of the material as they thought they did. If you wait until the day of the exam to monitor your learning, you won't have enough time left to learn the material you didn't know.

Plan Properly for Comprehensive Finals

What are comprehensive finals? Comprehensive finals are exams that cover either all previously tested material or some new material along with some previously tested material. They may include a few questions that come from older chapters or they may contain questions that cover all of the course material. You need to prepare differently for exams that are 25-percent comprehensive (25 percent of the questions come from old material and 75 percent come from new material) 50-percent, 75-percent, and 100-percent comprehensive finals.

Plan your study time correctly. If you had an exam that was composed of 100 multiple-choice questions covering twelve chapters, and it was 25-percent comprehensive (with new Chapters 10, 11, and 12), how would you set up your study plan? Take a look at the sample study plans in Figure 10.4. Which of these plans correctly reflects which chapters you should study for the first four days of your five-day

Figure 10.4 ● Sample
Study Plans

Plan 1		Plan 2		Plan 3	
Day 1	Ch 1–3	Day 1	Ch 10–12	Day 1	Ch 1–9
Day 2	Ch 4–6	Day 2	Ch 7–9	Day 2	Ch 10
Day 3	Ch 7–9	Day 3	Ch 4–6	Day 3	Ch 11
Day 4	Ch 10–12	Day 4	Ch 1–3	Day 4	Ch 12

plan? Remember that twenty-five questions on this exam will come from the old material and seventy-five will come from the new material. You need to use the same formula for planning out your study time that you used for taking an exam. Percentage of total points equals percentage of total time. If 25 percent of the points will come from Chapter 10, you need to spend 25 percent of your time preparing that material. In the same way, if only 25 percent of the points on the final will come from Chapters 1 to 9, only 25 percent of your preparation time should be scheduled for those chapters as a unit. Plan 1 is a great plan for either a 75-percent comprehensive final with Chapters 10, 11, and 12 comprising the new material or a 100-percent comprehensive final. Plan 2 works well for a 50-percent comprehensive final and Plan 3 will work nicely for the final described previously.

Study strategies for comprehensive finals. You've probably been thinking, how can you prepare nine chapters in only 2 hours? Well, you can't. That's why it's so important to find out early in the term whether or not your exams will be comprehensive and exactly how comprehensive they will be. If you knew that you were going to have a comprehensive final covering those first nine chapters in addition to three new chapters, you should save all of the word cards, questions, study sheets, and self-tests that you made for those early exams. Instead of preparing new material on Day 1, you could use that time to begin quizzing yourself on the old material to find out which information you still need to review again on the following days. If you did well on the first three exams, for example, you may find that much of that information comes back rather quickly. If you didn't do as well, you would need to start reviewing and keep reviewing each day since you covered that material so long ago. For the new material, you could prepare your word cards, questions, and study sheets on each day of the plan or you could prepare some of the material the week before. In any case, you need to use the same active preparation and active review strategies that you used for your regular exams.

If you've been working with a study group during the semester, you'll be able to help each other prepare for the final. Getting together each day of your Five-Day Study Plan to share materials, talk about the course material, predict possible test questions, and quiz each other is a great way to help everyone in the group be more successful on the exam. However, unless you also spend some time working on your own, you won't have those materials to share or questions to ask. If you work on a chunk of the material on your own before meeting with your study group, you can make better use of the time you spend as a group. You need to work on your own after meeting with the group, too. During that study session, you need to practice working on any material you didn't know that came up during the group discussion or any information that you didn't get correct during the group tests.

WORKSHOP 10-1   Set Priorities for Finals

In this workshop, you'll have an opportunity to practice calculating course grades and setting priorities for finals. Once you've completed the practice activities, calculate your own course grades and set priorities for your finals.

1. Calculate the current course grade for each of the following classes. In this example the student has four exams in each course (the final is Exam IV), which all count equally.

Course	Exam I	Exam II	Exam III	Current Grade
A	82	84	83	_____
B	81	76	79	_____
C	74	84	85	_____
D	14	40	56	_____

2. Rank the courses to set priorities for study. Put a 1 on the line for Rank for the course that is your highest priority and 2 for the next highest and so on. Then explain your reasoning for assigning the ranks in the space labeled Rationale.

COURSE A

RANK _____

RATIONALE _____

_____

_____

COURSE B

RANK _____

RATIONALE _____

_____

_____

COURSE C

RANK _____

RATIONALE _____

_____

_____

COURSE D

RANK _____

RATIONALE _____

_____

_____

3. Calculate the grade you would need to earn on each of the finals to earn the highest-possible grade.

Course	Grade Needed on Final	Highest-Possible Grade for Course
A	_____	_____
B	_____	_____
C	_____	_____
D	_____	_____

4. Calculate your current grade for each of your courses, the grade you need on the final, and the highest grade you can earn for each course. Then set a realistic grade goal and priority rank for each class.

Course Name	Current Average	Grade Needed on Final	Highest Grade Possible	Realistic Grade Goal	Priority Rank

5. Which is your highest priority class? Why?

_____

_____

_____

6. Which course is your next priority? Why?

_____

_____

_____

WORKSHOP 10-2 Critique Final Exam Study Plans

In this workshop, you'll have a chance to critique some final exam study plans and then develop a revised study plan for one of the students. *Note:* All of the study plans have major problems.

1. Look at Joel's Final Exam Planning Calendar in Figure 10.5. What mistakes did Joel make?

_____

_____

_____

_____

_____

_____

_____

_____

2. What changes would you make in Joel's plan to make it more useful?

_____

_____

_____

_____

_____

_____

_____

_____

3. Look at Tanya's Final Exam Planning Calendar in Figure 10.6. What mistakes did Tanya make?

_____

_____

_____

_____

_____

_____

_____

_____

4. What changes would you make in Tanya's plan to make it more useful?

_____

_____

_____

_____

_____

_____

_____

_____

_____

5. Now look at Jodi's Final Exam Planning Calendar in Figure 10.7. What mistakes did Jodi make?

_____

_____

_____

_____

_____

_____

_____

_____

_____

_____

6. What changes would you make in Jodi's plan to make it more useful?

_____

_____

_____

_____

_____

_____

_____

_____

_____

7. Work as a group to create a new study plan for Jodi. Use the Revised Final Exam Planning Calendar in Figure 10.8 for this activity.

Figure 10.5 ● Joel's Final Exam Planning Calendar

	Wednesday	Thursday	Friday	Saturday	Sunday	Monday	Tuesday
8:00 A.M.	Get up/ Dressed		Get up/ Dressed			Get up/ Dressed	
9:00 A.M.	Lift Weights	Get up/ Dressed	Lift Weights			Computer Literacy Final	Get up/ Dressed
10:00 A.M.	Weight Training	Computer Literacy	Weight Training				
11:00 A.M.				Get up/ Dressed	Get up/ Dressed		
12:00 P.M.	College Algebra	Comp 1	College Algebra				
1:00 P.M.	Lunch	Lunch	Lunch	Lunch	Lunch	Lunch	Lunch
2:00 P.M.							
3:00 P.M.		Soc		Lift Weights	Lift Weights	Soc Final	Algebra Final
4:00 P.M.							
5:00 P.M.	Dinner	Dinner	Dinner	Dinner	Dinner		
6:00 P.M.		Lift Weights					
7:00 P.M.							
8:00 P.M.		Day 1 Algebra	Day 2 Algebra	Day 3 Algebra	Day 4 Algebra	Day 5 Algebra	
9:00 P.M.	Day 1 Soc	Day 2 Soc	Day 3 Soc	Day 4 Soc	Day 5 Soc		
10:00 P.M.	Day 1 Computer Literacy	Day 2 Computer Literacy	Day 3 Computer Literacy	Day 4 Computer Literacy	Day 5 Computer Literacy		

Note: This plan contains some common planning mistakes.

Figure 10.6 ● Tanya's Final Exam Planning Calendar

	Monday	Tuesday	Wednesday	Thursday	Friday	Saturday	Sunday	Monday	Tuesday	Wednesday	Thursday
8:00 A.M.	Get Up/ Dress, etc.	Get Up/ Dress, etc.	Get Up/ Dress, etc.	Get Up/ Dress, etc.	Get Up/ Dress, etc.	Sleep	Sleep	Get Up/ Dress, etc.	Get Up/ Dress, etc.	Get Up/ Dress, etc.	Get Up/ Dress, etc.
9:00 A.M.	Trig 2.7–3.1 →	Class →	Review APP	APP Final	Read Econ	Sleep	Sleep	Recite Note Cards	Recite Note Cards →	Do Test Ch 2 →	Trig Final
10:00 A.M.	→	→	→		Chs 28, 30 & 33 →	Get Up/ Dress, etc.	Sleep	Econ	→	→	
11:00 A.M.	Biology Ch 13 →	Class →	Lunch	Biology Final	→	Lunch	Get Up/ Dress, etc.	Lunch	Lunch	Do Test Ch 3 →	
12:00 P.M.	→	Lunch	Trig 4.1–4.4 →	Lunch	Lunch	Review Econ →	Lunch	Do Formulas Econ	Trig 3.2–3.6 →	→	
1:00 P.M.	Lunch	Review	→	Review 4.1–4.4	Review Econ	→	TV		→	Lunch	
2:00 P.M.	Trig 4.3 →	Trig 4.4 →	APP Review →	Quiz Trig 4.1–4.4	Ch 5–7 →	→	TV		→	Do Test Ch 4 →	
3:00 P.M.	→	→	→	Bowling →	→	→	TV		Recite Note Cards	→	
4:00 P.M.	Biology Ch 14 →	Biology Ch 15	→	→	→	→	TV	Dinner	Dinner	Recite All Formulas	
5:00 P.M.	Dinner	Dinner	→	→	→	→	TV	Recite Note Cards	Recite Note Cards	→	
6:00 P.M.	Class →	Class →	Dinner →	Dinner	Dinner	Dinner	Dinner	Econ Final	Computer Literacy Final	Dinner	
7:00 P.M.	→	→	APP Review →	Out	Out	Out	Make Note Cards Econ →			Ch Review 2.1–2.8	
8:00 P.M.	→	→	→	Out	Out	Out	→			Ch Review 3.1–3.6	
9:00 P.M.	APP Review	Review Trig	Trig Review →	Out	Out	Out	Recite Note Cards	Make Note Cards	Trig 4.1 to 4.3 →	Ch Review 4.1–4.4	
10:00 P.M.	Study Sheet 6 →	Secs. 4.1–4.4 →	Biology Review →	Out	Out	Out	→	Computer Literacy	→	Sleep	
11:00 P.M.	→	→	→	Out	Out	Out	→	→	→		

Note: This plan contains some common planning mistakes.

Figure 10.7 ● Jodi's Final Exam Planning Calendar

	Wednesday	Thursday	Friday	Saturday	Sunday	Monday	Tuesday	Wednesday	Thursday
7:00 A.M.	Get up/Dress	Sleep	Sleep	Sleep	Sleep	Sleep	Sleep	Sleep	Sleep
8:00 A.M.	Composition Class	Get up/Dress	Sleep	Sleep	Sleep	Get up/Dress	Sleep	Sleep	Sleep
9:00 A.M.			Get up/Dress	Get up/Dress	Sleep		Get up/Dress	Get up/Dress	Get up/Dress
10:00 A.M.	Psychology Class		Psychology Class	Study Psychology	Get up/Dress		Study Psychology		
11:00 A.M.	Lunch	Lunch	Lunch	Lunch	Lunch	Lunch	Lunch	Lunch	Lunch
12:00 P.M.						Review History	Review CSS		
1:00 P.M.	CSS Class	History Class	CSS Class		Study CSS	History Final			
2:00 P.M.			Study History	Study History	Study CSS				
3:00 P.M.			Study History	Study History					Psychology Final
4:00 P.M.	Band								
5:00 P.M.	Dinner								
6:00 P.M.	Dinner	Dinner	Dinner	Dinner	Dinner	Dinner	Dinner	Dinner	Dinner
7:00 P.M.		Study CSS	Study CSS	Study CSS	Study Psychology	Study Psychology	CSS Final		
8:00 P.M.	Study History				Break	Break		Study Psychology	
9:00 P.M.		Study History			Study History	Study CSS			
10:00 P.M.					Sleep	Sleep			
11:00 P.M.								Sleep	

Note: This plan contains some common planning mistakes.

Figure 10.8 ● Jodi's Revised Final Exam Planning Calendar

	Wednesday	Thursday	Friday	Saturday	Sunday	Monday	Tuesday	Wednesday	Thursday
7:00 A.M.									
8:00 A.M.	Composition Class								
9:00 A.M.									
10:00 A.M.	Psychology Class		Psychology Class						
11:00 A.M.	Lunch	Lunch	Lunch						
12:00 P.M.		History Class							
1:00 P.M.	CSS Class		CSS Class						
2:00 P.M.									
3:00 P.M.						History Final			Psychology Final
4:00 P.M.	Band								
5:00 P.M.							CSS Final		
6:00 P.M.	Dinner								
7:00 P.M.									
8:00 P.M.									
9:00 P.M.									
10:00 P.M.									
11:00 P.M.									

WORKSHOP 10-3 **Create Your Own Final Exam Planning Calendar**

In this workshop, you'll have an opportunity to create your own Final Exam Planning Calendar to schedule your study time for your exams.

1. Write your classes and other fixed commitments on your blank Final Exam Planning Calendar in Figure 10.9. Do not list meal times on the calendar until you've planned out your study blocks. If you plan to study after 2 A.M., add blocks to the bottom of your calendar.

2. Write in the time blocks for each of your final exams and color code each one using a different-colored highlighter or marker.

3. List each of your finals in the space below and rank them with 1 as your highest priority, 2 next highest, and so on.

_____

_____

_____

_____

_____

_____

_____

_____

4. Now count back from each of your final exam blocks to determine Day 1 of each study plan.

5. Set up Five-Day Study Plans for each of your exams. Be sure to leave at least a 1-hour break between each study session.

6. Do you have any comprehensive finals? _____ If so, how do you plan to divide the material for each of them?

_____

_____

_____

_____

_____

_____

_____

7. Did you have any problems setting up your plan?

_____

_____

_____

_____

_____

_____

_____

8. What changes did you have to make in your regular schedule to set up overlapping Five-Day Study Plans?

_____

_____

_____

_____

_____

_____

_____

9. Exchange your plan with one of your classmates. What suggestions would you make to your classmate to improve his or her study plan?

_____

_____

_____

_____

_____

_____

10. Now that you've looked at a classmate's plan and received feedback on your plan, what changes do you plan to make? Use the extra Final Exam Planning Calendar in Figure 10.10 to make any revisions to your plan.

_____

_____

_____

_____

_____

_____

_____

Figure 10.9 ● Final Exam Planning Calendar

	Wednesday	Thursday	Friday	Saturday	Sunday	Monday	Tuesday	Wednesday	Thursday	Friday	Saturday
6:00 A.M.											
7:00 A.M.											
8:00 A.M.											
9:00 A.M.											
10:00 A.M.											
11:00 A.M.											
12:00 P.M.											
1:00 P.M.											
2:00 P.M.											
3:00 P.M.											
4:00 P.M.											
5:00 P.M.											
6:00 P.M.											
7:00 P.M.											
8:00 P.M.											
9:00 P.M.											
10:00 P.M.											
11:00 P.M.											
12:00 A.M.											
1:00 A.M.											

Figure 10.10 ● Revised Final Exam Planning Calendar

	Wednesday	Thursday	Friday	Saturday	Sunday	Monday	Tuesday	Wednesday	Thursday	Friday	Saturday
6:00 A.M.											
7:00 A.M.											
8:00 A.M.											
9:00 A.M.											
10:00 A.M.											
11:00 A.M.											
12:00 P.M.											
1:00 P.M.											
2:00 P.M.											
3:00 P.M.											
4:00 P.M.											
5:00 P.M.											
6:00 P.M.											
7:00 P.M.											
8:00 P.M.											
9:00 P.M.											
10:00 P.M.											
11:00 P.M.											
12:00 A.M.											
1:00 A.M.											

WORKSHOP 10-4 What Would You Do?

In this workshop, you'll have a chance to consider a case study and make suggestions that Rick could use to improve the outcome of his final exams.

Rick is a Geology major with a 1.89 GPA. He is in his second term in college and has been working hard to improve his grades and get off academic probation. After attempting to calculate his current grade in each course, he set up an appointment with each of his instructors to review his grade. With all grades calculated prior to finals, he has the following grades: Physical Geology 92%, English 72%, College Algebra 85%, Art History 48%, and Learning Strategies 79%. Rick is concerned that his Art History grade will pull down his average, so he has decided to make that his top priority. He has two exams on Tuesday of finals week (Physical Geology and Art History), and then one on each of the following days. He's not very concerned about his Geology grade since he has an A in the course and the final is comprehensive and covers the same material he was tested on already. He feels confident that he can score well enough to keep his A, or at least earn a B, in Geology. He has decided to spend all day Monday studying for the Art History exam. It covers some old material and only four chapters of new material. He'll stay up all night preparing if necessary to pass that class. Once the Tuesday exams are over, Rick thinks that his plan to study for one exam each day will work well and help him achieve his goals.

1. Which courses should have been Rick's priority for finals? Why?

_____

_____

_____

_____

_____

_____

_____

_____

_____

2. What mistakes did Rick make in planning his study time?

_____

_____

_____

_____

_____

_____

_____

_____

_____

3. What changes should Rick make to achieve his goal of getting off probation?

_____

_____

_____

_____

_____

_____

_____

_____

_____

_____

_____

_____

_____

_____

_____

Now think about the final exams that you have this term. What are your high-priority classes? What are your grade goals?

4. How can setting priorities and planning your time help you be more successful on your final exams?

_____

_____

_____

_____

_____

_____

_____

_____

_____

_____

_____

_____

_____

_____

_____

_____

_____

Credits

Figure 5.1, p. 123. From *Communication Mosaics: An Introduction to the Field of Communication*, 3rd edition by WOOD. 2004. Reprinted with permission of Wadsworth, a division of Thomson Learning: www.thomsonrights.com Fax: 800-730-2215.

Figure 5.2, p. 124. From *Essentials of Oceanography*, 3rd edition by GARRISON. 2004. Reprinted by permission of Brooks/Cole, a division of Thomson Learning: www.thomsonrights.com Fax 800-730-2215.

Figure 5.3, pp. 127–128. From *World History: Volume II: Since 1400*, 4th edition by DUIKER/SPIELVOGEL. 2004. Reprinted with permission of Wadsworth, a division of Thomson Learning: www.thomsonrights.com Fax: 800-730-2215.

Figure 6.3, p. 143. From *World History: Volume 1: to 1400*, 4th edition by DUIKER/SPIELVOGEL. 2004. Reprinted with permission of Wadsworth, a division of Thomson Learning: www.thomsonrights.com Fax: 800-730-2215.

Figure 6.4, p. 145. From *Psychology: Themes and Variations* (Brief, Paperbound edition with Concept Chart and InfoTrac), 6th edition by WEITEN. 2005. Reprinted with permission of Wadsworth, a division of Thomson Learning: www.thomsonrights.com Fax 800-730-2215.

Figure 6.5, pp. 149–150. From *Media/Impact: An Introduction to Mass Media*, 7th edition by BIAGI. 2005. Reprinted with permission of Wadsworth, a division of Thomson Learning: www.thomsonrights.com Fax 800-730-2215.

Figure 6.6, p. 152. From *Principles of Economics*, 3rd edition by MANKIW. 2004. Reprinted with permission of South-Western, a division of Thomson Learning: www.thomsonrights.com Fax 800-730-2215.

Figure 6.7, p. 153. From *Living in the Environment*, 13th edition by MILLER. 2004. Reprinted with permission of Brooks/Cole, a division of Thomson Learning: www.thomsonrights.com Fax 800-730-2215.

Figure 7.1, p. 166. From *Horizons, Exploring the Universe* (with the Sky CD-ROM, AceAstronomy and Virtual Astronomy Labs) 9th edition by SEEDS. 2006. Reprinted with permission of Brooks/Cole, a division of Thomson Learning: www.thomsonrights.com Fax 800-730-2215.

Figure 7.7, pp. 179–180. From *World History to 1500*, 3rd edition by DUIKER/SPIELVOGEL. 2001. Reprinted by permission of Wadsworth, a division of Thomson Learning: www.thomsonrights.com Fax 800-730-2215.

Figure 7.8, pp. 183–184. From *Living in the Environment*, 11th edition by MILLER. 2000. Reprinted with permission of Brooks/Cole, a division of Thomson Learning: www.thomsonrights.com Fax 800-730-2215.

Matching test, p. 243. From *New English Handbook*, 2nd edition by GUTH. 1985. Reprinted with permission of Wadsworth, a division of Thomson Learning: www.thomsonrights.com Fax 800-730-2215.